D1135113

# Such Sweet Thunder

*Beside the groves,*
*The skies, the fountains, every region near*
*Seem'd all one mutual cry. I never heard*
*So musical a discord, such sweet thunder.*

—A Midsummer Night's Dream
Act IV, Scene 1

Other books by Whitney Balliett

*The Sound of Surprise*
*Dinosaurs in the Morning*

# Such Sweet Thunder

Forty-nine
Pieces
on Jazz

# Whitney Balliett

The Bobbs-Merrill Company, Inc.

A Subsidiary of Howard W. Sams & Co., Inc.
Publishers:     Indianapolis     New York     Kansas City

ML
3561
J3
B255

*First printing, 1966*

Copyright © 1962, 1963, 1964, 1965, and 1966, by *The New Yorker Magazine, Inc.*
All rights reserved
Library of Congress catalog card number 66–28030
Designed by Martin Stephen Moskof
Printed in the United States of America

For N.

# Contents

# Contents

# Note

This book consists of a selection from the seventy-odd pieces I have written on jazz between 1962 and the present for *The New Yorker*. They are in roughly chronological order, although the Ellington pieces, done over a two-year period, have been put together in an effort to give a composite picture of an extraordinary career. I have eliminated obvious repetitions, but I have left some intact —the review of the celebrated 1963 Earl Hines concert and the opening of the Hines profile—simply to preserve the design of the pieces. The book continues the chronicle— critical and biographical—of the music begun in 1954 and previously collected in *The Sound of Surprise* and *Dinosaurs in the Morning*. I hope that it proves that jazz, which is now passing through one of its periodic revolutions and seasons of discontent, continues to unfold its unique beauties.

The title of this collection is a tribute to Duke Ellington, who used it in 1957 for some witty pieces based on Shakespeare's characters. It is a choice description of his music and, for that matter, of jazz itself.

My gratitude to William Shawn and Rogers E.M.F. Whitaker of *The New Yorker* is undiminished.

W. B.

1962

# New Fig

The professional jazz traditionalist, or moldy fig, is becoming serpentine. He now cloaks his mustiness in ethical-religious arguments (*The Heart of Jazz*, an astonishing book written by William L. Grossman and Jack W. Farrell, and published in 1956), or blandly deifies his idols (a more recent and equally dumbfounding effort by H. O. Brunn, *The Story of the Original Dixieland Jazz Band*). He no longer rants or excoriates but sidles up beside the enemy (anyone born after 1900) and withers him with faint praise. He has also become adept at omission, at seemingly valid musical analysis, and at oblique downgrading. The high-water mark of this new-figgism has just been reached in *Jazz: A History of the New York Scene* (Doubleday), by Samuel B. Charters and Leonard Kunstadt. Charters, the author of pioneering new-fig chronicles of New Orleans jazz and rural blues singers, has done the—well, writing ("The music of the bands, as well as the instrumentation, was greatly influenced by the music the men were playing" and "They are both short, a little plump, wearing glasses, and looking like very unpretentious but pleasant men"), and Kunstadt, an assiduous jazz scholar, has done the research. The result is a three-hundred-and-sixty-page polemic dis-

3

guised as a definitive history of jazz in New York from the ragtime days to the present. It easily outfigs Brunn, and Grossman and Farrell. In fact, Charters—with his footnotes (Grossman, too, is a footnote man), his myriad reproductions of pertinent documents, his statistics, and his sagacious, unruffled tone—even bests himself.

Nearly two-thirds (two hundred and thirty-eight pages) of the book is an admirable display of how to write full-bodied history about practically nothing, for this section deals with the period from 1900 to 1930 (the traditionalist's favorite playground), when jazz was centered not in New York but in New Orleans, St. Louis, Chicago, and points southwest and southeast. (New York pretty much invented the Harlem stride pianists and the adolescent swing bands, but the Original Dixieland Jazz Band, Bessie Smith, Freddie Keppard, Louis Armstrong, Bix Beiderbecke, and Jelly Roll Morton were transient, if stimulating, out-of-towners.) Nonetheless, Charters, an unflagging historian, abhors vacuums. The new-fig fill he uses consists of intense appreciations of Clarence Williams, Charlie Johnson's Paradise Band, the Louisiana Five, Paul Whiteman, the "Rhapsody in Blue," Johnny Dunn, Henry Goodwin, Ed Allen, and Bub (Bubber to you and me) Miley. The Fletcher Henderson band is evaluated, found wanting, and dismissed as of 1929, five years before it coalesced; Ellington is slyly labelled an opportunist who was overrecorded; and Luis Russell, who had *the* band in New York in the twenties, is given, in the best new-fig manner, a brief, if favorable, paragraph.

New York has been the headquarters of jazz since 1930, and Charters is magnanimous. He allots fifty-three pages to the thirties, forty-eight pages to the forties, and, in a final burst of largess, seventeen pages to the fifties and early sixties. His vision of the swing era embraces Chick Webb (and Ella Fitzgerald), Jimmy Lunceford, Cab Calloway, Benny Goodman, and Count Basie. Left almost entirely on the bench are Benny Carter, Ellington, Coleman Hawkins, Lester Young, Billie Holiday, Bill Coleman, Frankie Newton, Dickie Wells, Red Allen, J. C. Higginbotham, Ben Webster, Art Tatum, Sidney Catlett, Roy Eldridge, Jack Teagarden, and Sidney Bechet. Left out, too, is the founding, in the late thirties, of the important Blue Note and Commodore recording firms. Basie gets a full six and a half pages, but they are subtly askew: "The band Basie had [in 1935] was probably the best he ever had," and Buster Smith "was one of the greatest alto men in jazz." (Few people, outside of John Hammond and some avant-garde citizens of Kansas City, heard the unrecorded Basie band of 1935, and Smith, one of its sidemen, is chiefly regarded as a workmanlike performer who had some influence on the young Charlie Parker—a fact that Charters bypasses.) Charters' omissions and near-omissions swell in the forties. He rockets past Fifty-second Street (the most concentrated and vigorous jazz factory in the music's history), ignores both Café Society Uptown (Teddy Wilson's matchless small band) and Café Society Downtown (Pete Johnson, Albert Ammons, Meade Lux Lewis, and Joe Turner), and all but sideswipes Duke Ellington's unparalleled 1940 band. Charlie Parker, Thelonious Monk, Dizzy Gillespie, and Miles Davis whip by, and are followed, in the fifties, by cooljazzhardbopfunky-jazz, the Modern Jazz Quartet, and Charlie Mingus. We come to rest in the present, on Ornette Coleman and Cecil Taylor, who share one sentence (downgrading). The

5

book's last sentence is the perfect summation: "The story of jazz in New York [read: *our* story of jazz in New York] is in many ways the story of jazz itself."

Charters has edited a companion record, "A History of Jazz: The New York Scene" (Folkways), which includes reissues by Jim Europe's Society Orchestra, the Original Dixieland Jazz Band, Mamie Smith, Henderson, Clarence Williams, Charlie Johnson, Miff Mole, the Louisiana Sugar Babes, Ellington, the Missourians, Cab Calloway, Lunceford, Coleman Hawkins, and Dizzy Gillespie. Since none of the selections is first-rate and only a few are even second-rate, the record reflects the book perfectly.

# Non-Spectrum

The First International Jazz
Festival, sponsored by the Music Committee of the President's People-to-People Program, and recently held in
Washington, was all potatoes and no meat. One of those
paternal-visionary affairs, it was designed, according to the
official program, "to provide national recognition of jazz
through the creation of a Festival in the nation's capital
which will explore the full spectrum of jazz and indicate
its influence throughout the world." Well, of the ten main
events six were peripheral—a program of symphonic jazz,
a jazz liturgical service, a gospel-music program, a jazz ballet, a program of "jazz for a young audience," and a chamber concert showing the supposed influence of jazz on
classical music. Three of the rest were, aside from other
faults, largely inaudible; straight jazz programs, they were
held in the Washington Coliseum, a small, barrel-vaulted
Madison Square Garden with the acoustics of the Penn
Station concourse. And the last, devoted to small groups,
was, give or take a few performances, merely dull. Woven
throughout these ten were incidental appearances by the
remarkable Eureka Brass Band, of New Orleans; a continuous showing of jazz films at the National Gallery (including Gjon Mili's fine "Jammin' the Blues" and Bessie Smith's

"St. Louis Blues"); and a display at the Smithsonian of jazz memorabilia—photographs, old records, books, posters, paintings, drawings, one of Lester Young's tenor saxophones, and the prehistoric cornet that Louis Armstrong played in the Colored Waifs' Home, in New Orleans.

What this cornucopia failed to produce was good journeyman jazz, of whatever school. Indeed, the entire festival had a pretentious, marginal air. Thus, the Dave Brubeck quartet and the Charlie Bell ensemble were present, but the Modern Jazz Quartet was not; George Russell and a Dadaist named John Benson Brooks were there, but Ornette Coleman, Cecil Taylor, and Charlie Mingus were not; the jazz ballet, performed by Lee Becker and a group of ten or twelve dancers, with the great Baby Laurence tacked gratuitously on, was chosen in place of Al Minns, Leon James, John Bubbles, Honi Coles, and Pete Nugent; swing was represented by Lawrence Brown, Harry Carney, and Johnny Hodges (present as members of the Ellington band), and, in just four numbers, by Ben Webster and Roy Eldridge, but Pee Wee Russell, Red Allen, Coleman Hawkins, Benny Carter, Jo Jones, Vic Dickenson, Jack Teagarden, Benny Morton, Buddy Tate, and Doc Cheatham were absent; Dinah Washington and the Clara Ward Singers were on hand, but Jimmy Rushing, Mahalia Jackson, and Joe Turner were not; the international note was struck by Chris Barber (from England) and the Wreckers (from Warsaw), instead of by Martial Solal (from France). In short, almost every performer had superior ghosts peering over his shoulder— ghosts that grew, after a time, to formidable proportions.

Probably the most contrived spectacles were the jazz ballet and the evening of symphonic jazz. The ballet, which consisted largely of decorous bumps-and-grinds, was ac-

companied partly by musicians and partly by records, and now and then an Abstract Expressionist painter, Paris Theodore, appeared and whipped off an inspirational work on a huge canvas with black paint and a ten-foot brush. Baby Laurence, in trim condition, thankfully danced by himself to two Charlie Parker records and again, for twenty seconds or so, in the finale. The symphonic-jazz evening was sweltering (Constitution Hall) and often pompous. The National Symphony Orchestra was onstage, and so, at various times, were the Duke Ellington band and such instrumentalists as Don Ellis, Ron Carter, Eddie Costa, Charlie Persip, and J. J. Johnson. Ellington and the N.S.O. played his "Night Creature" (1955), a three-part descriptive piece, notable principally for the marvellous caricatured boogie-woogie bass at the beginning and end of the second movement. Costa, on vibraphone, read his way through a short, metallic concerto for the instrument by André Hodeir, and the program closed with J. J. Johnson's "Scenario for Trombone and Orchestra," a porous jumble of Tchaikovsky effects, Spanish melodies, Gil Evans orchestrations, and brief rhythmic passages. The single worthwhile event during the evening was a shortened version of James P. Johnson's "Yamekraw," written as a piano work in 1927 and newly orchestrated by Gunther Schuller, who also conducted. A charming period piece, based largely on the blues and full of lullaby string passages and pleasantly dumpy rhythmic sections, "Yamekraw" in many ways captures what ultimately escaped Gershwin in the "Rhapsody in Blue." Schuller was also on hand, as composer and conductor, during the young folks' jazz program, when the première of his "Journey Into Jazz"—a "Peter and the Wolf" piece, with fragmentary, elusive music and a Golden Book narration written by Nat Hentoff—was presented.

9

(Music cannot be raised or lowered to fit certain ages; the audience itself must fall short of, match, or outgrow what it hears.)

Some of the rare exceptions to this non-spectrum occurred during the small-ensemble program, where Sonny Rollins, in company with Jim Hall, played two long ballads, in which he soloed brilliantly and at length. Gerry Mulligan, relaxed, if repetitive, offered six creditable numbers with Bob Brookmeyer. And the pianist-composer John Benson Brooks, along with an alto saxophonist and a drummer (equipped only with a snare drum and cymbal), performed a couple of atonal pieces in which moans and thumps were endlessly exchanged. The remaining exceptions were buried in the Luxor-steam-bath atmosphere of the Coliseum concerts. An excellent Mississippi blues singer, Howlin' Wolf, was submerged by the amplification system. (Sonny Rollins, though, battled it and won.) The Oscar Peterson trio accompanied Roy Eldridge and Ben Webster, who were nervous but rewarding, and Thelonious Monk, accompanied by Charlie Rouse, Art Davis, and Billy Higgins, played three superb numbers. (Higgins took two exceptional drum solos.) The Ellington band tired after five excited and exciting instrumentals.

On Sunday morning, four groups of gospel singers appeared at the Coliseum and demonstrated that gospel singing is sliding rapidly from an irresistible amateurism down to a glossy professionalism of noisy handclapping, self-conscious growl-singing, dancing, and racing up and down the aisles. Several members of the audience worked hard at hearing the call, but it never quite reached them— a shorting-out in keeping with the rest of the weekend.

# The Inheritors

From the audience's point of view, the Platonic ideal for a jazz festival runs in threes —three concerts, each limited to around three hours and to three stylistically different groups, and held in a place that affords intimacy between the performers and the three-thousand-only listeners. This ideal materialized stirringly at the first Great South Bay Festival, in 1957, but, inexplicably, not enough customers did, and after a second, equally idealistic attempt the next year, the G. S. B. went under. The Newport Jazz Festival courted this ideal in its first couple of years (1954-55), and then abandoned it for Growth. As a result, it died in its seventh year, of overweight and social pressure—the now celebrated Newport Riot. Last year, a popular-music festival was substituted in Newport. Law and order prevailed, and the town fathers, nudged by the local merchants, who are said to clear upward of a million dollars on festival weekends, asked George Wein, the founder of the Newport Jazz Festival, to resurrect it, and he did, over the Fourth of July weekend. The festival was not Platonic. There were five concerts, most of them too long; there was dross; and the audiences, sometimes twelve thousand strong, were again herded into Freebody Park, a corral the size of Yankee Stadium. But the festival was trimmer, purer, and more light-footed than it has been since its opening years. Indeed, it had one concert of the kind that becomes legendary the next day and that is described with first-hand relish years later to children and grandchildren by people who were not even there.

This graceful and affecting event, on Saturday afternoon, was given over largely to jazz tap-dancing, a classic American art long obscured by the belly-and-bottom modern dance beloved by Broadway, Hollywood, and television. The dancers were Baby Laurence, Bunny Briggs, Pete Nugent, Charlie Atkins, and Honi Coles, and there was a loose narration by Marshall Stearns, who was responsible several years back for reviving Al Minns and Leon James, the masters of "ballroom" jazz dancing. Stearns pointed out, among other things, that tap-dancing resulted from the slow fusion of Irish jigs and clogs and various soft-shoe dances, like the Sand, invented by American Negroes. The dancers demonstrated—singly, in pairs, in trios, and all together—the formidable intricacies of "time" steps, the many "wing" steps (saw wings, pump wings, double-back wings), and "flash" steps, such dances as the trenches-and-over-the-top and the soft-shoe "class" acts, and the styles of originators like Eddie Rector, John W. Bubbles, and Bill Robinson. Coles and Atkins performed a delicious class act. At a slow, slow tempo, they slid across, around, and up and down the stage, mixing in offhand gull turns, polite double toe-taps, hip wiggles, and arm movements ranging from cold-engine propeller motions to weighty pumping. It was that rarity—an immensely serious performance that never takes itself seriously for an instant. The afternoon came to a climax in two dances—one by Briggs and one by Laurence. Briggs, short, slim, and shaggy-headed, is a fey, airborne dancer whose steps and motions are an exquisite balance of comic exaggeration and almost fussy precision. In the Paddle-and-Roll (a Midwestern dance that arrived in New York in the forties), he began with a long sequence of abrupt, irregular heel beats, punctuated by silences and quick, stiff head-and-arm motions, broke into a barrage of military-type flam strokes, and settled into soft, dizzying heel-and-toe beats (his torso and head now motionless) that carried him smoothly all over the seemingly ice-coated stage. Gradually, he brought his body into action with swaying motions, high-kneed walking (the clickclickclickclick of his feet never ceasing), and drawn-out slides, and then released loud, fast staccato beats, sometimes with both feet and sometimes with first one and then the other (this was astonishing), and returned suddenly to his opening pattern. Laurence unenviably followed with a bop dance, and, though exceptional, did not quite match Briggs. (Laurence's style—intense, direct, overbearing—is the opposite of Briggs'.) At the close of the afternoon, all five men did an uproarious takeoff on rock-and-roll and the Twist. The program was helped immeasurably by the accompaniment of Jo Jones and Roy Eldridge (plus bass and piano), both of whom equalled what they were watching. Saturday evening, before a far larger audience, Briggs and Laurence, accompanied by the Duke Ellington band, did variations of their afternoon performances and then danced together and *at* each other; this time, it was a draw.

There were other delights during the weekend. Sunday night, Wein, crowning his managerial functions, sat down at the piano and, in an engaging Jess Stacy-Fats Waller-Teddy Wilson fashion, led a group consisting of Ruby Braff, Pee Wee Russell, Marshall Brown, Bud Freeman, John Neves and Buzzy Drootin through six numbers. These

13

included a relaxed, selfless rendition of Waller's "Crazy 'Bout My Baby," a "Blue and Sentimental" notable for its tempo (molasses dripping) and for Braff's gorgeous playing, and a slow blues in which Russell delivered four lower-register choruses just as good as any of the countless uncanny blues solos he has tossed to the winds these four decades. Wein's group, which has worked together off and on for several years, represents a type of jazz that is rapidly disappearing. Relaxed, emotional, unpretentious, and of no school, it firms the heart and brightens the eye, and it will be a gloomy day when it is gone. Still other beauties were scattered about. Eldridge, accompanied by a rhythm section including Jones, opened the festival, on Friday evening, with three exemplary numbers, and, later in the evening, Coleman Hawkins joined Gerry Mulligan's quartet for "Sunday" and a remarkable "Body and Soul," complete with a leonine coda. Mulligan never worked harder. The next evening, Charlie Mingus set forth six or so strange, congested numbers, and unpardonably took no solos. Sonny Rollins appeared on Sunday afternoon with Jim Hall, Bob Cranshaw, and Ben Riley, and played two long and imaginative numbers, and that evening Thelonious Monk sat in with the Ellington band, which hummed "Monk's Dream" and a blues. Monk, who learned much from Ellington, suggested a witty, kindly, and ingenious parody of his master. Monk then led his quartet through four numbers, soloed brilliantly, and, during his colleagues' contributions, stood up and worked out a series of slow, breezy dances that were, in their way, as fresh as the Briggs-Laurence displays. The last of the weekend's blessings, though mixed, was startlingly funny. It was offered by Roland Kirk, a blind tenor saxophonist and flutist who doubles on a number of horns, some of his own design (he occasion-

ally plays three instruments at once). They are the man-
zello and the stritch, early forebears of the saxophone; a
pocket-sized nose flute; the poor man's piano, or melodica,
a kind of accordion that is blown, not pumped; and the
swarellophone, a small trombone with a horizontal bell and
a vertical slide. Kirk produces a hellish combination of
sounds from these instruments, but his clowning, which is
embellished by comic introductory remarks and a physical
intensity that threatens to hurl him from the stage, dis-
guises a first-rate musician. One hopes he will not sink
wholly into the easy mists of eccentricity.

The rest of the weekend was mechanical, silly, or
plain inept. Most mechanical were the various lady singers
(Louise Tobin excepted), Oscar Peterson (the best cock-
tail pianist in the business), and Dave Brubeck (the worst
c. p. in the business). The sillies were displayed by Max
Roach, who appeared with a sextet and an eight-voice
choir plus conductor, which thrummed like a theremin.
The inept and/or weary will be nameless. It would be cruel
to link them with Briggs and Laurence and Atkins and
Nugent and Coles, who should inherit the earth.

# Pure

A couple of years ago, writing about Benny Carter, the arranger, composer, bandleader, alto saxophonist, trumpeter, and clarinettist, I said that he "is a puzzling figure. . . . Despite its ease and fluidity, his saxophone style has, except in his earliest work, always had an academic ring. He has a round yet colorless tone; his phrasing . . . is . . . often predictable; and his approach to improvisation invariably suggests lofty reflections on, rather than reworkings of, the melody." The rest of my comment was sown with such derogations as "careful," "schoolmarm," and "prim." Well, I have just spent several illuminating days getting reacquainted with Carter's recordings, which run from 1928 to now, and they offer indisputable evidence that Carter's sustained combination of skill, versatility, and imaginativeness is very nearly unmatched in jazz. Few of his contemporaries continue to play or arrange or compose as well as he does, and none of them plays as many instruments *and* arranges *and* composes with such aplomb. Carter, indeed, belongs to that select circle of pure-jazz musicians who tend to represent the best of their times. His work is an unfailing balance of technique, emotion, freshness, and taste. Moreover, it is succinct, oblique, flexible, and cheerful. Carter knows, within his own terms, exactly what to play and how to play it. This is not to say that such pure-jazz musicians as Bix Beiderbecke, Nat Cole, Sidney Catlett, Joe Thomas, Lester Young, and John Lewis are unrivalled. Some of the greatest jazz musicians have been *im*pure, and have made virtues of being excessive, eccentric, or even erratic. But they flare up and flicker out, leaving the Carters to carry tradition from decade to decade.

When I said, in my earlier remarks, that Carter is puzzling, I should have said that his public, or lack of public, is puzzling. For Carter, a man for all seasons, has had an oddly unattended career. Born in New York in 1907, he began his second-banana life with Fletcher Henderson. During the time (1928-31) Carter played and arranged for Henderson, he turned out possibly the best arrangements the Henderson band ever used. But it was Don Redman's and Fletcher and Horace Henderson's more ordinary scores that gave the band its stamp. In 1932, after fleeting appearances with Charlie Johnson, McKinney's Cotton Pickers, and Chick Webb, Carter formed his own big band, and it became law among New York musicians that you had arrived if you were hired by Carter. But the depression was on, and Carter's band soon went under. For the next couple of years, he subsisted as a free-lance arranger and by doing pick-up recordings. (Carter made a steady succession of such small-band recordings between 1930 and 1946, and some of them are classics. These were done with Pete Brown, Lionel Hampton, several Chocolate Dandies groups, and Coleman Hawkins.) Then, in despair, he left for Europe, to record in London, Stockholm, Amsterdam, Copenhagen, and Paris. Lionized in Europe, he was shelved in America. But he returned in 1938 and put together a big band that included such men as Joe Thomas,

17

Vic Dickenson, Coleman Hawkins, Bill Coleman, Sandy Williams, Jonah Jones, Sidney de Paris, Doc Cheatham, Emmett Berry, J. C. Heard, J. J. Johnson, and Max Roach. It was a first-rate band, but Carter's luck was still out; Benny Goodman and Artie Shaw had the public by its lapels, and two other bands—Duke Ellington's and Count Basie's—were just reaching still unequalled apogees. Carter drifted into Hollywood studio work in the mid-forties, big bands disappeared, bebop sprang up, and it wasn't until five or six years ago that he began edging back toward jazz.

Carter has an unstudied middle-of-the-road tone on the alto saxophone; in fact, his sound is as close to the ideal one as any alto saxophonist has come, barring the young John Handy—smooth and almost transparent, it has a light, slightly remote quality. Tonally, Carter's contemporaries and descendants fall neatly on one side or the other of him. Hilton Jefferson is decorous and waxy, and Paul Desmond is ethereal. The heavier-toned men include Willie Smith, whose sound is sharp and gesticulating; Tab Smith (no relation), who is all butterballs and cherubim; Pete Brown, a fat man with a fat, jumping tone; Johnny Hodges, who is Bristol Cream; and Charlie Parker, who was simply careless, often allowing his tone to slip halfway to the tenor saxophone's. In many ways, Carter's approach to improvisation forms a link between Coleman Hawkins and Lester Young. At slow and medium tempos, Carter is apt, in Young fashion, to hover around the melody, or ghosts of the melody, using legato sliding phrases, frequently fitted into lazy descending patterns, and a vibrato that is not really a vibrato but a nod toward one. The effect is a succession of orderly arabesques in slow motion. At faster speeds, Carter folds this method into a more rhythmic, Hawkinslike attack. (Carter is not an imitator of Hawkins or Young; he and Hawkins, self-taught rookies, went their own ways in the Henderson band, and in the early thirties, when Carter's style was pretty well set, Young was still an unknown sideman in King Oliver's last, disaster-ridden band. Carter has mentioned learning from Bubber Miley, Cuban Bennett [a trumpeter], Beiderbecke, and Frankie Trumbauer, the last two of whom are just beginning to be credited with the wide influence they had on Negro musicians in the late twenties.) He will open an up-tempo improvision by constructing a fleeing quasi-melodic line, which he breaks only to catch his breath, and which is full of intervals, riff figures, and pitching runs. Then, abruptly going languorous, he fashions a series of brief descending planes, each of which pours over into the next plane, lulling listeners into a calm that he will shatter by picking up fistfuls of notes and returning to a near-staccato rhythm-bound approach. Whether Carter rides his notes or barely touches them, he tints each one with his presence, his special touch; any two, or perhaps three, Carter notes make him immediately identifiable. But the singular things about his most energetic alto solos are their seemingly pre-arranged unity and their steady undercurrent of emotion. He is like a deer; one first is struck by his grace and light-ness, then by the tensions that govern such beauty.

Carter's trumpet playing, which he began recording in the mid-thirties, is a delight. It has much in common with the spare and melodious style developed by such men as Joe Thomas, Frankie Newton, Shorty Baker, and Doc Cheatham. Since it is not his chief instrument, Carter approaches it the way Babe Ruth played golf—proficiently, but largely for kicks. His legato style, parcelled out among short, easy phrases, is tinged with a nice vibrato, and his tone is bright and direct. Carter displays more emotion on the trumpet than he does on the saxophone; perhaps it is because he can ignore his "p"s and "q"s—a relaxed attitude that also occasionally leads him into mild and attractive disarrays of fluffed notes. Carter has played trumpet sparingly in his recent recordings. But the results are as of old, and this is especially agreeable at a time when such laissez-faire trumpet playing has all but vanished.

One of the persistent sorrows of jazz is Carter's abandonment of the clarinet, which he played through the thirties. (Lester Young, equally lamented, quit the instrument before 1940.) Carter's clarinet on the celebrated Chocolate Dandies sides made in 1930 has a timeless air, and so have the bits and pieces of it that pop winningly to the surface of his big-band records of ten years later. These recordings suggest that Carter might easily have been *the* jazz clarinettist. His tone was new. It had none of the unctuous liquidity of the New Orleans men and none of the manly woodenness of the later white clarinettists. It fell handsomely between, and—like his saxophone—it offered the ideal sound for the instrument. His attack was close to his saxophone one. Fertile double-time runs dominated his saxophone and trumpet plane phrases, but there was never any urgency. (There is nothing more racking than a clarinettist playing beyond his means.) The clarinet is a demanding instrument, but Carter handled it with an assured looseness that gave the impression he was using it for beautiful doodles.

Carter's songs often have a blue, minor cast, but his arranging is an extension of his instrumental buoyancy. His arrangements for Henderson were in a sense done for the wrong band. They demand a flowing rhythm section and precise execution by the horns, neither of which the Henderson band had until the mid-thirties. Nonetheless, the spareness of these Carter arrangements suggested for the first time how a big jazz band could get around its Prussian tendencies. Unlike Ellington, who often blends all his instruments, Carter regards a big band as made up chiefly of saxophones, with trumpets-trombones-and-rhythm in attendance. He doesn't pit the sections against one another; instead, he often uses them in pastel sequences whose colors and timbres are homogeneous. Carter insinuates with a big band rather than startles. He builds his arrangements around his saxophones, which he supplies with resilient passages, and these, perhaps unwittingly, are generally close approximations of his alto-saxophone solos. These leavening figures are enclosed or underlined by salutary trumpet accents or riffs, frequently muted, and occasional trombone choir effects. His arrangements, particularly for his second big band, have an improvised air; the writing is as spontaneous as the solos. Unfortunately, Carter's arranging methods have never caught on. The long-prevalent Henderson vein was finally worked out by Stan Kenton, while Ellington's ingenuity has resulted largely in the lugubrious chants of Gil Evans. For a time, Basie reflected some of Carter's tricks (there was considerable similarity between the two bands in the late thirties), but he has given them up, leaving the big band in general pretty much where it was in 1940.

Carter almost always sounds at ease on records. This is true to such an extent on his "Further Definitions: Benny Carter and His Orchestra" (Impulse!) that, with a couple of notable exceptions, his compatriots (Coleman Hawkins, Phil Woods, Charlie Rouse, Dick Katz, John Collins, Jimmy Garrison, and Jo Jones) seem strained or sluggish. More often than not, Hawkins lumbers, which depresses Jones, who drags the beat. Garrison swings uneasily back and

forth on his bass between far-out notes and twanging traditional ones. Woods is emotional, Rouse hesitant, and Katz
unswinging. But this is all to the good, since it sets off
Carter's solos (alto saxophone), which are perhaps the
freest, most jubilant ones he has recorded. Listen to him
in "Honeysuckle Rose," "Cherry," and "Doozy." And listen
to his longest, most sustained written passage on the record,
which comes at the end of his "Blue Star" and which is a
distillation of all his solos. Indeed, "Blue Star" is, a few
blank spots notwithstanding, close to a classic performance.
It is a lovely tune, and Hawkins, well pulled together (as
he is in his magnificent coda in "Body and Soul"), plays
the melody against handsome Carter ensemble figures in
that bravura, intense, frontal way he uses these days. And
Carter's solo matches Hawkins'. Rouse and Woods also
have their moments, mainly in "Doozy," an infectious Carter medium-tempo blues. Carter's written and improvised
contributions to the record have a *beginning* air, and the
only things that are missing are his trumpet and clarinet.
But perhaps he will take them up next time around.

# Even His Feet Look Sad

In hopes of finding out how Pee Wee Russell, the unique and imperishable jazz clarinettist, has survived a notably exhausting profession so well and so long, I telephoned him at his apartment, on King Street, not long after his fifty-sixth birthday to ask if I could visit him. I called late in the afternoon, when jazz musicians, like most nocturnal creatures, are beginning to stretch and stir about. The phone rang seven or eight times, and I had started to hang up when a brusque, deep woman's voice answered. It was Russell's wife, Mary. An old friend of the Russells had told me that she is shy but peppery. "Wait a minute till I get my hat off," she said. I apologized for hurrying her. "Don't be silly, I haven't worn a hat for twenty years, but I just came in the door." There was a thump, a dog barked, and Mrs. Russell said, "All right." Before I had finished explaining my call, she interrupted me. "Do you know Pee Wee? I mean what do you *think* of him? Oh, not those funny sounds that come out of his clarinet. Do you *know* him? You think he's kindly and sensitive and sweet?" I said I'd met him only briefly but that those words seemed to fit. "Yes. Well, he's intelligent and he doesn't use dope and he is sensitive, but Pee Wee can also be *mean*. In fact, Pee Wee's the most egocentric man I know." Mrs. Russell laughed, abruptly but pleasantly. "Anyway, he's in Pittsburgh on a job. He finishes Saturday and he'll be home the day after. I'll tell him to call you when he gets back."

Russell belongs to a special group of people. Despite the nimbuses their admirers paste on them, and despite the lightning pleasures their work occasionally gives them, jazz musicians generally lead bedevilled lives. The best of them, though artists, keep upside-down white-collar hours for white-collar pay—when there is work to be had, that is—but without the usual white-collar props of paid vacations and the like. Their working conditions are often noisome and they are by necessity semi-nomads who sometimes subsist for weeks on blue-plate specials and the kind of sleep you get in buses and damp hotel beds. They are part of the entertainment world, but they enjoy little of the renown and pampering granted many of even its most ephemeral figures. As a minority group made up of representatives of old-line minority groups (Negroes, Jews, Italians, Irish), they are, moreover, caught between a fickle public and a mossy body of middlemen—night-club owners, booking agents, impresarios, disc jockeys, recording directors, and union officials. Worst of all, they are at the mercy of a particularly demanding music. Improvisation, the core of jazz, insists that a performer be an instant and non-repetitive poet, not simply an assiduous reader of orchestrations, and that he be this lyric creature several hours a night, six nights a week, year in and year out. The emotional and physical abrasion of such a creative schedule is unparalleled in the performing arts. (This is why there is so little true improvisation; most jazz soloists patent a reliable set of mannerisms—certain phrases, certain timbres, even entire solos—that they fall back on when their imaginations stall, and some of them hobble through whole careers on such crutches.) Not surprisingly, the number of middle-aged jazz musicians still working fruitfully and freshly is small and select. Of these marvels, Russell is at once the most scarred and the most triumphant. He has weathered a long and near-fatal illness. He has borne a clownlike face and figure and an inborn timidity that have type-cast him as a beloved freak. He has been afflicted (or blessed) since the twenties with an iconoclastic style of playing that is still widely misunderstood and even hooted at. Russell's instrument itself is a problem; in many ways it is the most difficult one in jazz, and, on top of that, it is now just about out of fashion. For all this, Russell is more robust than ever before in his forty-year career. He now works pretty much when he wants and has money in the bank. He has outlived or outstripped such contemporary clarinettists as Sidney Bechet, Benny Goodman, Artie Shaw, Edmond Hall, Irving Fazola, Buster Bailey, Joe Marsala, and Barney Bigard. Most important, his playing has taken on in recent years a subtlety, serenity, and poignance that few jazz musicians, let alone clarinettists, have ever achieved.

Diffidence and economic need persuaded Russell to play with Chicago, or Eddie Condon-style, musicians for most of that career, but the lumping together has never been comfortable. Indeed, since 1929 his best recordings have attested that he is not a Dixieland clarinettist but a kind of swing musician with modern overtones. The clarinet is a precise, small-toned instrument, and it is not easy, without sounding peevish or pendulous, to transmit emotion through it. But this problem has never bothered Russell, who, in a sense, has long since *absorbed* his instrument. His style is restless, furtive, unpredictable, eloquent, and mildly sardonic. Unlike mose jazz clarinettists, he has several tones. In the lowest register, which he seems increasingly to prefer, he gets a hushed, edgeless sound. In the middle range, his tone becomes more explicit, suggesting soft, highly polished wood. In the high registers, where the clarinet tends to dwindle into a flute, Russell sounds remote and thin. (He has all but set aside the derisive, discontented growl that once coated his middle- and low-register tones.) He is particularly affecting in a medium- or slow-tempo blues. He often starts such a solo in the lower (or chalumeau) range with a delicate rush of notes that are intensely multiplied into a single, unbroken phrase that lasts the entire chorus. Thus, he will begin with a pattern of winged double-time staccato notes that, moving steadily downward, will be abruptly pierced by adolescent falsetto jumps. When he has nearly sunk out of hearing, he reverses this pattern, keeping his myriad of notes back to back, and then swings into an easy uphill-downdale movement, topping each rise and fall with an oddly placid vibrato. By this time, his first chorus is over, and one has the impression of having just passed through a crowd of jostling, whispering people. Russell takes what appears to be his first breath, and, breaking the tension momentarily, opens the next chorus with a languorous, questioning phrase, made up of perhaps just four notes, at least one of which will be a spiny dissonance of the sort favored by Thelonious Monk. A closely linked variation follows, and Russell may fill out his chorus by reaching behind him and producing an ironed-out paraphrase of the chalumeau first chorus. In his final chorus, he moves snakily up toward the middle register with a series of tissue-paper notes and placid rests, adopting a legato attack that allows the listener to move back from the edge of his seat. Then, lest the listener nod, he finishes the solo with an abrupt cluster of flatted notes. An unmistakable gladdening quality pervades much of Russell's work at faster tempos and on standard materials. He uses fewer notes, leans to runs and legato musings, and uses a shiny, declarative tone. He is also courtly, paying the composers of the tunes he uses the compliment of showing that they have inspired in him new melodies that often unintentionally match and sometimes surpass the originals.

On Sunday evening, Russell called me, and we arranged to meet on Tuesday morning at his apartment. "I'm kind of bushed," he said. "Give me a day to catch my breath." Russell lived then on the third floor of a peeling brownstone. When I stepped out of the elevator, he was standing in his door, a pepper-and-salt schnauzer barking and dancing about behind him. "Shut up, Winkie, for God's sake!" Russell said, and made a loose, whirlpool gesture at the dog. A tall, close-packed, slightly bent man, Russell has a wry, wandering face, dominated by a generous nose. He has down-slanting eyes and arched eyebrows, a brush mustache, and a full chin. A heavy trellis of wrinkles holds the features in place. His gray-black hair is combed absolutely flat. Russell smiled, without showing any teeth, and led the way down a short, bright hall, through a Pullman kitchen, and into a dark living room, brownish in color, with two day beds and two easy chairs, a bureau, a television, and several small tables. The corners of the room were stuffed with suitcases and fat manila envelopes. Under one table were two clarinet cases. The shades on the three windows were drawn, and only one lamp was lit. The room was suffocatingly hot. Russell, who was dressed in a tan, short-sleeved sports shirt, navy-blue trousers, black socks, black square-toed shoes, and dark glasses, waved me to one of the day beds and sat down in a huge red leather chair. "Mary was embarrassed about your coming here," Russell said, taking off his glasses and lighting a cigarette. "We've lived in this cave six years too long. Mary's no housekeeper, but she tries. Every time a new cleaning gadget comes out, she buys it and stuffs it in a closet with all the other ones. I bought an apartment three years ago in a development on Eighth Avenue in the Chelsea district, and we're moving in. It has a balcony and a living room and a bedroom and a full kitchen. We'll have to get a cleaning woman to keep it respectable." Russell laughed—a sighing sound that seemed to travel down his nose. "Mary got me up at seven this morning before she went to work, but I haven't had any breakfast, which is my own fault. I've been on the road four weeks—two at the Theatrical Café, in Cleveland, with George Wein, and two in Pittsburgh with Jimmy McPartland. I shouldn't have gone to Pittsburgh. I celebrated my birthday there, and I'm still paying for it, physically and mentally. And the music. I can't go near 'Muskrat Ramble' any more without freezing up. Last fall, I did a television show with McPartland and Eddie Condon and Bud Freeman and Gene Krupa and Joe Sullivan— all the Chicago boys. We made a record just before it. They sent me a copy the other day and I listened halfway through and turned it off and gave it to the super. Mary was here, and she said, 'Pee Wee, you sound like you did when I first knew you in 1942.' I'd gone back twenty years in three hours. There's no room left in that music. It tells *you* how to solo. You're as good as the company you keep. You go with fast musicians, housebroken musicians, and you improve."

Russell spoke in a low, nasal voice. Sometimes he stuttered, and sometimes whole sentences came out in a sluicelike manner, and trailed off into mumbles and down-the-nose laughs. His face was never still. When he is surprised, he opens his mouth slightly and pops his eyes, rolling them up to the right. When he is thoughtful, he glances quickly about, tugs his nose, and cocks his head. When he is amused, everything turns down instead of up— the edges of his eyes, his eyebrows, and the corners of his mouth. Russell got up and walked with short, crabwise steps into the kitchen. "Talking dries me up," he said over his shoulder. "I'm going to have an ale."

While Russell was in the kitchen, I took a look at the four framed photographs hung on the walls. Two of them show what is already unmistakably Russell, in a dress and long, curly hair. In one, he is sucking his thumb. In the other, an arm is draped about a cocker spaniel. The third shows him at about fifteen, in military uniform, standing beneath a tree, and in the fourth he is wearing a dinner jacket and a wing collar and holding an alto saxophone. He looks demure and pleased in this one. Russell came back, a bottle of ale in one hand and a pink plastic cup in the other. "Isn't that something? A wing collar. I was sixteen, and my father bought me that saxophone for three hundred and seventy-five dollars." We sat down. Russell filled his cup and put the bottle on the floor. "My father was a steward at the Planter's Hotel, in St. Louis, when I was born, and I was named after him—Charles Ellsworth. I was a late child and the only one. My mother was forty. She was a very intelligent person. She'd been a newspaper-woman in Chicago, and she used to read a lot. Being a late child, I was excess baggage. I was like a toy. My parents, who were pretty well off, would say, You want this or that, it's yours. But I never really knew them. Not that they were cold, but they just didn't divulge anything. Someone discovered a few years ago that my father had a lot of brothers. I never knew he had *any*. When I was little, we moved to Muskogee, where my father and a friend hit a couple of gas wells. I took up piano and drums and violin, roughly in that order. One day, after I'd played a school recital, I put my violin in the back seat of our car and my mother got in and sat on it. That was the end of my violin career. 'Thank God that's over,' I said to myself. I tried the clarinet when I was about twelve or thirteen. I studied with Charlie Merrill, who was in the pit band in the only theatre in Muskogee. Oklahoma was a dry state and he sneaked corn liquor during the lessons. My first job was playing at a resort lake. I played for about twelve hours and made three dollars. Once in a while, my father'd take me into the Elks' Club, where I heard Yellow Nunez, the New Orleans clarinet player. He had a trombone and piano and drums with him, and he played the lead in the ensembles. On my next job, *I* played the lead, using the violin part. Of course, I'd already heard the Original Dixieland Jazz Band on records. I was anxious in school—anxious to finish it. I'd drive my father to work in his car and, instead of going on to school, pick up a friend and drive around all day. I wanted to study music at the University of Oklahoma, but my aunt —she was living with us—said I was bad and wicked and persuaded my parents to take me out of high school and send me to Western Military Academy, in Alton, Illinois. My aunt is still alive. Mary keeps in touch with her, but I won't speak to her. I majored in wigwams at the military school, and I lasted just a year. Charlie Smith, the jazz historian, wrote the school not long ago and they told him Thomas Hart Benton and I are their two most distinguished nongraduates." Russell laughed and poured out more ale.

"We moved back to St. Louis and I began working in Herbert Berger's hotel band. It was Berger who gave me my nickname. Then I went with a tent show to Moulton, Iowa. Berger had gone to Juárez, Mexico, and he sent me a telegram asking me to join him. That was around the time my father gave me the saxophone. I was a punk kid, but my parents—can you imagine?—said, Go ahead, good riddance. When I got to Juárez, Berger told me, to my surprise, I wouldn't be working with him but across the street with piano and drums in the Big Kid's Palace, which had a bar about a block long. There weren't any microphones and you had to blow. I don't know what I used for a reed. It must have been a board. Three days later there were union troubles and I got fired and joined Berger. This wasn't long after Pancho Villa, and all the Mexicans wore guns. There'd be shooting in the streets day and night, but nobody paid any attention. You'd just duck into a saloon and wait until it was over. The day Berger hired me, he gave me a ten-dollar advance. That was a lot of money and I went crazy on it. It was the custom in Juárez to hire a kind of cop at night for a dollar, and if you got in a scrape he'd clop the other guy with his billy. So I hired one and got drunk and we went to see a bulldog-badger fight, which is the most vicious thing you can imagine. I kept on drinking and finally told the cop to beat it, that I knew the way back to the hotel in El Paso, across the river. Or I thought I did, because I got lost and had an argument over a tab and the next thing I was in jail. What a place, Mister! A big room with bars all the way around and bars for a ceiling and a floor like a cesspool, and full of the worst cutthroats you ever saw. I was there three days on bread and water before Berger found me and paid ten dollars to get me out." Russell's voice trailed off. He squinted at the bottle, which was empty, and stood up. "Let's get some lunch around here."

It was a crisp, sunny day, and the light outside was

blinding. We headed west on King Street, turned up Varick Street and into West Houston. Russell pointed at a small restaurant with a pine-panelled front, called the Lodge. "Mary and I eat here sometimes evenings. The food's all right." We found a table in the back room, which was decorated with more panelling and a small pair of antlers. A waiter came up. "Where you been, Pee Wee? You look fifteen years younger." Russell mumbled a denial and something about his birthday and Pittsburgh and ordered a Scotch-on-the-rocks and ravioli. I ordered a Martini and spaghetti with mushrooms. We sipped for a while in silence, studying the tablecloth. Then Russell looked up and said, "Did you know for ten years I couldn't eat *any*thing? All during the forties. I'd be hungry and take a couple of bites of delicious steak, say, and have to put the fork down— finished. My food wouldn't go from my upper stomach to my lower stomach. I lived on brandy milkshakes and scrambled-egg sandwiches. And on whiskey. The doctors couldn't find a thing. No tumors, no ulcers. I got as thin as a lamppost and so weak I had to drink half a pint of whiskey in the morning before I could get out of bed. It began to affect my mind, and sometime in 1948 I left Mary and went to Chicago. Everything there is a blank, except what people have told me since. They say I did things that were unheard of, they were so wild. Early in 1950, I went on to San Francisco. By this time my stomach was bloated and I was so feeble I remember someone pushing me up Bush Street and me stopping to put my arms around each telegraph pole to rest. I guess I was dying. Some friends finally got me into the Franklin Hospital and they discovered I had pancreatitis and multiple cysts on my liver. The pancreatitis was why I couldn't eat for so many years. They operated, and I was in that hospital nine months. People gave benefits around the country to pay the bills. I was still crazy. I told them Mary was after me for money. Hell, she was back in New York, minding her own business. When they sent me back here, they put me in St. Clare's Hospital under an assumed name—McGrath, I think it was—so Mary couldn't find me. After they let me out, I stayed with Eddie Condon. Mary heard where I was and came over and we went out and sat in Washington Square park. Then she took me home. After three years."

Russell started in on his ravioli and ordered two coffees. He looked mournful, and to get his mind off what he had told me, I asked him what he thought about when he improvised. His face cleared, and he picked up a spoon and twiddled the ends of his long, beautifully tapered fingers on it, as if it were a clarinet. "You take each solo like it was the last one you were going to play in your life. What notes to hit, and when to hit them—that's the secret. You can *make* a particular phrase with just one note. Maybe at the end, maybe at the beginning. It's like a little pattern. What will lead in quietly and not be too emphatic. Sometimes I jump the right chord and use what seems wrong to the next guy but I *know* is right for me. I usually think about four bars ahead what I am going to play. Sometimes things go wrong, and I have to scramble. If I can make it to the bridge of the tune, I know everything will be all right. I suppose it's not that obnoxious the average musician would notice. When I play the blues, mood, frame of mind, enters into it. One day your choice of notes would be melancholy, a blue trend, a drift of blue notes. The next day your choice of notes would be more cheerful. Standard tunes are different. Some of them require a legato treatment, and others have sparks of rhythm you have to bring out. In lots of cases, your solo depends

33

on who you're following. The guy played a great chorus, you say to yourself. How am I going to follow *that*? I applaud him inwardly, and it becomes a matter of silent pride. Not jealousy, mind you. A kind of competition. So I make myself a guinea pig—what the hell, I'll try something new. All this goes through your mind in a split second. You start and if it sounds good to you you keep it up and write a little tune of your own. I get in bad habits and I'm trying to break myself of a couple right now. A little triplet thing, for one. Fast tempos are good to display your technique, but that's all. You prove you know the chords, but you don't have the time to insert those new little chords you could at slower tempos. Or if you do, they go unnoticed. I haven't been able to play the way I want to until recently. Coming out of that illness has given me courage, a little moral courage in my playing. When I was sick, I lived night by night. It was bang! straight ahead with the whiskey. As a result, my playing was a series of desperations. Now I have a freedom. For the past five or so months, Marshall Brown, the trombonist, and I have been rehearsing a quartet in his studio—just Brown, on the bass cornet, which is like a valve trombone; me, a bass, and drums. We get together a couple of days a week and we *work*. I didn't realize what we had until I listened to the tapes we've made. We sound like seven or eight men. Something's always going. There's a lot of bottom in the group. And we can do anything we want—soft, crescendo, decrescendo, textures, voicings. What musical knowledge we have, we use it. A little while ago, an a.-and-r. man from one of the New York jazz labels approached me and suggested a record date—on his terms. Instead, I took him to Brown's studio to hear the tapes. He was cool at first, but by the third number he looked different. I scared him with a stiff price, so we'll see what happens. A record with the quartet would feel just right. And no 'Muskrat Ramble' and no 'Royal Garden Blues.' "

When we left the Lodge, the sunlight seemed to accelerate Russell, and we got back to King Street quickly. He unlocked the door, and Winkie barked. "Cut that out, Winkie!" Russell shouted. "Mary'll be here soon and take you out." He removed his jacket, folded it carefully on one of the day beds, and sat down in the red chair with a grunt.

"What did you do after Juárez?" I asked.

"What? Oh, Juárez. I wish Mary was here. She knows more about me than I'll ever know. Well, I went with Berger to the Coast and back to St. Louis, where I made my first record, in 1923 or 1924. 'Fuzzy Wuzzy Bird,' by Herbert Berger and his Coronado Hotel Orchestra. The bad notes in the reed passages are me. I also worked on the big riverboats—the J. S., the St. Paul—during the day and then stayed at night to listen to the good bands, the Negro bands like Fate Marable's and Charlie Creath's. Then Sonny Lee, the trombonist, asked me did I want to go to Houston and play in Peck Kelley's group, Peck Kelley's Bad Boys. At this time, spats and a derby were the vogue, and that's what I was wearing when I got there. Kelley looked at me in the station and didn't say a word. We got in a cab and I could feel him still looking at me, so I rolled down the window and threw the derby out. Kelley laughed and thanked me. He took me straight to Goggan's music store and sat down at a piano and started to play. He was marvellous, a kind of stride pianist, and I got panicky. About ten minutes later, a guy named Jack Teagarden walked in, took a trombone off the wall, and *he* started to play. I went over to Peck when they finished and said, 'Peck, I'm in over my head. Let me work a week and make my fare home.' But I got over it and I was with Kelley several months." Russell went into the kitchen to get another bottle of ale. "Not long after I got back to St. Louis," he said when he got back, "Sonny Lee brought Bix Beiderbecke around to my house, and bang! we hit it right off. We were never apart for a couple of years—day, night, good, bad, sick, well, broke, drunk. Then Bix left to join Jean Goldkette's band and Red Nichols sent for me to come to New York. That was 1927. I went straight to the old Manger Hotel and found a note in my box: Come to a speakeasy under the Roseland Ballroom. I went over and there was Red Nichols and Eddie Lang and Miff Mole and Vic Berton. I got panicky again. They told me there'd be a recording date at Brunswick the next morning at nine, and don't be late. I got there at eight-fifteen. The place was empty, except for a handyman. Mole arrived first. He said, 'You look peaked, kid,' and opened his trombone case and took out a quart. Everybody had quarts. We made 'Ida,' and it wasn't any trouble at all. In the late twenties and early thirties I worked in a lot of bands and made God knows how many records in New York. Cass Hagen, Bert Lown, Paul Specht, Ray Levy, the Scranton Sirens, Red Nichols. We lived uptown at night. We heard Elmer Snowden and Luis Russell and Ellington. Once I went to a ballroom where Fletcher Henderson was. Coleman Hawkins had a bad cold and I sat in for him one set. My God, those scores! They were written in six flats, eight flats, I don't know how many flats. I never saw anything like it. Buster Bailey was in the section next to me, and after a couple of numbers I told him, 'Man, I came up here to have a good time, not to work. I've had enough. Where's Hawkins?'

"I joined Louis Prima around 1935. We were at the Famous Door, on Fifty-second Street, and a couple of hoodlums loaded with knives cornered Prima and me and said they wanted protection money every week—fifty bucks from Prima and twenty-five from me. Well, I didn't want any of that. I'd played a couple of private parties for Lucky Luciano, so I called him. He sent Pretty Amberg over in a big car with a bodyguard as chauffeur. Prima sat in the back with Amberg and I sat in front with the body-guard. Nobody said much, just 'Hello' and 'Goodbye,' and for a week they drove Prima and me from our hotels to a midday radio broadcast, back to our hotels, picked us up for work at night, and took us home after. We never saw the protection-money boys again. Red McKenzie, the singer, got me into Nick's, here in the Village, in 1938, and I worked there and at Condon's place for most of the next ten years. I have a sorrow about that time. Those guys made a joke of me, a clown, and I let myself be treated that way because I was afraid. I didn't know where else to go, where to take refuge. I'm not sure how all of us feel about each other now, though we're 'Hello, Pee Wee,' 'Hello, Eddie,' and all that. Since my sickness, Mary's given me confidence, and so has George Wein. I've worked for him with a lot of fast musicians in Boston, in New York, at Newport, on the road, and in Europe last year. I'll head a kind of house band if he opens a club here. A quiet little group. But Nick's did one thing. That's where I first met Mary."

At that moment, a key turned in the lock, and Mary Russell walked quickly down the hall and into the living room. A tall, slightly stooped, pretty, black-haired woman in her forties, she was wearing a green silk dress and black harlequin glasses.

"Did Winkie bother you?" she asked me, plumping herself down and taking off her shoes. "She's the kind of dog that's always barking except at burglars. Pee Wee, you forgot to say, 'Did you have a hard day at the office, dear?' And where's my tea?"

Russell got up and shuffled into the kitchen.

"I work in the statistics and advertising part of Robert Hall clothes," she said. "I've got a quick mind for figures. I like the job and the place. It's full of respectable ladies. Pee Wee, did I get any mail?"

"Next to you, on the table. A letter," he said from the kitchen.

"It's from my brother Al," she said. "I always look for checks in letters. My God, there *is* a check! Now why do you suppose he did that? And there's a P.S.: 'Please excuse the pencil.' I like that. It makes me feel good."

"How much did he send you?" Russell asked, handing Mrs. Russell her tea.

"You're not going to get a cent," she said. "You know what I found the other day, Pee Wee? Old letters from you. Love letters. Every one says the same thing: I love you, I miss you. Just the dates are different." Mrs. Russell, who speaks in a quick, decisive way, laughed, and turned to me. "You know, Pee Wee and I had an awful wedding. It was at City Hall. Danny Alvin, the drummer, stood up for us. He and Pee Wee wept. I didn't, but *they* did. After the ceremony, Danny tried to borrow money from me. Pee Wee didn't buy me any flowers and a friend lent us the wedding ring. Pee Wee has never given me a wedding ring. The one I'm wearing a nephew gave me a year ago. Just to make it proper, he said. That's not the way a woman wants to get married. Pee Wee, we ought to do it all over again. I have a rage in me to be proper. I don't play bridge and go to beauty parlors and I don't have women friends like other women. But one thing Pee Wee and I have that no one else has: we never stop talking when we're with each other. Pee Wee, you know why I love you? You're like Papa. Every time Mama got up to tidy something, he'd say, Clara, sit down, and she would. That's what you do. I loved my parents. They were Russian Jews from Odessa. Chaloff was their name. I was born on the lower East Side. I was a charity case and the doctor gave me my name, and signed the birth certificate—Dr. E. Condon. Isn't that weird? I was one of nine kids and six are left. I've got twenty nephews and nieces. Did Pee Wee tell you about Pretty Amberg?"

I nodded.

"He worships those inchbrows. Lucky Luciano was his dream man."

"He was an acquaintance," Russell snorted.

"I'll never know you completely, Pee Wee," Mrs. Russell said. She took a sip of tea, holding the cup with both hands. "Sometimes Pee Wee can't sleep. He sits in the kitchen and plays solitaire, and I go to bed in here and sing to him. Awful songs like 'Belgian Rose' and 'Carolina Mammy.' I have a terrible voice."

"Oh, God!" Russell muttered. "The worst thing is she knows *all* the lyrics."

"I not only sing, I write," she said, laughing. "I wrote a three-act play. My hero's name is Tiny Ballard. An Italian clarinet player. It has wonderful dialogue."

"Mary's no saloon girl, coming where I work," he said. "She outgrew that long ago. She reads about ten books a week. You could have been a writer, Mary."

"I don't know why I wrote about a clarinet player. I hate the clarinet. Pee Wee's playing embarrasses me. But

I like trombones: Miff Mole and Brad Gowans. And I like Duke Ellington. Last New Year's Eve, Pee Wee and I were at a party and Duke kissed me at midnight."

"Where was I?" he asked.

"You had a clarinet stuck in your mouth," she said. "The story of your life, or part of your life. Once when Pee Wee had left me and was in Chicago, he came back to New York for a couple of days. He denies it. He doesn't remember it. He went to the night club where I was working as a hat-check girl and asked to see me. I said no. The boss's wife went out and took one look at him and came back and said, 'At least go out and talk to him. He's pathetic. Even his feet look sad.'"

Russell made an apologetic face. "That was twelve years ago, Mary. I have no claim to being an angel."

She sat up very straight. "Pee Wee, this room is hot. Let's go out and have dinner on my brother Al."

"I'll put on a tie," he said.

1963

# His Lordship

Jazz, an organic music, invariably corrects its deficiencies. When the New Orleans ensemble began to pall, the first great soloists emerged, to provide contrast and an ensemble-soloist tension. When the big bands finally proved militaristic, they simply vanished, making way for a host of flexible small units. When the steady four-four beat, an improvement on the lopsided two-four beat, became tyrannical, Sid Catlett, Jo Jones, and Kenny Clarke broke it up and inspired the free-rhythm drummers led by Max Roach. Improvisation, too, has been steadily remodelled. Melodic embellishment was replaced by improvisation on chords, which was set aside for melodic-rhythmic improvisation, which in turn is going down before free, or abstract, improvisation. But one of the major failings in jazz—thin materials—is only now being remedied. To be sure, composers like W. C. Handy, Jelly Roll Morton, and Duke Ellington have furnished a long list of substantial and original jazz compositions. In the main, though, the jazz repertory has up to now been restricted to the blues, standards by the likes of Gershwin, Kern, and Porter, and nonsense novelty numbers; jazz has been how and not what. This is no longer true. A compositional revolution, begun when bebop musicians altered the chords and structures of certain evergreens, is now being led by such composers as Charlie Mingus, John Lewis, George Russell, Jimmy Giuffre, Thelonious Monk, and Ornette Coleman. Though the written jazz these men have contributed in the past ten years naturally varies in intent and quality, it has common characteristics: it has *content* (sometimes emotional, sometimes intellectual, sometimes both), it often borders on atonality, it is complex, rhythmically and melodically, and is difficult to play, and it is—within its scope—a new Western music. One of the most absorbing and daring of these composers is Ornette Coleman, the alto saxophonist.

Not long ago, Coleman gave a brilliant Town Hall concert, in which ten of the eleven numbers were his; the eleventh was an unaccompanied bass solo. Eight of his works were performed by him along with David Izenzohn, bass, and Charles Moffett, drums; one was played by a string quartet, three of whose members, refreshingly, were Negroes; and in the last the trio was augmented by a rhythm-and-blues group made up of piano, guitar, and bass. By and large, Coleman's compositions are intricate investigations of certain moods, rhythmic patterns, and tonal areas. They are not really melodic structures, nor are they predictable rhythmically, for their rhythm centers shift continually, occasionally from phrase to phrase. A single number may contain long ad-lib passages, marching rhythms, shuffle rhythms, furious four-four passages, and dozen-layered polyrhythms. Coleman's slow pieces are often magnificent. They have a thick, grieving quality that is spelled out in heavy legato phrases, which move all over the scale and which include patches of pure, sky-blue melody. At faster tempos, the music is compressed into lightning lines that demand at least three listenings before they can be appreciated. Two of Coleman's statuesque slow studies were on view at Town Hall—"I Don't Love You," which has a spooky melodic line composed of drawn-out, bullying slides and high, tight, clenched notes, and "Sadness," a blues that, with its long-held notes and ad-lib tempo, is one of the lowest blues ever invented. Coleman played just three choruses, developing—in no more than a minute or two—an almost visible mood. With the exception of his piece for the string quartet (a witty distillation of some of his jazz ensemble devices) and the tongue-in-cheek "Blues Misused" (done with the rhythm-and-blues group), the rest of the numbers were mercurial medium-fast compositions, most notable for a series of Coleman glisses (in "The Ark") in which all the notes, though slurred, were as identifiable as a row of toes under a blanket.

Coleman's playing, which has not been heard for nearly a year, was stunning. Much of his earlier madness and diabolic sounds has been harnessed into soft, subtle, understated phrases—a glancing, dodging approach suggestive of Benny Carter and Ben Webster. His accompanists, however, were less celestial. Izenzohn is a virtuoso arco performer, and Moffett, while bulging with ideas, is short on technique and taste. The rhythm-and-blues trio was mostly inaudible, and the string quartet played with energy and understanding, if not precision.

# Anti-Music

The avant-garde is the last refuge of the untalented. But it can also be a quicksand for the talented. Jimmy Giuffre, the gifted clarinettist, saxophonist, and composer, regrettably proves the latter proposition. Giuffre's pioneering has not been accidental. He started boldly, in the early fifties, with experiments in free improvisation, ad-lib rhythmic patterns, and odd instrumentations. In 1956, he stepped back a few paces and fashioned a delicate trio (himself, a guitar, and a bass) that seemed farther out than it actually was. It used unconventional rhythms and harmonies and fresh, partly written and partly improvised ensembles, but its materials, composed largely by Giuffre, were safe old blues and downhome compositions that ultimately gave the group its stamp. Then, heading on again, Giuffre began listening to Thelonious Monk, Sonny Rollins, and Ornette Coleman. Unfortunately, they absorbed him and by 1960 his playing had become a strained mélange of theirs. His composing also stiffened. This disturbing sense of strain suggested that Giuffre was going against his own sweet lyrical grain. He was and still is.

The newest Giuffre, glimpsed at a concert at Town Hall, has shed the 1960 Giuffre. The long-gone 1956 Giuffre was a soft version of Lester Young, particularly on the clarinet, which Giuffre played almost completely in the chalumeau register. The 1963 Giuffre is splintered Coleman, or the untamed Coleman of two years ago. Indeed, Giuffre, who plays only the clarinet now, doesn't have a style any more. His attack is a dismaying crazy quilt of Coleman runs (upanddown upanddown upanddown, each one faster than the last), freakish squeaks and growls, and hard, atonal fragments. His new compositions merely float these raw clumps of sound. The three numbers played at Town Hall by Giuffre and his present group (Steve Swallow on bass and Paul Bley on piano), who followed performances of Sammartini, Mozart, and Schubert by the New Chamber Orchestra and other hands, could easily have been run together into a single work. They were wholly abstract and free. There were no set rhythms and keys, and very little form. The emotion that invariably underpins Coleman's most wayward solos was absent. It was to all intents and purposes an anti-music. In the first number, "A Tryst," Giuffre introduced a rapid, jerky figure, which was echoed by Bley and Swallow. A series of Giuffre squeaks and arpeggios followed. Bley struck a chord, and Giuffre switched to a quiet ad-lib melodic fragment, backed by otherworldly Bley chords. More Giuffre anti-music; a short solo from Swallow, and that, in seven minutes, was it. Giuffre's accompanists left the stage and he played by himself for three minutes. The audience tittered. In the final number, Giuffre's "Composition for Trio and String Orchestra," the trio went through an approximation of the first number, and here and there executed unison or contrapuntal passages with the New Chamber Orchestra. Along the way, Swallow took a brief, agile solo and Bley outlined some mock Debussy. In the background, Giuffre, momentarily reverting to himself, played pleasant, old-fashioned clarinet hums. In the circumstances, they sounded revolutionary.

# The Street

By and large, jazz is manfully unmindful of its surroundings. During the thirty years New York has been its headquarters, the music has been played in ballrooms, theatres, supper clubs, night clubs, hotels, Macy's, museums, concert halls, stadiums, Madison Square Garden, classrooms, school and college auditoriums, Central Park, churches, subways, radio and television studios, in the street, and on the floor of the Stock Exchange. It has, though, centered on three areas—Harlem, Broadway and the Fifties, and Greenwich Village. In the twenties, jazz was simply utilitarian; in New York, it could be found in the Harlem and Broadway ballrooms and behind the floor shows in night clubs like Connie's Inn, the Kentucky Club, and the Cotton Club. After prohibition, the focus shifted gradually to Fifty-second Street, between Fifth and Seventh Avenues, where the music was almost entirely for listening. (The Savoy, the Apollo, Minton's, and Monroe's remained essential outposts in Harlem.) Fifty-second Street, or The Street, as it came to be known, was spotted by the realtors after the Second World War, and the music began a retreat to the Village, where a few jazz night clubs had existed since the late thirties, and to a handful of places in the East Fifties. At present, there is no center; jazz has been scattered.

48

# The Street

Fifty-second Street was the most brilliant of the communes. The first club on it was the Onyx, an upstairs speakeasy, which later moved downstairs and across the street, and the only remaining one is the Hickory House. The Street was in its glory between 1940 and 1945. Its clubs —the Onyx, the Three Deuces, the Club Downbeat, Jimmy Ryan's, the Spotlite, and the Famous Door—were clustered toward the west end of the block between Fifth and Sixth (Kelly's Stable was, and Hickory House still is, in the next block), and they frequently changed hands and names and swapped locations. These vanished clubs occupied the ground floors of seedy brownstones and had interchangeable interiors. There was a small vestibule, with a coffin-sized coatroom, and, beyond, a bar along one wall. This area, which on Saturday nights resembled a football rally, gave onto a forest of postage-stamp tables, and at the end of the room, flanked by rest rooms and a nominal kitchen, was a tiny bandstand on which four men were comfortable and five a crowd. The décor ran to stamped-tin ceilings, tinted mirrors, maroon velours hangings, and water-stained plaster. The clubs were dark and smoky, the liquor was bad but cheap, and they smelled like abandoned caves. But they were perfect places to hear jazz. Although sheer human density sometimes muffled the music, you could see the performers from anywhere in the house, even at the bar, and there was an intimate give-and-take between the audience and the musicians. (A front table might be three feet from Art Tatum's right elbow.) Even better, the musicians flowed from club to club, so that you'd hear in three or four places the same two or three musicians in three or four bands. Visiting musicians also sat in frequently, as did nonprofessionals without union cards. Sadly, this fertile crossbreeding has just about disappeared in New York. The esoteric, coded manner of much modern jazz doesn't encourage sitting in, and neither does the union, which feels that musicians should not play without pay—even for pleasure.

The music on Fifty-second Street included New Orleans and Chicago jazz, small- and big-band swing, be-bop, and the early cool groups, and because of competition, crossbreeding, variety, and the intense atmosphere of the place and the times, it was often uncannily good. Between December and February of 1944-45, for example, The Street displayed Hot Lips Page, Ben Webster, Barney Bigard, Stuff Smith, Wingy Manone, Art Tatum, Joe Marsala, Coleman Hawkins, Trummy Young, Benny Morton, Art Hodes, Oscar Pettiford, Dizzy Gillespie, Max Roach, Don Byas, Tiny Grimes, Charlie Shavers, and Billie Holiday. Best of all were the sometimes classic Sunday-afternoon jam sessions at Jimmy Ryan's. Musicians of every persuasion sat in with two basic bands, and during an afternoon the parade might include Bill Coleman, Pee Wee Russell, James P. Johnson, Edmond Hall, Vic Dickenson, Sid Catlett, Frankie Newton, Morton, Pete Brown, Jack Teagarden, Sidney Bechet, J. C. Higginbotham, Red Allen, Hawkins, Claude Jones, and Roy Eldridge. (I recall particularly a very slow "Sunny Side of the Street," played by Coleman, Hall, Eddie Heywood, and Newton, the last of whom also sang. It was an empyrean performance that lasted, I think, over twenty minutes.) Unfortunately, none of the Ryan's sessions were recorded, although similar ones in Harlem were. At the close, every musician in the house squeezed onto the bandstand for the "Bugle Call Rag." The results, though untidy (there might be fifteen men on the stand), were often stunning.

Columbia has seen fit to celebrate Fifty-second Street in a four-record set, "Swing Street" (Epic). The album contains sixty-four titles (sixty-three, actually, since one record, Bobby Hackett's "Bugle Call Rag," is inadvertently repeated), recorded between 1931 and 1947. It is, however, a lopsided celebration, for only eighteen numbers were recorded after 1939. During the war, Columbia, discouraged by the unfashionableness of jazz and by two long union bans on recording, went pretty much off the jazz standard. The slack was taken up by small labels—Blue Note, Commodore, Keynote, Dial, Savoy, Manor, Guild, Apollo, Signature, Session, Delta, Continental, and many others. Because of apathy and procedural complications, only a few of these recordings, many of which were superb, have been reissued. Nonetheless, the Epic album, despite some odd choices from what *is* available to Columbia, contains pleasant and even valuable material and is a reasonably accurate picture of the warming-up days on The Street. There are four selections by the Spirits of Rhythm, a guitar-tipples-bass-and-drums group, notable for the guitarist Teddy Bunn and the Surrealistic scat singing of Leo Watson; all of a 1933 Eddie Condon session, played by Sid Catlett, Pee Wee Russell, Floyd O'Brien, and Max Kaminsky; two good small-band Henry Allen sides, "Every Minute of the Hour" and "Lost"; two good numbers by Frankie Newton's Uptown Serenaders (which contained the nucleus of the John Kirby band) that have snatches of Newton's irreplaceable legato trumpet; Fats Waller, Art Tatum, and Teddy Wilson piano solos; three average John Kirby sides (why not the un-reissued "Blue Skies" and "Royal Garden Blues"—the band minus its customary veil and gloves?); a couple of fine Billie Holidays, "I Hear Music" and "Practice Makes Perfect"; two welcome 1940 Basie numbers, "Love Jumped Out" and "Five O'Clock Whistle"; Roy Eldridge's "That Thing"; and two Dizzy Gillespie dates from the Manor label (Columbia now owns the masters), "I Can't Get Started" and "Good Bait," the second of which contains a shouting, jolting bridge by Gillespie that is the most exhilarating moment in the album. The rest of the material, which ranges from the academic to the poor, is by—among others—Mildred Bailey, Red Norvo, Frankie Froeba, Wingy Manone, Toy Wilson, Sidney Bechet, Clarence Profit, Louis Prima, Hot Lips Page, Stuff Smith, and Red McKenzie. There is a lengthy booklet, with excellent photographs and a slow-breathing memoir by Charles Edward Smith. There is also a short note by John Hammond, who points out that The Street was Jim Crow for many years (the Columbia album is proof) and that the salaries paid the performers were often minimal.

The sound reproduction, by the way, is poor—inexplicably, since many of the original 78 r.p.m.'s were well recorded.

Hickory House, a steakhouse and jazz club on the first floor of a twelve-story loft-and-office building on West Fifty-second Street, opposite the Americana Hotel, is celebrating its thirtieth anniversary, and is, since the recent defection of Small's Paradise, in Harlem, the oldest nonstop jazz club in the city. One icy day I stopped in at Hickory House around lunchtime to talk with John Popkin, its owner and founder, and discovered that it hadn't changed a bit since my last visit, six or seven years before. A deep, high-ceilinged room with stained-glass windows and panelled walls, broken here and there by heroic oil paintings of such as Babe Ruth, Jack Dempsey, Red Grange, and Bobby Jones, Hickory House is built chiefly around an oval bar, some forty feet long, which contains a bandstand and is covered by an oval wooden canopy. A dozen or so wrought-iron chandeliers frame the canopy, and at the back of the room are several open grills, where steaks and chops are broiled. Booths line one wall, and the rest of the floor is taken up by large, indifferently arranged tables. I spotted Mr. Popkin at a table near the bar, and found that he hadn't changed, either. An amiable, medium-sized man with thinning hair and a crinkled, pleasantly worn face, he greeted us and introduced us to Joe Morgen, his publicity agent.

Morgen, who is short and melancholy-looking, pulled a thick sheaf of newspaper clippings from an envelope and dumped them on the table. "Duke Ellington sent these from England, John," he said. "He's on tour, you know. In fact, I spoke to him this morning. On the phone."

"You spoke to him in *England?*" Popkin asked, raising his eyebrows. "A call like that costs! I've known Duke thirty or thirty-five years. He's been coming in here since I opened. That man works too hard, but he eats nothing but proteins."

Morgen nodded solemnly, and said, "He spends hundreds of dollars a month here feeding himself and his family and friends."

Popkin nodded with equal solemnity, and turned to me. "I haven't had breakfast yet, so all I'm going to have is a medium egg and orange juice," he said. "But you better eat some shrimps and a junior sirloin and a salad."

I asked Popkin about the early days of the Hickory House.

"I rented the place with three other men in 1933 and rebuilt it," he said. "It was a second-hand-car salesroom, and the idea to make it a steakhouse was mine, and so the name, which is based on the fact that we cook our steaks entirely over hickory logs—two-foot hickory logs shipped special from a farmer up at Cornwall on the Hudson, and another man, up in Durham, Connecticut. In November, 1934, after I'd bought out my partners, I got the idea to bring in jazz, so I hired Wingy Manone, who had the Marsala brothers with him and Eddie Condon. Not long after that, the Three Ts—Jack and Charlie Teagarden and Frankie Trumbauer—came in from Paul Whiteman's band, and when they left, Joe Marsala formed his own group. Marsala was in and out of here right into the early forties, and had people like Adele Girard, the harpist, who became his wife; Joe Bushkin; Flip Phillips; George Wettling; Bobby Hackett, on guitar and cornet; and Buddy Rich. I brought Rich in from Brooklyn myself. He was playing in a little place right on the edge of Washington Cemetery, facing Ocean Parkway. Right on the edge, surrounded by stones. I heard music coming out of there one night—it was eerie—and went in, and this kid was playing. He was sensational. 'How old are you, sonny?' I asked him during the intermission, and he said, 'Seventeen, but I'll be eighteen soon.' I told him I wanted to hire him, but he wouldn't believe me, so later I drove him home and we woke up his father at four in the morning, and he *did* believe me. Then it took me a week to persuade Marsala to use him. I can't tell you, in order, all the rest of the bands I had in the thirties. My memory used to be like a telephone book, but it skips on me now. Anyway, there was Red Norvo and Mildred Bailey; Red McKenzie; Bud Freeman; Red Allen; the Adrian Rollini Trio; John Kirby; Louis Prima; Riley and Farley, who wrote 'The Music Goes 'Round and Around'; Bunny Berigan; and all sorts of intermission pianists— Hazel Scott, Frances Faye, Irving Fields, Toy Wilson, Pearl Williams, and Frankie Froeba. Fats Waller, who was in a floor show next door at the Yacht Club, came in every evening just to play what he wanted to play, and they'd have to send somebody over to get him when his next set began. Around 1935, I started Sunday-afternoon jam sessions. Everybody dropped in—Basie, Teddy Wilson, Art Tatum, Hot Lips Page, Chu Berry, Roy Eldridge, the Dorseys, Artie Shaw, Goodman, and Nat Cole, who was across the street at Kelly's Stable. Frank Sinatra and Frankie Laine used to hang around in that back booth, waiting for a chance to sing. Beer was thirty-five cents and whiskey fifty, and the customers would be three-deep around the bar, some of them nursing one drink for the entire afternoon. I stopped hiring horns in the late forties. The food side had become very important, and the horns made too much noise. Since then, I've had small, quiet groups, a lot of them led by women, like Mary Osborne, the guitarist; Jutta Hipp and Toshiko; Marjorie Hyams, the vibraphonist; and, of course, Marian McPartland, who's a fixture, and who gave Joe Morello his start. George Shearing started here, too, and so did Peter Nero, in 1959. He was Bernie Nierow then, and an intermission pianist."

Popkin finished his egg and took a sip of coffee. What had he done in his pre-Hickory House days? "I was born—real name of Pupko—in Vilna, Russia, in 1895, and came over in 1907 on a cattle boat from Latvia," he said. "My father had been in New York three or four years, and owned a fish cart. I didn't go to school; I started right away as a newsboy. Then I worked for Postal Telegraph and became Eva Tanguay's personal messenger boy. At seventeen, I took a job as a salesman with United Cigar, and after that as a men's-clothing model in a store on Fourteenth Street. My father and I had a fish market down on Ludlow for a while, and at twenty-one I went into the auction business. On Lispenard Street. I made a little money and bought

55

a duck ranch in Yardley, Pennsylvania. I was the only Jewish duck raiser at that time, and I lived in an old house that George Washington had had as his headquarters. The keys to the doors were all a foot long. I got married in that house. A very historical wedding. I gave up the ranch after I lost most of my ducks in an epidemic, and worked for the Commission for Relief in Belgium, under Herbert Hoover, during the First World War. Then I opened the Little Club, a speakeasy on Forty-fourth, between Broadway and Eighth Avenue. I always wanted to be in the theatrical and musical line. I quit the Little Club in 1925 and went into perfumes. I was very successful until 1929, when I went broke on Wall Street. I didn't want to go back with my father, and I was having a hard time when I started this place. I can't retire. If I do, I'm afraid I'll die. I'm here fourteen, fifteen hours a day. I meet people and talk. Time flies. There are always problems to occupy my mind. People keep telling me, 'Modernize the place, John. Pep it up.' Maybe I'll do some fixing this spring, but I won't change it much. I'm too old-fashioned."

# His Master's Voice

The arts have long come in two grades—the original and its popularization. Jazz is no exception. Almost every poll-winning big band, group, instrumentalist, or singer is a loose copy, adaptation, or even mockery of a lesser-known and often pioneering big band, group, instrumentalist, or singer. (Jazz is often called "popular music." It isn't. Popular music is Frank Sinatra and Doris Day, vocal groups, dance bands, hotel bands, and rock and roll. Some of these are remotely related to jazz, some are not.) Popularized jazz is more popular than jazz but not as popular as popular music. There are a good many jazz popularizers. Here are some of them—the originals on the left, their adapters on the right:

Fletcher Henderson = Benny Goodman
Chick Webb and Sidney Catlett = Gene Krupa and
    Buddy Rich
Jimmy Lunceford = Stan Kenton
Billie Holiday = Anita O'Day and June Christy
Lester Young = Stan Getz
Albert Ammons, Meade Lux Lewis, and Pete Johnson =
    Freddie Slack
Bix Beiderbecke = Red Nichols and Bobby Hackett
Art Tatum = Oscar Peterson and André Previn

Charlie Parker = Cannonball Adderley
Bud Powell = George Shearing

There are odd twists here. A few jazz pioneers have popularized themselves—that is, they have, because of wear and
tear, perfected easily prepared, easily digested versions of
their original selves. These include Louis Armstrong, whose
many imitators, however, have never become popular; Ella
Fitzgerald; Count Basie; and Erroll Garner, whose popular form—another odd twist—is identical with his original
form. The most obvious difference between the pioneers
and their adapters is racial. The Negro invents, the white
man borrows. Duke Ellington still struggles while Benny
Goodman retires. The other differences are subtler. The
popularizers tend to be better technicians and steadier performers (read: mechanical). At the same time, they are less
inventive, less high-minded about their work, more osten-
tatious, and perhaps because they are borrowers, less sure
of themselves. A few of these popularizers have come extremely close to equalling their models. One of them is the
celebrated Stan Getz, the thirty-six-year-old tenor saxophonist from Philadelphia.

Getz is the poll winners' poll winner. He won the
*Metronome* poll eleven years in a row and would probably
still be winning if the magazine hadn't gone out of business.
He won the *Down Beat* readers' poll eleven times and its
critics' poll six times. He topped the *Playboy* poll seven
years and is one of *Playboy's* All Stars' All Stars. And yet
Getz will always be several notches beneath his chief
model, Lester Young, who pulled down just two *Esquire*
polls, one *Down Beat* readers' poll, and a posthumous elec-
tion to *Down Beat's* Hall of Fame. Continuous poll winners
breed admirers, and Getz's are legion and often inter-

changeable. Some of them are Zoot Sims, Allen Eager, Brew Moore, Herbie Steward, Al Cohn, Dick Hafer, and Bill Perkins. Lester Young, late in life, was therefore in the lamentable position of being unable to turn around without hearing a Getz-filtered facsimile of himself, and the less knowledgeable among his audiences frequently mistook him for just another Getz admirer.

Getz looks like a country boy. He is of medium build, with the bland, homogeneous handsomeness that belongs with plenty of milk and regular sleep. Like many other white musicians, he shows the strain of trying to keep up with the Joneses when he plays. He clamps his eyes shut, contorts his face, stoops and stands up, stoops and stands up. His style is romantic, and this makes him an alien in jazz, where softness and sentiment have little honor. His tone is a moist, primped version of Lester Young's, which was dry and nasal. It is, at first, a lovely tone, the kind of tone one would want to go home to. But after repeated hearings one notices a whining quality, a note of self-pity. Coleman Hawkins and Ben Webster, by comparison, are dark, tough, and intense; they are affecting because they express what they feel, not what they think they ought to feel. Getz's tone is at the mercy of his romanticism, which is a yearning after those blues emotions natural to Webster, Hawkins, and Young. In a slow blues or a ballad, he exhibits all the paraphernalia jazz musicians use to convey emotion. He grows husky, he plays blue notes, he goes soft and sinuous, and he preaches. But his effects come through as quavery and genteel and falsetto, particularly when he ascends into the upper register, which he does frequently in heated moments. The exterior is flawless, but the guts are missing. This emotional anemia is to an extent disguised, for Getz is a formidable technician. In fast tempos, he uses many-noted lines that gallop around the scale (and sometimes off it), short, peremptory riffs, a trim vibrato, complex staccato intervals, and down-low honks. He becomes liquid, and he hounds the beat—until, that is, he runs out of patterns, when he slips behind the beat into a legato refuelling passage. But many of these thousands of notes, though well chosen, accented, and joined, are merely excited and compulsive. (Getz made an absorbing record five or six years ago with Dizzy Gillespie; on it, he is largely rhetorical, while Gillespie is witty, precise, and passionate.) Getz approaches fulfillment in slow ballads. He has an unmistakable gift for inventing sweet and graceful melodies, which, though stated fulsomely, are original. These lyric flights, however, do not wear well. One or two close hearings do them justice; after that they grow transparent.

Getz's career has been divided between being a sideman in big bands (the forties) and the leader of small groups (the fifties, the sixties), both here and in Scandinavia. In 1957, though, he toured with a black-tie Jazz at the Philharmonic group that was recorded in action at the Chicago Opera House. Getz's portion of the concert, "Stan Getz and J. J. Johnson at the Opera House," has now been reissued by Verve. It is well recorded, the crowd sounds are not objectionable, and, all in all, it is probably the best record Getz has made. (He has recorded prolifically, and at the moment is hip-deep in *bossa nova*. Some of his *bossa-nova* efforts are best-sellers, and they may suitably shape him, after all these years, into a purely popular musician.) Oscar Peterson, Herb Ellis, Ray Brown, and Connie Kay accompany Getz and Johnson. There are two blues and four standards. "Billie's Bounce," a Charlie Parker blues, is in a medium-fast tempo, and is an excellent example of Paganini-Getz, who takes a dozen choruses, each more heated and hollow than the last. Getz is nearer his peak in the medium-tempo "My Funny Valentine," in which he controls his moony tendencies and displays a firmness of tone and an invention that come close to Ben Webster's. "Crazy Rhythm" is a very fast and predictable flag waver, and the slow "Yesterdays" is given over to Johnson. In "It Never Entered My Mind," Getz plays just one chorus, in an ad-lib tempo. It is a saintly demonstration of how to woo fragile embellishments from an even more fragile melody. "Blues in the Closet," which takes the tempo up again, is notable for Getz's tribute to Lester Young. Toward the end of a dozen choruses, he discards all pretense and plays a couple of choruses straight from the Master's mouth. The rhythm section, with Connie Kay in command and Oscar Peterson heard only as an accompanist, is first-rate.

# Hear Today, Gone Tomorrow

Jazz has always been bedevilled by certain audiences— the social-protesters, the Beats, and the hard thinkers who use the music as a weapon or smoke screen, and the eccentrics who spend lifetimes squabbling over the merits of spent musicians and unearthing the matrix numbers of forgotten, third-rate recordings. The chatty illiteracy of the occasional bulletins published by these archeologists calls to mind the nudist magazines whose editorials are apt to lead off, "Hi ya, skinfolks!" One reason for this condition, though, is the music itself, which changes too much and too fast. No sooner has a style or school begun to attract an audience (this usually takes two or three years) than a new style or school smothers it. First came the primitives (the rural singers and instrumentalists). They were followed by the classicists (New Orleans and Dixieland), who were toppled by the romantics (the first great soloists). These were supplanted by the neo-classicists (the big swing bands), who went down before the neo-romantics, or first moderns (bebop). Out of the moderns grew the avant-garde (abstract jazz) and, indirectly from that, the—well, neo-avant-garde (third-stream music). One trouble with these changes of skirt length is their increasing frequency. In the past fifteen years, jazz has suffered two thorough revolutions (bebop, abstract jazz). Apprentice musicians, watching idol after idol diminish, are left with half-formed, polyglot styles, and the often gifted idols are unemployable at the advanced age of thirty-five. Record companies, trying to keep up, concentrate on the New, and so force the very thing they pursue to accelerate. Thus the jazz student who grew up in the relatively stable days of 1940 has had, since his first enthusiasms, to absorb Charlie Parker and Dizzy Gillespie, then Lennie Tristano, then the Modern Jazz Quartet, then Charlie Mingus and Sonny Rollins, then John Coltrane and Cecil Taylor and Ornette Coleman. And while the rug is repeatedly pulled from under him, he is asked to be alert, broadminded, judicious, sympathetic, and eager.

Consider the concert given at the Carnegie Recital Hall under the title of "Recent Developments in Jazz." Organized by Gunther Schuller, who conducted, the evening was a *potage* of third-stream compositions (André Hodeir and Lalo Schifrin), atonal jazz (George Russell), and Duke Ellington, plus three numbers by the Eric Dolphy quartet that fell between hard bop and abstract jazz. One of Hodeir's four pieces, "Jazz Cantata," has seven movements, and it shuttles between written solos, fairly conventional ensemble scoring, and passages of up-tempo scat singing, which were read with astonishing aplomb by a soprano, Susan Belink. Schifrin's "The Ritual of Sound" is a jumpy study of timbres, and employs staccato clumps of sound and passages in which a bass clarinet, playing a ground, is pitted against a flute and French horn, then against a tuba and unison trumpets, and so on. Schifrin's program notes, written in Sanskrit, explain: "The thirteen-piece instrumental ensemble is used so as to achieve textures which are determined by serially derived degrees of density and timbral associations, both singly and in combination. In order to locate this sound material in sound space, registral displacement was determined on the basis of a numerical series derived from the original pitch series." After Schifrin's serially derived density, George Russell's "Lydian M 1," seven years old, sounded old-fashioned. The last composition of the evening was a transcription, by Schuller, of Ellington's pioneering "Reminiscin' in Tempo," a twelve-minute tone poem written in 1935. Ellington's piece is—for me, anyway—a static, almost effete work, and it suggests the probable fate of the works of Hodeir, Schifrin, and Russell.

The selections by Dolphy's quartet (the leader on alto saxophone, flute, and bass clarinet, with Edward Armour on trumpet, Richard Davis on bass, and J. C. Moses on drums) were notable for Dolphy's arpeggio flute (his work on the bass clarinet, though, trampled that instrument's deep-pile tone). Charlie Parker's "Donna Lee" ("Indiana") was then performed in a straightforward ensemble-solos-ensemble fashion by ten of the eighteen musicians on hand during the concert. As they neared the final chorus, however, all the horns, improvising collectively, stumbled on a marvellous, shattering chord that had the Furies in it and a moment-of-truth intensity that had been hidden all evening.

# Supreme Tickler

It has become clear only in the past decade that the up-the-river-from-New Orleans story is merely a rib or two of jazz history. Long before this over-celebrated migration, itinerant blues guitarists and pianists washed back and forth across the Southwest, the Southeast, and the Midwest. Jelly Roll Morton, a one-man vanguard, had travelled from coast to coast, sowing as he went, and by the time the New Orleans-to-Chicago migration was complete, independent and equally important jazz movements were entrenched in Kansas City, the Southwest, Baltimore, and New York. Perhaps the most influential and under-valued of these movements involved the Harlem "stride" pianists, who began to appear during the First World War and flourished in the twenties and thirties. Stride piano is characterized chiefly by an oompah left hand (a two-beat seesaw, whose ends are a powerful mid-keyboard chord and a weaker single note played an octave or a tenth below) and by an arabesque of right-hand chords and arpeggios, fashioned in counter rhythms. Stride piano, unlike New Orleans jazz, did not pop from one mythical man's forehead. It grew slowly out of ragtime, a unique piano form that lasted from about 1900 to about 1920. Though ragtime had similar features, it was not jazz. It was a complex, rococo *composed* music that evolved, as far as anyone knows, from the music used in the eighties and nineties to accompany Southern dances like the cakewalk. It employed the oompah left hand, syncopation, and elaborate treble figures, and each number was built on three or four distinct themes, arranged in *abacd, abcd,* or rondo form. It was a brittle, spirited, elegant music which had considerable lyric charm, and in its highest form (the work of Scott Joplin, James Scott, and Joseph Lamb) it demanded a Lisztian technique. Recorded on widely bought piano rolls, it was the first machine-fostered musical fad. It was also the first musical fad to be destroyed by overexposure. (Its lack of development helped cause its death, too; the late rags, though often fancier, do not differ much from those written in 1900.) The stride pianists, however, were busy remodelling ragtime long before it sank, and by the time it did they had perfected a full-bodied replacement—an improvised music, at once telescoped and loosened. The multiple themes of the typical ragtime composition gave way to the *aaba* structure of the thirty-two-bar chorus; the oompah left hand was supplemented by four-four chords, broken-rhythm chords, and single-note melodic lines; the right-hand figures became less garrulous; longer rests and behind-the-beat legato phrases were added; and there were fewer tremolos and trills, although the arpeggios and sudden breaks persisted. Like the ragtime pianists, the stride men were orchestral pianists, and they most often played by themselves or in "cutting" contests, which took place in cabarets, in back rooms, and at rent parties. At their height, the stride pianists formed a glittering, ritualistic duchy. James P. Johnson, the dean of the Harlem "ticklers" (one of those *mots justes* that only jazz musicians seem able to fashion about their music), recalled several of its rules of etiquette in the *Jazz Review* a couple of years before his death, in 1955:

When a real smart tickler would enter a place, say in winter, he'd leave his overcoat on and keep his hat on, too. We used to wear military overcoats or what was called a Peddock Coat, like a coachman's; a blue double-breasted, fitted to the waist and with long skirts. We'd wear a light pearl-gray Fulton or Homburg hat with three buttons or eyelets on the side, set at a rakish angle. . . . Then a white silk muffler and a white silk handkerchief in the overcoat's breast pocket. Some carried a gold-headed cane, or if they were wearing a cutaway, a silver-headed cane. A couple of fellows used to wear Inverness capes, which were in style in white society then. . . .

When you came into a place you had a three-way play. You never took your overcoat or hat off until you were at the piano. First you laid your cane on the music rack. Then you took off your overcoat, folded it and put it on the piano, with the lining showing.

You then took off your hat before the audience. Each tickler had his own gesture for removing his hat with a little flourish; that was part of his attitude, too. You took out your silk handkerchief, shook it out and dusted off the piano stool.

Now, with your coat off, the audience could admire your full-back, or box-back, suit, cut with very square shoulders. The pants had about fourteen-inch cuffs and broidered clocks.

Full-back coats were always single-breasted, to show your gold watch fob and chain. Some ticklers wore a horseshoe tiepin in a strong single-colored tie and a gray shirt with black pencil stripes.

We all wore French, Shriner and Urner or Hanan straight or French last shoes with very pointed toes, or patent-leather turnup toes, in very narrow sizes. . . . They cost from twelve to eighteen dollars a pair. . . . [Fred Tunstall] was a real dandy. I remember he had a Norfolk coat with eighty-two pleats in the back. When he sat down to the piano, he'd slump a little in a half hunch, and those pleats would fan out real pretty. That coat was long and flared at the waist. It had a very short belt sewn on the back. His pants were very tight.

He had a long neck, so he wore a high, stiff collar that

came up under his chin with a purple tie. A silk handkerchief was always draped very carefully in his breast pocket. His side view was very striking.

Johnson stands with Duke Ellington, Count Basie, and Jelly Roll Morton among the seminal jazz figures. Johnson's principal admirers and pupils in the early twenties were Ellington and Fats Waller. Ellington is now an institution, and as both pianist and composer he has affected Thelonious Monk, who in turn has spawned a host of lesser pianist-composers. Waller, an ironic master of self-parody, taught Count Basie, who became head of the Kansas City school as well as an unmistakable influence on John Lewis, another institution. Waller also made a lasting imprint on Art Tatum, a genuine virtuoso, and Tatum inspired—among countless others—Bud Powell, the widely followed bop pianist. For all this, Johnson was passé when he died. Seventy-five people attended his funeral. His career was a string of quick successes and slow-burning failures. Born in 1894, in New Brunswick, New Jersey, of a poor but solid family, Johnson picked up the piano from his mother and other informal teachers, and in his early teens became a reasonably good tickler. By the mid-twenties, he was a master pianist, songwriter ("If I Could Be with You One Hour Tonight," "Charleston," "Carolina Shout," "Old Fashioned Love"), and piano-roll maker. He was also writing music for revues and Hollywood shorts, playing in pit bands and onstage, making records as a bandleader and soloist, and performing in vaudeville. But Johnson, in the manner of the comedian lusting after the role of Hamlet, had dreams, and around 1930 he retired to a house he had bought in Jamaica, Long Island. There he composed a couple of symphonies, an orchestral suite based on the "St. Louis Blues," and a one-act opera with a libretto by Langston Hughes. Some of these were performed, but none were recorded. In the late thirties, John Hammond's Carnegie Hall "From Spirituals to Swing" concerts brought Johnson out of retirement, and he made a fine series of solo and small-band jazz recordings. In 1940, he suffered a stroke. Several years later, he was back again, appearing on some classic Blue Note recordings, as well as with desultory Dixieland groups. In 1951, a second stroke permanently disabled him.

Although Johnson metamorphosed from a slim, dapper man with a long, narrow head into a bear with a profusion of lips and double chins, his style—give or take a little elaboration—remained much the same. All in all, he was the steadiest and most refined Harlem stride pianist. Luckey Roberts, who taught Johnson, was and is more showy, and there is a Fragonard quality in his slow playing. Willie the Lion Smith, a contemporary of Johnson, has a frightening rhythmic bark but not much melodic bite, which was generally true of Waller, a first-rate second-rate pianist. Many of Johnson's compositions reflect the Old South church-meeting atmosphere of his home when he was a child. His "Carolina Shout" and "The Mule Walk" are *dances*, and they have an exuberant, extrovert air. This cheerful openness flowed into Johnson's playing, which has little of the dark, in-turning concentration of Southern jazz musicians. Indeed, his piano often suggests the bounce of polkas and schottishes. In contrast to Jimmy Yancey, who wore his soul on his sleeve, Johnson played *at* the blues; he never seemed to take them seriously—an attitude shared by Waller and Art Tatum, both Northerners. But the emotional caution of Johnson's composing and playing was balanced by the glistening architecture of his style. When necessary, his left hand produced oompah patterns equalled only by Waller and Smith. These figures, though, were constantly relieved by offbeat chords, rests, and little melodic lines, all of which gave his oompah twice as much force. His right hand was brilliantly casual. He liked broken arpeggios (Monk, Bud Powell), and generously spaced chords (Tatum) that outlined the melody and then floated off. He liked to decorate the melody with a furze of staccato, single-note lines, and he liked the ring of the upper registers and the boom of the deepest octave. But he was never predictable. His chords were oddly placed (Monk again), and, just at the right moment, they dissolved into single notes or runs that in turn fell before brief, virtuoso breaks and arhythmic interludes (Tatum again). No matter how fast the tempo, Johnson never hurried (John Lewis). And no matter how slow the tempo, he never dragged (Basie). Most important, Johnson's solos, of whatever length, were not bound by measures and bridges and reprises but were wholes—an improvisational skill only recently rediscovered by the young abstract performers.

Two welcome sets of Johnson reissues have now been put out—"Backwater Blues: The Stride Piano of James P. Johnson" (Riverside) and "James P. Johnson: Father of the Stride Piano" (Columbia). They stretch from 1920 to 1939, forming a nearly complete picture of Johnson's career. The twelve numbers on the first record were done between 1920 and 1927 as piano rolls. Four ("Charleston," "Daintiness Rag," "It Takes Love to Cure the Heart's Disease," and "Caprice Rag") are by Johnson. By and large, the record reveals the flashy, stylized Johnson of the rent parties. Ragtime influences are still strong, particularly in "Daintiness Rag," "Caprice Rag," and "Baltimore Buzz." More impressive, though, are Johnson's left hand in "Vampin' Liza Jane," when he matches runs and single notes against right-hand slurs; his left-hand tremolos and right-hand staccato figures in "Don't Tell Your Monkey Man"; and, in "Gypsy Blues," his heavy right-hand chords and the plopping left-hand single notes. "Backwater Blues," made in 1927, has a boogie-woogie bass, tremolos, and the porous stride attack that Albert Ammons and Pete Johnson sometimes used a decade later. It is an excellent example of Johnson balancing a blues on one finger and saying, in a mock-melancholy way, "Ah, yes, those *sad, sad* blues."

There are sixteen selections on the Columbia record. Five are piano solos from the twenties; one is a funny 1930 duet with Clarence Williams; five are 1939 piano solos; and five are small-band sides from the same year. The 1939 solos show Johnson at his peak. He is less mannered and fussy than he was in the twenties, and he uses more pronounced dynamics and rhythms. "If Dreams Come True," the best of the lot, has glassy out-of-tempo interludes and irresistible oompah passages, and "The Mule Walk" rolls with poly-rhythms. "Blueberry Rhyme" has a rhapsodic Tatum quality. The small-band sides, made with Red Allen, J. C. Higginbotham, Gene Sedric, Al Casey, Johnny Williams or Pops Foster, and Sidney Catlett, fall below the small-band efforts Johnson made with Frankie Newton for Victor and with Sidney De Paris and Ben Webster for Blue Note. But there are good moments from Allen and Higginbotham and Catlett, the last of whom adopted an attack when he played with Johnson that was a delicate mixture of spoofing and respect. The piano solos from the twenties are creditable, though poorly recorded. Fortunately, Ellington's short eulogy of Johnson in the liner notes has none of the customary lollipop flavor of his public effusions. James P., a disciplined man, would be pleased.

# The Well

The best place to hear jazz is a matter of accident. Sometimes it is outdoors, beneath trees or in the sun. Sometimes it is under a circus tent during a thunderstorm. Sometimes it is in a classroom (Thelonious Monk, with Louis Bellson on drums and Jimmy Hamilton on clarinet, demonstrating how "Tea for Two" sounds as written and in Monk fashion), and sometimes it is in an abandoned Elks' hall or a living room (Pee Wee Russell, sitting in a curved-back Pennsylvania Dutch rocker —his profile to his listeners—and playing the blues, with George Wein on the piano). Once in a great while it is in a concert hall, which tends to separate the musicians and the audience and which inflicts echoing amounts of space on the musicians. It is never in a recording studio, whose clinical confines and now-or-never pressures cage the musician. And sometimes it is in the night club, which, for better or worse, has nurtured the music for many years.

Since the disappearance of the ideal, longhouse-shaped clubs on West Fifty-second Street, the downtown New York jazz clubs have sprouted in cavernous basements (some of them like swimming pools and some of them like old-fashioned hotel lobbies), in reconverted stores, in old dance halls, in bars, and in cafeterias. One of the most satisfactory of these was the Five Spot, a plain Third Avenue bar, at the foot of Cooper Square, that took on jazz in the mid-fifties simply by adding a piano and a small bandstand. It was small and unpretentious and you could see and hear from anywhere in the room. As a result, it was intricately awash with music and reaction, reaction and music. Then the building it occupied was torn down and it vanished. But in March a new Five Spot opened, three blocks north, on Third Avenue and Eighth Street, in a reconverted cafeteria.

The new one comes in three sections. Behind its glass front is a kind of arcade filled with small tables. This is separated from the main room by a wall punctuated with four archways, and the main room, which is about thirty by fifty and has a long bar down one side, is partly divided by a row of mirror-encased pillars. The bandstand is at right angles to the bar. The tables are cafeteria tables, the walls are a heavy red, and the ceiling is literally carpeted in matching red. It is a spacious room, with good sound and little atmosphere. Thelonious Monk, fresh from a tour of Japan, was at the new Five Spot with his quartet (Charlie Rouse on tenor saxophone, Butch Warren on bass, and Frankie Dunlop on drums) when I stopped in a while back. During the past three or four years, Monk has gone through a curious transformation: he has retreated physically from the world while his music has grown increasingly aggressive and explicit. He now generally performs in a disguise that consists of a hat (the other night, he was wearing a narrow-brimmed Tyrolean model, its crown pushed out in in a sawed-off stovepipe effect), dark glasses, two blunderbuss-sized rings, one on each hand, and his beard, which is slowly increasing in length. He never speaks to his audiences, nor does he face them when, at least once in every

73

number, he gets up from the piano and—his arms outspread and groping, his torso erect, his feet flapping—performs a unique soft-shoe. Thus, even though he is unmistakably there, it is difficult to *see* him. At the same time, his playing, once an equal mixture of sound and silence, has become extraordinarily busy. Savory dissonant chords dwindle abruptly into stiff, purposely crooked arpeggios. Repeated single-note figures end in crossed-hands chords or in upper-register splats effected with his right elbow. Stride-piano basses appear and disappear. And his backing-up, which includes his dancing and is both a fun-house mirror of and a prod for the soloist, is just as busy. All this was apparent when I heard him, particularly in a slow solo version of "Don't Blame Me" (Monk, noted for his tardiness, was on time for his first set, which was delayed by a late Charlie Rouse); "Crisscross"; a fine, lingering "I'm Getting Sentimental Over You," in which he played, almost note for note, Tommy Dorsey's celebrated solo, and then—after a quick, tantalizing pause—parodied it; "Well, You Needn't"; "Epistrophy"; and "Blue Monk," in which he stayed close to the melody, while repeatedly reorganizing its rhythmic structure. (Monk's sets are at least an hour long, and usually contain half a dozen numbers.) His quartet is satisfactory. Rouse is an intense, often affecting saxophonist whose hard-bop outlines have gradually softened, and Butch Warren is another of the gifted bassists who have appeared in the wake of Charlie Mingus. Dunlop is a measured, careful soloist and a measured, careful accompanist (Monk, though, loves a drummer who will occasionally war with him). But his accompanists matter little; his music is a well, and at its bottom—alone and furiously digging—is Monk himself.

# The Ladies

By releasing "Billie Holiday: The Golden Years" and "Mildred Bailey: Her Greatest Performances," three-record sets, each containing forty-eight selections, the first made between 1933 and 1941 and the second between 1929 and 1946, Columbia, aside from doing a public service, has raised again the apparently permanent question of why there have been so few genuine jazz singers. (Taste largely decides who is and who isn't a jazz singer. To my ears, Ella Fitzgerald and Anita O'Day are not jazz singers, but Edith Piaf, who has nothing to do with jazz, is, and so are Earl Hines and Johnny Mercer.) Logically, there should be countless jazz singers. Jazz, which grew out of vocal music, primarily attacks the emotions, and the human voice conveys emotion more readily than any instrument. When instrumental jazz superseded vocal jazz, it copied its predecessor, and jazz singers suddenly sounded as if they were emulating their imitators. Of course, they weren't. Billie Holiday and Bessie Smith, the two greatest jazz singers, attained with nothing more than their voices a majesty and wit and emotion that few instrumentalists have matched. Indeed, they suggested the direction in which jazz singing might go, but the talents of their admirers and of their admirers' admirers have simply not been up to the

75

task. And a change isn't likely; jazz, in its newest forms, has become unsingable. It is not too late, though, to ponder again the miraculous work of Billie Holiday, which has not dated, and to ponder Mildred Bailey, who was just about unclassifiable.

In spite of their differences, the two women had strikingly similar careers and even personalities. Both attracted and held small, vociferous coteries, and both were unsuccessful commercially. Both had appearances that went against them—Mildred Bailey was fat and plain, and Billie Holiday was a Negro. Partly for these reasons, both were emotional cripples. Mildred Bailey was addicted to food and Billie Holiday to drugs. Both made good money at times and died poor. Both had unsatisfactory relations with men and lavished their affections on pets. Both had sharp tongues and sharp tempers. Both had a sense of humor and delighted in kidding inferior material into superior material. Both lived to the age of forty-four, and both died puzzled, bitter women.

Mildred Bailey's singing had set by the late twenties, and it never changed. She was already a sizable woman, and, like many fat people, she had a little voice, a trapped voice. It gave the impression of being a miniature one, with everything in scale. It was also pure and neat. She used her vibrato (which was quite pronounced in the twenties) sparingly, her diction was absolutely clear, and she never went off pitch. She generally placed her notes on or a trifle behind the beat, and she always placed them perfectly. She never growled or allowed any huskiness in her voice, and she rarely indulged in blue notes. She had a finished, sweet, china-doll voice, and she sang as well at the end of her career as she did at the beginning. But Mildred Bailey had no real style. Her *voice* was unmistakable, but the conscious imbalances and flourishes and original colorations that are the marks of style were missing. She might have become a good comic singer. This is suggested by the Betty Boop scat passages she sometimes slipped into and by her funny, bouncy handling of ridiculous lyrics. She sang the blues the way she sang "There's a Cabin in the Pines"—directly, discreetly, assuredly, and with small emotion. Indeed, the emotional content of her singing was turned inward. One had the feeling that if she let it out, she knew it would shake her to pieces. So she was not emotional and she was not sentimental; a good jazz singer must be the first and a good popular singer the second. She was caught between.

This plight is clear all through the Columbia album. Again and again, on the fine sides made in 1935 with Bunny Berigan and Johnny Hodges, and on those made later with Mary Lou Williams, she inches up to the verge and seems about to tip over into jazz singing, but then she retreats into what she *knows* she can do. And there are many instances, in numbers like "Thanks for the Memory," "Heaven Help This Heart of Mine," and " 'Tain't What You Do," when she just misses a plain, rousing popular vocal. After a time the no man's land in which Mildred Bailey ran continually and hopelessly from side to side palls. Each vocal sounds like the last; not even material and tempo make a difference. One turns for relief to her accompanists, among them Red Norvo, Benny Goodman, the John Kirby band, a Basie contingent, Coleman Hawkins, Chu Berry, Roy Eldridge, and Teddy Wilson, but they, too, never rise past a predictable level. All is polite, polished, and, despite the frequent outward show of "swinging," a little dull.

Billie Holiday had everything Mildred Bailey lacked. In fact, it was a superabundance, and when she discovered this she tried to control it, but with disastrous results. She

77

simply hardened a marvellously intuitive style and almost overnight turned it into mannered torch singing, and when her voice gave out, around 1950, there was nothing left but a stylized skeleton. But it is always astonishing to return to the records she made before 1939. They are superb jazz recordings, and a few—"I Must Have That Man," "What a Night, What a Moon, What a Girl," "It's Too Hot for Words," "Miss Brown to You"—are possibly without peer. No matter how many times they are heard, they remain fresh, and even when one hums her melodic lines from memory they magically retain their surprise. This surprise comes from her effortless refashioning of the melody; her remarkable simultaneous stretching and reshaping of the lyrics, which nonetheless are never garbled (listen to the way she makes one long, bumpy word out of the first twelve words of "Them There Eyes" in the Columbia album: "Ifell-inlovewithyouthefirsttimeIlookedinto—them there eyes"; once heard, never forgotten); her wit and humor; the continually changing colors in her voice, effected through her use of vibrato, huskiness, and bent notes, and by playing hob with the beat; and her steady, enclosing warmth. All these qualities are apparent on the first two records of the Columbia set, which begin with her extremely creditable 1933 début and which end in 1939. And the accompaniment, particularly when Teddy Wilson, Lester Young, and Buck Clayton are on hand, is as good as she is. (Such is not the case on three previously unreleased air shots made in 1937 at the Savoy Ballroom, when she was with the Basie band, which sounds like the rabble marching off to Quebec.) The rest of the album distinctly falls off. Self-consciousness had set in, and many of the post-1938 numbers are strained. The tempos drag and the brilliant fun of the early sides is gone. Numbers like "Gloomy Sunday," "I Cover the Waterfront," "Time on My Hands," and "Body and Soul" are depressing.

Both the Bailey and Holiday albums come with booklets that have good photographs, complete discographies, and varyingly fulsome appreciations. The Bailey booklet, though, includes three sentences by Irving Townsend that amount to an epitaph: "I remember watching her late one night at her farm in upstate New York while she listened to a record of Duke Ellington's 'Black Butterfly.' She sat at the kitchen table with a single candle blowing in the wind from the open door. The shadows of the leaves on the maples outside the door danced all over the kitchen walls, and Mildred played the record over and over again as if afraid the trees might stop blowing if the band did."

# Evans vs. Evans

The most impressive of modern pianists is Bill Evans, a pale, shy, emaciated figure who wears glasses and long hair combed flat, and who, when he plays, hunches like an S over the keyboard, his face generally turned away from his audience, as if the struggle of improvisation were altogether too personal to be practiced in public. For Evans, improvisation is obviously a constant contest—a contest between his intense wish to practice a wholly private, inner-ear music and an equally intense wish to express his jubilation at having found such a music within himself. When Evans edged into sight five years ago, as a sideman in experimental and modern-jazz groups (one was led by Miles Davis, who has long waged a war similar to Evans'), his extrovert tendencies were uppermost. Already a finished pianist, with a sure touch, perfect rhythm, and a superb dynamic sense, Evans was marked by Bud Powell and Lennie Tristano. At medium and fast tempos, he played long, uniquely shaped single-note phrases that were distinguished by staccato figures, sudden on-the-beat or double-time clusters, and short, purposeful arpeggios. (Most jazz pianists exude arpeggios the way a squid exudes ink; by the time the clouds of sound clear, a new idea has been found and the danger is over.) These three attacks were rhythmically and melodically exciting because they were beautifully juxtaposed, and they were the means of building within each solo a series of bright climaxes. That is, Evans would play six or seven close-together, ascending, on-the-beat notes, abruptly accenting the last one, and perhaps repeating it several times; he would then quickly fall into a little run, would pause, and would begin climbing another slope of the hill, this time in a staccato onetwothree-fourfive manner, until he again reached the top note, which he would again accent before lightly rolling away through both soft and loud notes. These undulations had a wind-blown sound, and their most insistent sections pulled tenaciously at his listeners, making them strain to hear what surely came from Evans' depths. At slow tempos, he turned inward, playing pedalled Debussy chords, and his single notes were filigree. It was a wistful, aeolian-harp music.

When Evans formed a trio, late in 1959, with Scott La Faro on bass and Paul Motian on drums, a peculiar thing happened: The burden of being *the* soloist instead of *a* soloist appeared too much for him, and he became increasingly ruminative and withdrawn. He experimented endlessly with slow, cloudy numbers, and the singing climaxes all but vanished. Then, in the spring of 1961, La Faro, a stunning musician who tried to draw Evans out by working contrapuntally with him and by playing daringly executed solos, was killed in an accident, and Evans' work became even more closeted and gloomy. The irony was uncomfortably plain: Evans, shy to the point of pain, had become a young Werther. But in the past year Evans has unexpectedly made three quite different recordings—a duet with Jim Hall, a trio effort with Shelly Manne and Monty

Budwig, and a small-band date with Freddie Hubbard, Hall, Percy Heath, and Philly Joe Jones—which suggest that he is again doing battle with himself.

"Undercurrent" (United Artists), which he recorded with Hall, resembles two close friends talking quietly late at night. There are six standards, one of them Hall's "Romain," and each consists of gentle ensemble passages, sometimes with and sometimes without a lead voice, and brief solos in which the accompanist moves into the background. Nobody bothers about steady tempos, but if one seems appropriate, it is sounded and then abandoned before it becomes assertive. "Romain" and John Lewis's "Skating in Central Park" work out best; the two men are in clearest accord, and Evans even goes through the motions of setting up and knocking down several climaxes. These moments invigorate Hall, who in turn cheers Evans.

Unlike Elvin Jones and Philly Joe Jones and Billy Higgins, who use the drums as polyrhythmic engines, Shelly Manne accomplishes his infinite colorations through implication. His work, particularly behind pianists and bassists, abounds in odd, pleasant, oblique sounds—fingers and hands on cymbals, a silver dollar spinning on a drumhead, ruffling wire brushes, and occasional tom-tom or cymbal-top pongs. In four of the six numbers (all standards) in "Shelly Manne/Bill Evans with Monty Budwig: Empathy" (Verve), Evans responds to these touches with vigorous solos, full of up-and-down figures, startling rhythmic and harmonic turns, and an iron concentration. Manne takes a couple of delightful solos ("The Washington Twist" and "With a Song in My Heart"), which, as is usual with him, are partly contrapuntal exercises with either piano or bass and partly pure solo. Indeed, they are refreshing offshoots of the ensemble rather than look-Ma exhibitions. Budwig is a skilled bassist and a sufficient soloist. And, near the end of "With a Song in My Heart," Evans reveals a new side by dropping in a heavy, mock-pompous statement of the melody that comically evokes everything from Victor Herbert baritones to Erroll Garner.

Evans responds almost as well to Philly Joe Jones in "Interplay: Bill Evans Quintet" (Riverside) as he does to Manne. Jones can be overweening, but he restricts himself here to precise pushing. (His loudness is caused by recording imbalance.) Listen to his worrying but exact ride-cymbal patterns behind Hall in "Interplay," an ingenious medium-tempo blues by Evans (the five other numbers are standards), and to his pumping high-hat work during the ensembles. Hall is in good form, and Heath, as always, is safe and polished. Unfortunately, Hubbard, who is still an overblowing admirer of Miles Davis and Art Farmer, tends to jar the easy communion of the rhythm section. His presence, in fact, induces wishful thinking. Had either Davis or Farmer been on hand, Evans, who has made some of his best recordings with them, might have shaken off the last of his melancholia.

Since the release of these recordings, Evans' new trio (Gary Peacock on bass and Paul Motian on drums) has been taken on as the house band at the Village Vanguard. On the basis of its showing one night recently, it is an intense, welling-up group. It works contrapuntally a great deal of the time, with both Peacock, a superb bassist in the tradition of La Faro, and Motian developing their own "melodic" lines instead of acting as mere timekeepers. Evans, more of a ghostly figure than ever, seems freer and has perhaps found the median between his Werther musings and open, selfless playing. In a long, medium-slow rendition of Monk's " 'Round Midnight," which has the sort of imperious melody that almost commands note-for-note repetition, he attacked from every point—with loose chords, rising and falling single-note clusters, and excited rhythmic turns. The tune gradually softened under these pressures, and became a perfectly harmonious composition by Monk *and* Evans. Similar happy collaborations took place during the evening, giving the impression, all in all, that Evans' celebration of himself has resumed.

# Herd After Herd

One of the oddest contagions in jazz was the outpouring of big quasi-jazz bands that proliferated from 1935 to 1950. The most celebrated of the countless dozens that could be found in every ballroom, movie house, hotel, and college gym in the country in the late thirties and early forties were led by Glen Gray, Benny Goodman, Artie Shaw, Jan Savitt, Bob Crosby, Glenn Miller, Will Bradley, the Dorsey brothers, Harry James, Les Brown, Charlie Barnet, Bob Chester, Woody Herman, and Stan Kenton. These bands crowded the sizable gap between, on the left, the genuine jazz bands led by Duke Ellington, Count Basie, Jimmie Lunceford, and Benny Carter and, on the right, the out-and-out dance bands of Shep Fields, Russ Morgan, Guy Lombardo, and Alvino Rey. Indeed, it is difficult not to think of them in political terms. Their leaders, in the main, were smiling, affable businessmen, bent on pleasing all of the people all of the time. Their organizations were polished, predictable, and popular, and were capable of rabble-rousing and speaking softly. They were dead center musically, avoiding the heresies of the left and the Mickey Mouse tendencies of the right. Sometimes they were pompous (Artie Shaw) and sometimes they were just folks (Glenn Miller). Either way, they were dull. In short, they were paragons of conservatism, and while they were in office they ruled with a becalming moderation. The most agile and durable of these all but extinct bands is Woody Herman's, now in its twenty-eighth year of public service. Herman has tried to please not only his fellow-conservatives but also impressionable listeners on both flanks. He has done this by discreetly adapting the more accessible experiments of the left and mixing them with the least gluey ones from the right. As a result, the various Herman bands, or Herds, as they are called, have always sounded fresh and up-to-date. But, like the insistently *au courant,* the Herds tend to falter under a hard contemporary stare, and even worse things happen when they are subjected to hindsight.

Such is the case with the First and Second Herds, many of whose records have been reissued by Columbia in an album titled "Woody Herman: 'The Thundering Herds.' " Its three L.P.s contain forty-five numbers, and the years covered are 1945 to 1948. The First Herd evolved from the Infant Herd, an almost forgotten group that, in 1936, grew out of the Isham Jones orchestra. In the manner of the early bands of Tommy Dorsey, Bob Crosby, and Artie Shaw, the Infant Herd tried to inflate Dixieland to big-band proportions. It used two-beat rhythms, and its arrangements suggested the collective interplay of the Dixieland ensemble. It played pop songs and novelty numbers, and a lot of blues, which it handled in the self-conscious gut-bucket fashion of Dixieland bands. Now and then, however, the warm winds of Basieland washed over the band, causing it to play fast, stick-legged numbers that were full of bad piano solos and flat-chested ensembles. Aside from Cappy Lewis, an estimable Bunny Berigan student, and Neal Reid, a Jack Teagarden-flavored trombonist with an enormous range, its soloists were unprepossessing. Herman, a thin, short, pleasant-faced man from Milwaukee, played the clarinet like Jimmy Noone and the alto saxophone like Johnny Hodges. The band sank during the early years of the war, and then, in 1944, made a handful of records for Decca that showed a sudden fondness for Duke Ellington. (Hal McIntyre and Charlie Barnet had been seized by similar enthusiasms.) Ben Webster and Johnny Hodges and Juan Tizol sat in on some of these recordings, illuminating otherwise gray efforts. Another quiet period followed; then, early in 1945, the First Herd roared over the horizon. It was a nineteen-piece band made up of a lot of fledglings (Sonny Berman, Pete Candoli, Ralph Burns, Billy Bauer, Chubby Jackson) and a few veterans (Flip Phillips, Bill Harris, Dave Tough), and at first it appeared to be travelling fast. It was noisy and excited and determined, and everyone pointed out how much it *swung*. Those good old Goodman days were back, people said. Then it became clear that the band's repertory consisted of just two basic patterns—one fast and one slow. The fast numbers, or flag-wavers, were based on blues and standards, and were played in loose, on-the-spot (or "head") arrangements, which, as the Columbia album reminds us, went something like this: a riff, repeated for sixteen bars by the saxophones and supported only by the rhythm section, followed by an eight-bar piano solo on the bridge; return of the riff, with background trumpet punctuations, and the first chorus ends; next, a broken-rhythm interlude, introducing trombonist Bill Harris, who plays one chorus, backed by a saxophone figure; another interlude, introducing Flip Phillips, who plays two tenor-saxophone choruses, backed by a trombone figure; a gathering of wind and steam; and two final, overheated ensemble riff choruses, which include a bridge played by Herman on clarinet, a bridge played by a high-noted trumpeter, whose effects are echoed, in floor-show fashion, by the drummer, and a rum-te-dum coda by the bassist or drummer. After a time, the flag-wavers ("Northwest Passage," "Apple Honey," "Caldonia," "Blowin' Up a Storm") became interchangeable, and only their tempos varied. However, Charlie Parker and Dizzy Gillespie, busy elsewhere, helped by continually putting forward new patterns, and so did Basie and Jimmie Lunceford. The slow numbers, adapted mostly from the right, were ballads and novelties and were built around vocals by Herman ("Put That Ring on My Finger") or Frances Wayne ("Happiness Is a Thing Called Joe") or around fulsome solos by Bill Harris ("Everywhere") or Flip Phillips ("With Someone New"). Harris specialized in staccato, circus-band phrases, and Phillips swam back and forth between Ben Webster and Lester Young. Both men said almost nothing but said it with emotion. The First Herd was also rife with humorists. There were funny vocals, mostly by Herman ("Caldonia"), cute trumpet licks ("Goosey Gander"), a lot of *in-medias-res* shouting, and catchy codas. Like the Shriners, the First Herd had a lot of harmless fun.

Late in 1946, however, it grew serious and recorded a three-part suite by Ralph Burns called "Summer Sequence," which was full of dappled guitar passages (Chuck Wayne) and lacy piano fills (Burns). It was the sort of impressionistic, finger-bowl piece that Billy Strayhorn sometimes exudes. The effort proved fatal, and not long afterward the First Herd disbanded. In 1947, the Second Herd galloped into view. The new band had digested bebop, and it also had a new saxophone section, made up of three tenors and a baritone, which together emitted a smooth, doughy sound. Lester Young, in the person of such admirers as Herbie Steward, Stan Getz, and Zoot Sims, was everywhere, and there was a drummer, Don Lamond, who dropped bass-drum bombs and accented each phrase with stop-the-music rim shots. (The one ornament of the First Herd, Dave Tough, had been responsible for whatever grace the band had. Using ingenious, liquid, perfectly pitched cymbal work and beautifully placed accents, he tricked more than one listener into believing it was the band, and not he, that was swinging so.) The slow-or-fast pattern of the repertory remained unchanged, but it was now coated with the multi-note melodic lines of bebop. Moreover, the flag-wavers ("Keen and Peachy," "The Goof and I," "Four Brothers") were more nonchalant, and the slow tunes were jazzier and often taken up by Herman vocals delivered in a husky, lowdown buzz.

This is roughly where the Columbia album ends, but the Secord Herd went on, with occasional personnel refuelling, until 1949. A year or so later, the Third Herd, an even cooler version of the Second, crossed the prairies, alternating between well-combed flag-wavers and sotto-voce riff numbers that recalled Lunceford's "Organ Grinder's Swing." For the rest of the fifties, the Third Herd continued, in reincarnation after reincarnation, in the same direction, although at one point it was reduced to a distilled but recognizable octet. In its present reincarnation, the band, which has lots of new young soloists who say nothing at great length with emotion, displays considerable affection for the high points of the Second and even the First Herd, as well as for Ellington, the blues, and the fashionable accents of gospel music. All the Herds have now been conveniently rolled into one, which should please the voters a good deal.

# A Burning Desire

A few weeks ago, I got a letter out of the blue from Vance Bourjaily, the novelist and assistant professor of English at the State University of Iowa, telling me that Lou Black, the original banjoist with the New Orleans Rhythm Kings, a seven-piece white group that set Chicago on its ear in 1921, was considering a part-time comeback. He went on to say that Black, who is a hunting and fishing companion of his, had retired from music in 1931 and had become a successful Midwestern businessman as well as a "legendary shotgun shooter and fly-caster"; that he had bought a new thousand-dollar banjo nearly a year ago and had been practicing ever since; and that the results were astonishingly good. He closed by saying that he and Black would be in New York soon, and suggested that I call Black at the Gramercy Park Hotel. I did, the other day, and arranged to meet him at the hotel. He sounded big and hearty on the phone, and before he hung up, he uttered these cautionary words: "One thing I want to make absolutely clear, sir. I wouldn't go back into the music business full time for all the tea in China. I'm sixty-two and have too much sense."

When I stepped off the elevator, I found that Black, who was standing outside the door of his room, *is* big and hearty—tall, bald, and ample-waisted, with an open, generous face and a wide smile. He was dressed in a short-sleeved white shirt, a brown tie, black slacks, and black shoes. He ushered me firmly into his room and into a comfortable chair, and sat down in a straight-backed one. "You know, I don't understand it," he said, rubbing his hands together as if he were sampling a clear, cold January day. "I went out this morning for breakfast in this shirt and a summer jacket, and people were wearing hats, and overcoats up to their ears. This is some place! I can go fishing on North Wind Lake in the big woods way up north in Ontario and not get turned around for a second. Here, I never know where I'm at or what's going to happen next. Last night, Vance and Jim Silberman, an editor, and I went over to Bourbon Street. I took my banjo and they asked me to play, and, by golly, we were there until four o'clock. I'm a small-town boy likes to go to bed early. Dick Wellstood was on piano and Ahmed Abdul-Malik was on bass, and Malik told me he'd never heard things like that on the banjo. I can tell you I was pleased. I hadn't touched the instrument for thirty years when one day, around last Christmas, my daughter Joyce—she's an accomplished pianist—said, 'I want you to teach me the banjo.' I said, 'You're crazy, a beautiful girl like you playing banjo.' My wife, Natalie, who's a darn good Dixieland pianist, said, 'Nonsense, Dad. Go ahead and teach her.' We were at it two or three weeks, and then I said, 'What we need is another banjo.' I went to Chicago and bought this Vega, and we played duets, and suddenly I discovered I'd been lonely for playing. Of course, I'm not completely happy with it yet. Some things I used to do on the instrument are still quite impossible. As soon as I get this new banjo working, I may try a recording, but there's no rush. If there's anything more pitiful than a has-been trying to make a comeback who isn't ready, I don't know it."

I asked Black when he had first taken up the instrument.

"When I was about seven," he replied. "I was born in Rock Island, Illinois, where I still live. My dad was a conductor on the Chicago, Rock Island & Pacific, and he played banjo, and he and my mother used to sing old songs like 'Nelly Gray.' I had a burning desire to play the banjo, and it was my brother started me on it. Oh, my, he was good! When I was around twelve, I met a banjoist named Homer Garber in Des Moines, through relatives, and he showed me some things. He was a clerk in a cigar store, and he was the best banjo player I've ever heard. I started professionally in 1917, with a dentist named Wrixon. He had a four- or five-piece outfit, and we played the Rock Island society parties, the country club, and a dance hall named the Coliseum, which is still going. My schooling—I'd been through twelve years in nine—was already over, and in 1919 I joined Carlisle Evans, a pianist and good, solid orchestra man. Evans' Original Jazz Band, his group was called. In 1920, we worked on the riverboat Capitol between St. Louis and St. Paul in the summer, and around New Orleans in the winter. Leon Rappolo, the clarinettist, was in the band, and so were Emmet Hardy, a marvellous cornettist who never recorded, and Leon Prima, Louie's brother. I left Evans in 1921 and went over to the New Orleans Rhythm Kings, which already had Rappolo, Jack Pettis on saxophone, Frank Snyder on drums, George Brunies on trombone, Paul Mares on cornet, and Elmer Schoebel on piano. Steve Brown, the bassist, joined after me. We were at the Friar's Inn for a couple of years, and when we'd finished work, or when there were no more customers to play for, we'd go over to the Dreamland and sit in with Pop Oliver and Louis Armstrong. You know why he was called Pop? When he played, his right eye came almost out of the socket from the force of his blowing. It was the damnedest sight I've ever seen. He had enormous lips, too, and his cornet mouthpiece would disappear right inside them. Once in a while, he'd stand up there in front of the band, cradle the cornet on its valves on a handkerchief in his left hand, put his right hand in his pocket, and play ten or eleven choruses of 'Tiger Rag' or 'Dippermouth Blues' without ever touching the valves with his right hand and without repeating himself. Nobody ever matched Pop Oliver, except Bix Beiderbecke, who sat in with us when he was in town. Once, someone wrote out one of Bix's solos note for note and, without letting on, put the transcription in front of him and asked him to play it. Bix, who was a grand kid, looked at the music and looked at him, and said, 'Hell, I can't play that fancy stuff!' Dave Tough and Jimmy McPartland and Bud Freeman used to hang around, and Jelly Roll Morton did too. Well, the Rhythm Kings broke up in 1923—largely for personal reasons—and some of us joined the Memphis Melody Boys. It was a dance band—an eight-forty-five-to-eleven-forty-five band. In 1925, I rejoined Carlisle Evans, and a few years later I began jobbing around, and then, because things were already beginning to fall apart, I took a job as a staff man with Station WHO, in Des Moines, where I stayed until 1931. Then I quit music and went to work for a roofing company, and in 1940 I joined John Deere, the farm-implement manufacturers. After the war, I was hired by the Moline Consumers Company, where I'm an outdoor-building-materials man. I'm never going to retire, and I've made my boss sign a statement saying he'll never make me. I'll retire when I fall right flat dead on my face."

Black got up, stretched, walked easily up and down

the room several times, and sat down. "I said my playing again would be a part-time thing, and that's just what it is. Since last August, I've been working two nights a week at the Arabian Room of the Holiday Inn, in Moline, with a trio. There wasn't anybody around those parts who remembered who Lou Black the banjoist was, but now the place is packed. The banjo has been maligned, and I'd like to help set that right. Brian Rust, the English jazz critic, has been writing me, and he'd like me to come over to England and play. An English friend of Vance's says that in England everyone knows who Lou Black is."

# Uncharted

For purposes of orientation, I sometimes travel by mental helicopter over an imaginary relief map of Western music, which looks like this: On the right is a broad, old river, its many sources buried deep in Appalachian-type mountains. It is marked "Classical," and it has countless tributaries, some generally identified (Hungarian-Folk, Indian-Folk), some specifically (Monteverdi, Palestrina, Gluck). On the left of the map is a shorter, far narrower river, originating in a peak-encircled lake. These are the river Jazz and Lake European-African. The river courses through canyons and over dangerous rapids until it comes out on the same plateau as the Classical. It, too, has tributaries, some generally named (Spirituals, Field Cries, Blues), some specifically (Scott Joplin, Louis Armstrong, James P. Johnson). On the plateau separating the rivers, however, is a sizable stream fed by trickles from the rivers and called the Third Stream, or Schuller's Brook, after its discoverer, Gunther Schuller. This stream heads toward and perhaps feeds into—I am not always sure—a swampy, unexplored area. At any rate, during much of a third-stream concert given by the Orchestra U.S.A. at Hunter College, I found myself hovering between the brook and the swamp. It is a luxuriant terrain, but I saw little sign of life.

95

The Orchestra U.S.A. is a twenty-nine-piece coöperative group made up about half and half of jazz and classical musicians, and directed by John Lewis, the sometime musical director of the Modern Jazz Quartet. Lewis and Gunther Schuller act as conductors. According to an inclusive program note, the orchestra was "organized for the purpose of exploring fully the possibilities of the wide repertoire which the modern musician of all-around ability and understanding can perform." Last week, this repertoire consisted of a Bach fugue; two pieces by Miljenko Prohaska, a Yugoslavian jazz-and-classical musician; and six by Lewis. The Bach was the jazz counterpart of a Stokowski transcription, and used a light, ineffectual echoing of themes, supported by an occasionally sounded four-four beat. The rest of the repertoire had dimmer origins. Most had jazz rhythms, and most had solos of varying lengths by Gerry Mulligan (a guest), Eric Dolphy, Jerome Richardson, Joe Newman, and Lewis. The orchestrations suggested Gil Evans and Schuller and Jimmy Lunceford (Prohaska's "Intima"), and were overlaid here and there by strands dyed Debussy, Bartók, and Stravinsky. But, unlike some of the earlier and frequently exciting third-stream investigations by Schuller and Lewis, usually performed by less unwieldy groups, the selections played by the orchestra lacked the obvious qualities both of classical music (majesty, variety, complexity, passion) and of jazz (tone, timbre, improvisation, emotion).

The remainder of the evening was given over to seven straight jazz numbers played by Mulligan and such orchestra members as Jim Hall, Richard Davis, Connie Kay, and Lewis. All but one were standards, and all were distinguished by the work of Kay, Lewis, and Hall. Kay was a marvel. He was comfortable with both groups, and his cymbal work demonstrated that it is, with the exception of Dave Tough's, unprecedented in jazz. He uses thin, gorgeously toned cymbals, from which he gets a triangle-like ring, and he varies his patterns continually, often condensing the customary *da de-da* beat into a quick *da-da*. He never uses the expected cymbal, and he never plays at conventional volumes (thus his beautiful soft drumstick strokes behind the beginning of Mulligan's solo in "Poor Butterfly"; most drummers would have jumped in). Lewis was his succinct, impassioned self, and Hall played with a delicacy and thought that about dictate his abandoning the electric amplifier—a now superfluous device (guitarists adopted it during the big-band era simply to be heard) that distorts and cheapens the natural guitar sound. Mulligan was flawless and, for reasons beyond me, totally unaffecting. Perhaps the baritone saxophone, with its heavy tone, should not be played so *well;* Harry Carney and Serge Chaloff, though equally expert, purposely manhandle the instrument, breaking down its pomp and solemnity. Davis took a witty walking-bass solo in "The Way You Look Tonight," but elsewhere he used too many upper-register notes, which tended to jostle Kay's basically high-toned attack.

# Fortieth

The lot of the long-lived artist in this country is hazardous. He is fulsomely praised too soon, and then suffers from the inevitable swing of the pendulum. Or he is ignored during his life, and then guiltily canonized when he is dead. Or he is encircled by cultists, and then abruptly seized upon by the public and sentimentalized. Or he is teasingly paid middling compliments, and then, the gears skipping a couple of speeds, is taken for granted. The last of these alternatives has long since been thrust upon Duke Ellington, who, now sixty-four, is celebrating his fortieth anniversary as a composer-orchestrator-bandleader-pianist. There are explanations of this suspended status. Ellington is unique, and he has usually been praised by the wrong people for the wrong reasons. The world of classical music has compared him favorably (and condescendingly) to Ravel and Delius and Debussy, although the two musics cannot be compared. The world of jazz—when it has not downgraded him out of jealousy or ignorance—has deified him solely as a jazz musician, though he is far more. The Broadway musical world has nervously clapped him on the back but has rarely sought him out for a form that, given the chance, he might well revolutionize. And, of course, Ellington is a Negro.

But his originality, grace, durability, and variety demand that he be considered in relation to all American music. When that critical readjustment is made, it is immediately clear that Ellington, in his iconoclastic way, has constructed a musical organism without counterpart. This organism—built sometimes accidentally, sometimes consciously, but always painstakingly over the past four decades—functions something like this: Ellington composes a number, which may be a blues, a capsule concerto, a ballad, a program piece, a tone poem, a sly bit of portraiture, an up-tempo celebration of nothing in particular, or a reworking of a standard. It is tried out by the band, which makes suggestions, and an arrangement is developed. This arrangement is orchestrated and played over and over and, if it is found not wanting, passes into the band's repertory. Once there, it is far from static, for each time it is performed it is improvised upon, to different degrees, by both the ensemble and the soloists, among them the composer himself. Finally, a kind of composite rendition emerges, and a "Solitude" or "Mood Indigo" or "Never No Lament" takes permanent, though always malleable, shape. Thus Ellington is at once a classical and a popular-music composer, an interpretive classical musician, a conductor, and a jazz improviser.

How beautifully this organism functions at its best! Ellington is an extremely gifted melodist (he is comparable, in this respect, to Tchaikovsky). Moreover, unlike Gershwin and Berlin and Kern and Rodgers, whose finest tunes are discreet displays of subjective emotions, Ellington writes numbers that objectively suggest, with wit and poetry and subtlety and great taste, the *only* way to feel about a local train in the South, melancholy, the clatter in a Harlem air shaft, a beautiful woman, racism, a celebrated vaudevillian, a happy party, or a three-cent stamp, the last of which was immortalized in a number written in the forties and titled, naturally, "Three Cent Stomp." But Ellington is also a *composer*, whose miniature concertos are substantial in form and content as well as inimitable, and whose orchestrations, continually ruffled by the individualities of his sidemen, delight the ear and refresh the mind. The Ellington band, as the inseparable second half of this organism, is a remarkable democracy. Each member is a hero, yet each is beholden to the whole. The reason is brilliantly simple: Ellington, in shying away from such one-man bands as Armstrong and Lester Young and Charlie Parker, has chosen musicians whose originality stops at the eccentric rather than the iconoclastic. And yet these eccentrics—consider the varieties of sound and attack of such men as Cootie Williams, Jimmy Blanton, Lawrence Brown, Johnny Hodges, and Tricky Sam Nanton—have become a unit which is always a degree or two ahead of its marvellous parts.

These fortieth-anniversary thoughts have been provoked by Columbia's fitting release of "The Ellington Era: 1927-40." Although the album ends on the eve of Ellington's superb 1940-42 period (the property of Victor), it demonstrates, in many of its forty-eight numbers, just how Ellington readied himself and his band for that miraculous musical explosion. This preparation was accomplished in three bursts. The first, and faintest, lasted from 1925, when Ellington made his first records, to around 1928. The band was only on a par with Fletcher Henderson's and perhaps slightly below Jelly Roll Morton's various groups. It was distinguished by just two things—Ellington's already unmistakable talents as a composer ("Black and Tan Fantasy," "The Mooche," and "East St. Louis Toodleoo"), and the presence of Bubber Miley, Tricky Sam Nanton, Barney

Bigard, Harry Carney, and Johnny Hodges. From 1927 to 1932, the band played for dancing and the floor show at Cotton Club, and these functions are reflected in its sassy fast tempos ("Jubilee Stomp"), its occasionally dudish saxophone-section work, and Ellington's showy ragtime stride piano. Miley and his pupil, Nanton, were already imposing soloists who, with their plunger mutes and growling, were contributing wholly new musical sounds, and Hodges, Carney, and Bigard forcefully suggested their later selves.

The second period opened in 1929, with the departure of Miley and the arrival of Cootie Williams and Juan Tizol, and it ended in 1935, when the band had swelled to fourteen men, among them Rex Stewart and Lawrence Brown. Ellington's tunes in these years became virtual compositions—such things as "Rockin' in Rhythm," "Mood Indigo," "It Don't Mean a Thing," and "Drop Me Off in Harlem." These used varying chorus lengths, simultaneous solos, new harmonies (especially in the background saxophone figures, as in "Blue Tune"), the human voice as an instrument, swelling and subsiding brass-section chords ("Bundle of Blues"), and such rhythmic devices as unexpected breaks, double-time passages, and Afro-Cuban beats. Ellington's soloists developed with remarkable speed, and by 1935 Williams, Brown, Hodges (on soprano and alto saxophones), Nanton, and Stewart were first-rate improvisers, while the band, by virtue of Ellington's scoring and the originality of its ensemble sound, had a new texture and consistency. It could play anything and play it uniquely—a mock-mournful blues ("Saddest Tale"), fast blues, descriptive stomps ("Lightnin'," "Old Man Blues"), mood pieces ("Solitude," "Lazy Rhapsody"), and standards ("Sheik of Araby").

In 1936, the band blossomed into the marvel it has

been ever since. The rhythm section, long bedevilled by inadequate bassists and a general four-square approach, suddenly started to swing. Ellington began fashioning his perfect concertos around his sidemen ("Clarinet Lament" for Bigard, "Echoes of Harlem" for Williams, "Boy Meets Horn" for Stewart), and, in so doing, developed ensemble passages that were really collective alter-solos, often worthy of being expanded into whole numbers ("The Sergeant Was Shy"). Now and again, the entire band played together, in unison or in harmony—a rending, incredibly rich sound that is one of the delights of Western orchestral music. (Here is the nub of Ellington's success. Any proficient musician could transcribe such a passage and any proficient group of musicians could play it. But the results would not be the same, for no musician, regardless of his skill, could reproduce the timbre, tone, and inflections of Ellington's musicians. In short, their styles—massed into a single voice or heard alone—are as important to Ellington's music as his compositions.) In the six minutes of "Diminuendo in Blue" and "Crescendo in Blue," he proved once and for all that jazz can be a composed music, by letting the band roll through almost two dozen medium-tempo ensemble choruses of the blues, each completely different (an ingenious two-note saxophone riff, echoed by Cootie Williams—one chorus; a ripe-on-the-bough clarinet trio pitted against booming trombones—one chorus; and so forth). He went on writing gorgeous melodies—"I Let a Song Go Out of My Heart," "Prelude to a Kiss," "Subtle Lament," "Sophisticated Lady"—and his portraits of people took on an oblique and irresistible wittiness. The band, stimulated by these innovations, surpassed itself individually and collectively, and in turn stimulated Ellington. In 1939, when Billy Strayhorn, Ben Webster, and Jimmy Blanton were hired, the band reached perfection. One looked—and looks—for its match in jazz, on Broadway, and in the music of Copland and Virgil Thomson and Charles Ives. That this achievement—together with Ellington's sporadic echoes of it—should be taken for granted must distress him considerably. But gentlemen of genius never let on; they just keep working.

Jazz musicians are ultimately judged by their recordings, and in the past year or two Ellington has done uncommonly well. Moreover, he has done it by uncharacteristically stepping out of his band and recording as a piano soloist and with groups whose styles cover most of the rest of jazz. Four of these efforts are "Money Jungle: Duke Ellington-Charlie Mingus-Max Roach" (United Artists), "Duke Ellington: Piano in the Foreground" (Columbia), "The Great Reunion: Louis Armstrong and Duke Ellington" (Roulette), and "Duke Ellington and John Coltrane" (Impulse!). Why Ellington has all at once shed his modesty is not clear. Perhaps he has at last admitted his virtues as a pianist, hidden so long beneath the great bushel of his band, or perhaps he just wants to spell out some of his music *himself*, the way a director might suddenly take over his star's role. No matter which, the results have been beneficial, for we now know more about the origins of such revolutionaries as Thelonious Monk and Cecil Taylor, and we know a good deal more about Ellington. A master of circumlocution, he has never before spoken so clearly.

Ellington is a reformed stride pianist. Stride piano was as much a way of life as a way of playing, and Ellington's piano reflects this; it is accidental rather than calculated. His attack is orchestral and melodic. He uses a great many chords whose strangeness and richness summon up massed instruments. In between are generally brief single-note passages in the form of raggy arpeggios or spraddled rhythmic patterns. He has a clean, casual touch, and he never fluffs a note. Most pianists handle tempo as if it were a thermometer (slow equals cool, fast equals hot), but Ellington sees it as the means to varied moods. In slow tunes, he will rhapsodize, emitting romantic vapors and shadowy figures suitable for twilights and moon-blessed nights. He becomes pianistic in middle speeds, and instead of simply consorting with the melody, he will bear down, producing arabesques at once modern and Gothic. He does not take fast tempos seriously. He will fool around in the lower octaves with thunderous chords, rocking them heavily back and forth; he will ride for a chorus at a time on one or two notes, sending coded messages to another re-formed stride man, Count Basie; or he will pluck necklaces of notes out of the thin air of the upper registers. Urbanity keeps emotion at heel, and Ellington is a notably urbane man. (He was undeniably the first non-Uncle Tom Negro artist, and it is only recently that others have begun to catch up with him.) So it is not surprising, after all, that he has hidden his piano; for all its rococo quirks, it is basically primitive and very hot.

"Money Jungle" and "Piano in the Foreground" are solo excursions with rhythm accompaniment. The first, done with Charlie Mingus and Max Roach, is an almost warlike affair. Mingus and Roach, and many of their generation, have considerable respect for Ellington. Mingus, in fact, idolizes him, but an idolater brought face to face with his inspiration can, out of fear and/or excitement, turn into an unwitting combatant. Accordingly, in this recording Mingus sounds nervous and pushing and overwrought. Time and again he plays tight, obtrusive high notes, some of them with what appear to be his nails, and many of them in defiant staccato rhythms. He seems to be saying, I revere you and I shall prove it by demolishing you. Roach, on the other hand, reacts with confusion and uncertainty. His playing is muffled and lustreless, though Ellington *is* an extremely rhythmic pianist, and he frequently gets tangled up in Mingus's stridency. The result of this back-room free-for-all is a coarse thicket of sounds that do not bother Ellington at all. In "Money Jungle" and "Very Special," medium Ellington blues, he is firm and businesslike, but in "Caravan" he simply overrides his companions and out comes a stirring performance, full of big chords and brisk bass and tomtom work. And in the slow, pastel "Warm Valley" and "Solitude," Mingus and Roach slip nearly out of sight, leaving Ellington to marvellous ad-lib ministrations.

"Piano in the Foreground" is very different. Ellington is backed by Aaron Bell and Sam Woodyard, who are helpful and mostly self-effacing. Of the eleven selections, five are notable and one—"Summertime"—is a small masterpiece. An imitation Negro lament, "Summertime" generally brings out the worst in its interpreters. Ellington treats it with irony. After a hands-on-the-tomtoms introduction by Woodyard, he states the melody with lagging single notes. These soon fade into rocky, reiterated chords, decorated with jarring trills and off-notes. Heavy outright blues figures are hammered into this granitic procession, which grows increasingly intense. Then he suddenly relaxes the pressure, drifts back into mild single notes, and ends with a splintering Beethoven chord that is held until its last dissonance has lumbered out of sight. "It's Bad to Be Forgotten," a new Ellington tune, has a charming melody, and he approaches it with lightness and affection, using widely spaced notes and echoing upper-register plinks. "So," another new piece which is done slowly, is nearly equal to "Summertime." After a simple statement of the melody, Ellington drops into a thoughtful, possibly mocking low-register single-note passage reminiscent of Eddy Duchin at his best, then moves gradually up the keyboard and into a chorus of descending blues tremolos, and exits softly. "Yearning for Love," a regrettably forgotten Ellington tune, first recorded in 1936, is given a two-chorus rendition, which is enough to reveal its grace and to suggest that it should be recorded again by the band. The record closes with the newly composed "Springtime in Africa." It is the epitome of Ellington the impressionist; all is delicate, tingling, nebulous, barely stirring. There are, as well, fascinating reworkings of "I Can't Get Started" and "Body and Soul," the second of which has a bridge whose gorgeous, irregularly placed dissonances surpass Monk.

Ellington has recorded before with Louis Armstrong, and in "The Great Reunion" he sits in with Armstrong's group, which includes Trummy Young and Barney Bigard. Barring a fine solo in "Don't Get Around Much Anymore," he stays largely in the background. Armstrong, challenged by the all-Ellington material, plays and sings better than he has in years, and in his opening solo for "It Don't Mean a Thing" he fashions an annunciatory statement that recalls his celebrated introduction for "West End Blues."

Ellington's collaboration with John Coltrane is equally agreeable. Neither is frightened of the other, and their musical differences are easily resolved. When Coltrane gets involved in one of his Himalayan scalar exercises, Ellington drops out and listens, and when "In a Sentimental Mood" and "My Little Brown Book" are called for, Coltrane stays close to the melody, handling it with reverence. Ellington's occasional solos are good, and it is a treat to hear his composure when Elvin Jones, on drums, slips into interweaving streams of double- and triple-time accents. It's too bad that Jones, who is replaced in three numbers by Sam Woodyard, is not present all the way through. He understands Ellington's sly rhythmic complexities more thoroughly than most of Ellington's contemporaries.

Despite such delightful forays among his subjects, Ellington and his band are inseparable. "Afro-Bossa: Duke Ellington and His Orchestra" (Reprise), made a year or so ago, is proof. In spite of its title, the record has nothing to do with the *bossa nova;* instead, its twelve numbers, many of them new, are rendered in rhythms ranging from the bolero to belly-dance Egyptian. (Ellington began exploring such rhythms long before Xavier Cugat, Stan Kenton, the cha-cha, and the *bossa nova* were invented.) The band is in top condition, the arrangements are less fragmentary than in many recent Ellington band efforts, and all in all the record is the most impressive one the group has made since "Such Sweet Thunder." Especially appealing are "Purple Gazelle" (a handsome Harry Carney-led saxophone-section figure, loosed at leisurely wa-wa trumpets; a fine Cootie Williams plunger-mute solo), "Absinthe" (more fascinating saxophone writing), "Moonbow" (a Ray Nance plunger-mute trumpet solo over tomtoms and a clarinet trio and, eventually, a big ensemble hum), and "Sempre Amore" (Nance soloing on the violin, with a bow and pizzicato, against a wholly bewitching *chaconne* reed figure of the sort Ellington has been dropping into his backgrounds for thirty years). There are also wasted numbers, but these do not matter. The Ellington organism—from Ellington and Billy Strayhorn (who plays most of the piano) to Cootie Williams—is here in full armor.

## Such Sweet Thunder

Duke Ellington's band has something in common with the Supreme Court: its members tend to stay put for life. Harry Carney has been with him since the Coolidge administration; Johnny Hodges, except for a five-year stint of iconoclasm, has played for him since 1928; Lawrence Brown, another temporary individualist, has occupied his chair most of the time since 1932; Jimmy Hamilton has been with Ellington for twenty-one straight years; and Ray Nance has, with the exception of a year or so, been around for twenty-two years. Thus, when one of Ellington's sidemen quits, seismographs pick up the tremors. At least, that happened in 1940, when Cootie Williams left Ellington, after twelve years of service, to join Benny Goodman. Williams received hundreds of how-could-you-you-traitor letters, there were half-mast editorials, and the bandleader Raymond Scott wrote and recorded a lament called "When Cootie Left the Duke."

Well, Williams, after an absence of twenty-two years, has rejoined Ellington. I recently caught up with him and asked him how it felt to be back in the fold.

"It feels good," Williams said, in a deep, laconic voice. "My name is still on some of the parts in the arrangements, and that makes me feel specially good. Oh, the band have changed some. Jimmy Blanton, he's gone, and Sonny Greer and Ben Webster and Tricky Sam Nanton, and I think Duke builds the band more around arrangements now than around soloists. Of course, he had a lot of soloists to work with when I left. One reason I came back with Duke is he's the greatest man I ever knew. Everybody thought when I left I just jumped up and out. That's not true. When Benny Goodman wanted me, I told Duke, and he said, 'Let me handle everything. Let me see how much I can get for you. You deserve to make some money.' So he did—he handled the contract. And when I left, I said 'You have my job open when the contract is up?' and he said 'Your chair's always open.' "

Williams lit a cigarette and took a sip of coffee. A medium-sized, barrel-chested man with a square, imperious face, he was wearing a dark-blue suit, a pale-blue shirt, and a tie with broad red and black stripes. "I was born in Mobile, Alabama, in 1910—not 1908, like the history books say. My mother was a church organist, and my father ran a gambling house along with a man named Son Coin. When I was around three or four, my parents took me to a band concert in the park, and on the way home they asked me what did I hear. I said, 'Cootie cootie cootie.' It stuck. I took up drums when I was about five, and later, in the school band, I wanted to switch to trombone. But my arms were too short to reach the lowest position on the slide, so the bandmaster told me, 'You play trumpet.' I said I didn't like the trumpet, so he gave me a whooping, and I played the trumpet. Louis Armstrong has always been my idol, and I saw him first one summer when the school band went up to Chicago. A little kid, I stood outside the fence of the Oriental Garden, I think it was, and listened to Louis in King Oliver's band. When I got back that night, I got a whooping for that." Williams chuckled in a slow, easy way. "I worked around Mobile with Holman's jazz band and Johnny Pope's band, and then Edmond Hall, who was with Eagle-Eye Shields' band in Jacksonville, Florida, told Shields about me. Shields wanted to hire me, and Hall got hold of my father to see if it was all right. Well, Son Coin have relatives in Jacksonville, so my father say O.K. and put me in their care. Hall and I left Shields after two years and joined Alonzo Ross's band and toured all over Florida and Georgia. I believe we were the first colored band to play

109

Miami. I was making two hundred and fifty or three hundred dollars a week and I was only seventeen. I sent it home to my father. Then a ballroom in Brooklyn sent for Ross's band, and after the engagement Hall and I stayed on. We got a job playing at a dancing school in midtown, and after hours we used to jam at the Band Box, up at a Hundred and Thirty-first Street. They specialized in certain instruments on certain nights, and on the night of the trumpet I always went there. One time, somebody got Chick Webb out of bed, and he came and listened to me and asked me to join him. He was at the Savoy Ballroom, and this would have been about 1928. I worked with Chick a month, and then the union delegate came around, and since I didn't have my union card, he and Chick got in a big argument. We went down to union headquarters, and this union man said, 'All right, I'll tell you what I'll do, young fellow. Until you get your card, I'll let you work with anyone in New York *but* Chick Webb.' Chick didn't want me with anyone else, so he paid me a salary. Then Fletcher Henderson asked Chick could I come with him on a six-week road trip, and Chick said yes. It was rough at first. Big Green, Henderson's trombonist, used to sit right behind me in the band, and he'd lean over and say, 'Boy, I'm going to kill you, kill you, kill you,' and Bobby Stark, the trumpeter, sat next to me, and he'd say, 'Big, leave this boy alone. What's the matter with you?' Big Green scared me to death. I worked with Henderson for a while at the Roseland Ballroom when we got back, and then Johnny Hodges told Duke Ellington about me and I joined him at the Cotton Club. It was quite a different sound in music. I laughed out loud at first when I heard those weird wa-wa-wa jungle sounds. Then it seemed to me since I'd been hired to take Bubber Miley's place, I better learn to play the mute like him. I never heard Bubber in person, so I learned from Tricky Sam Nanton. Duke didn't tell me I had to learn. I just did, and it didn't take very long."

Williams leaned back, smoothed his shirt with his hand, expanded his chest, and exhaled slowly. "When my contract with Benny Goodman was up in 1941, I asked Duke for my job back, and he told me, 'You're too big for the job. You're bigger than you think you are. Go on your own.' So I did. I organized a big band, and for a while things were bad. But in 1943 I made two hundred and fifty thousand dollars. Half of that went to my backers. Everybody had backers in those days, or they would have sunk. Then I quit my backers and *I* sunk, and in 1948 I gave up the big band and took on a small one. In the fifties, we worked the Savoy Ballroom for seven years, until it closed. Then I toured as a single, and that was the hardest musical experience I ever had. Once, in Toronto, I played with a local group that had other jobs during the day, and we'd play 'Do Nothin' Till You Hear from Me'—that's what they called Duke's old 'Concerto for Cootie' after they put lyrics to it—and that group sound like they was playing something else. I had to learn to close my ears. I couldn't take it after that, so I got my own quartet, and then I was a musical director for a singer, and then I played for a month or so with Goodman, and finally I came back with Duke. And that's where I'll stay. My nerves are not good enough to go along with the crowd of musicians that are coming up. I went in Small's, in Harlem, a while back. A young tenor man—you'd know his name if you heard it—happened to be playing there. I listened. I thought, This can't be true. I left, and I came back and listened again, and it *was* true. I thought, He sound like a be*ginn*er to me." Williams chuckled. "Now, Charlie Parker and Bud Powell, they were *mu-*

*sicians.* Oh, they could play! I had both of them in my big band. But Charlie Parker was a bad influence on jazz. There never was a musician before that influenced all the instruments—saxophones, drums, trumpets, piano. Everybody had his own style in those days. Now everybody's Charlie Parker. Maybe in three or four months I'll write a book on the trumpet. I see so many young musicians don't even stand properly, don't know how to breathe. My power comes from breathing properly, from using my chest and my abdomen. Tomorrow we go to Newark, and then to Lowell, Massachusetts, and then to Europe. A musician have to travel to work."

Almost a year after I had interviewed Williams, Ellington, with Williams in striking evidence, gave a magnificent concert at Carnegie Hall. My report follows:

None of the trumpeters who replaced Williams in the Ellington band matched him, for he is—like such colleagues as Johnny Hodges, Lawrence Brown, and Harry Carney—unique. When he first joined Ellington, his style was already statuesque. He had a curiously dense tone, and he played with a deliberation and poise still new in jazz. He rarely left the middle register, he used few notes, and he conveyed a Percheron emotion. This style, though, was soon overshadowed by his adoption of the plunger mute. By 1940, Williams' plunger-mute playing had become one of the wonders of music. Its sounds seemed to bridge the twilight between thought and speech, and they evoked every emotion. There were crescendo growls (anger, happiness, jubilation), half-sounded sighs (sorrow, serenity), stuttering figures (surprise, laughter), and legato wa-wa's (compassion). He mixed these devices continually, forcing into them the same power that distinguished his open-horn work. Occasionally he put his mute aside, and with great effect. His tone swelled and rang, producing sounds that suggested anthems and whipping flags. Williams' abilities have diminished little since then. His tone has deepened and he uses even fewer notes. The dancing, tongued figures have slowed down and sometimes give way to rests or long-held notes, the last of which are literally pushed from his horn. His open-horn work remains pro-clamatory and final.

Williams is a fervent and delightful performer. At Carnegie Hall, he played throughout "Caravan" and a medium blues, exhibiting a singular mixture of shyness and bold professionalism. Standing stage front, he seemed to lift out his notes with his shoulders, which rose steadily during every phrase. At the same time, he listed slowly to port, and rocked easily back and forth, his face an intense whorl. During the interludes between his solos in the blues number, he went into a bear-like dance in which he spun, bowed, and shuffled, all the while mumbling loudly to himself. When the number ended, he clapped his horn to his side as if he were saluting, did an about-face, and was back in his seat before the applause began.

Williams appeared to ignite the whole band. The brass section played with an authority it hasn't had in twenty years, and the reeds and trombones were equally inspired. (When Jo Jones was once asked why he had turned down an invitation to join Ellington, he said, "The drummer sits right beside that brass section, and that brass section hits him right in the stomach night after night and kills him.") Ellington himself, got up in Edwardian style, looked buoyant. Aside from half a dozen throwaway numbers built around Paul Gonsalves, Hodges, Rolf Ericson (flugelhorn), and Cat Anderson, the program, in contrast to Ellington's recent wont, was varied and surprising. He introduced a five-part suite, "Impressions of the Far East," that was full of wit, Oriental harmonies and rhythms, and resplendent solos by Harry Carney and Lawrence Brown. There were several short new numbers, one written by Williams. He played "Harlem—A Tone Parallel," a first-rate program piece from the early fifties that has been re-scored and is dominated by rubato effects and stunning crescendos. And there were gentle, mocking reworkings of "Rockin' in Rhythm," "Satin Doll," "Black and Tan Fan-tasy," "Creole Love Call," and "The Mooche," the last three done as a medley. But for this evening, at least, the ma-terials did not matter as much as the superb orchestra that played them.

Duke Ellington has had a bullish year. The Pulitzer Prize Advisory Committee's refusal to honor him with a special long-term achievement award in music has brought him twice the attention the award would have. He has produced three well-received albums—witty reshapings of the "Mary Poppins" score, of some of the Beatles' music, and of old big-band hits—and last month he appeared at the Newport Jazz Festival; a week or so ago he conducted the New York Philharmonic in the world première of his "The Golden Broom and the Green Apple," and a few days later he was awarded the Bronze Medal of the City of New York. I missed the "Golden Broom" première, but was on hand at City Hall Plaza for the medal presentation. It was a hot, sunny day, and when I arrived, a five-piece Depart-ment of Sanitation band, stationed at one side of the plat-form, was doing wonders with Ellington's theme song, "Take the 'A' Train." I found an aisle seat on the platform beside a pleasant, bright-haired woman who introduced herself as Mrs. Wallace Lomoe, of Milwaukee, and as an old friend and fervent admirer of Ellington's. On her left was Willis Conover, of the Voice of America, and, on *his* left, Nesuhi Ertegun, vice-president of Atlantic Records.

"I'm staying at Delmonico's, and I'm having a fantastic week in New York altogether," Mrs. Lomoe told us. "On Friday night, I was at Philharmonic Hall for the première of 'The Golden Broom.' Duke made the Philharmonic *swing*. There were even some good solos, although the strings had trouble with a longish blues passage. And now I'm here at this marvellous ceremony. These are things that should happen often but do only rarely."

"There's Clark Terry and Billy Taylor and Bunny Briggs," Conover said. "And Jerome Richardson and Ben Tucker and Joe Benjamin. All the bass players in New York must be here. And there's Constance Baker Motley, the Manhattan Borough President, and Supreme Court Judge Edward Dudley."

Mrs. Motley and Judge Dudley took seats at the front of the platform.

"There's John Popkin, of the Hickory House," Conover said. "Hi, John!"

Popkin sat down across the aisle from us, and the Sanitation Department band broke into "Perdido." It stopped abruptly and started "Take the 'A' Train" again. Ellington, accompanied by his wife and by his sister Ruth and his nephew Stephen, had arrived and was approaching the platform. Shaking well-wishers' hands, he mounted the platform, where he shook more hands, delivered several embraces, and made his way over to Mrs. Lomoe and Conover. "I've got to get out of this sun," he said, looking at the sky and shutting his eyes. "It will give me a sunstroke." He leaned over and kissed Mrs. Lomoe, and waved at Conover. "Sweet kisses on you both," he said. "This scene is a complete shock to me. I thought they were calling me down here to some office to give me a certificate or something." Then he descended from the platform and, his family in tow, disappeared into City Hall. The Sanitation Department band took up "Perdido" again. It was hot and getting hotter. An elderly man with a kindly face, steel-rimmed glasses, and a wide-brimmed hat sat down in the front row.

"That's Arthur Spingarn, the president of the N.A.-A.C.P.," Conover said, leaning across Mrs. Lomoe. "And the big man with white hair next to him is Dr. Arthur Logan, Duke's personal physician and the chairman of the city's Council Against Poverty. Over there is Robert F. Wagner, Jr."

The music stopped, there was a cheer from the audience in the Plaza, which was a sizable one, and Ellington appeared at the top of the City Hall steps and posed with Mrs. Ellington for pictures. "Take the 'A' Train" started again. Ellington conducted the Sanitation Department band briefly and shook each member's hand. Then he mounted the platform with Acting Mayor Paul Screvane and sat down between Screvane and Mrs. Motley. He was dressed in a dark-blue-green suit with soft black stripes, a subtle blue-green shirt, a black tie, and black socks and moccasins.

"Have you noticed the cuffs on Duke's pants?" Mrs. Lomoe whispered to us. "They're at least four inches high. He's starting a new fashion."

Robert Dowling, the city's cultural executive, who was the m.c. for the occasion, took his place at the lectern and introduced Dr. Logan, who quoted a biological definition of the word "sport" as "a sudden spontaneous deviation or variation from type" and went on to say that Ellington was a biological sport, a psychological sport, a physiological sport, and a sport in human relations. Ellington, shielding his head from the sun with a square, flat, gold-wrapped package, beamed. Mr. Dowling introduced Billy Taylor, pianist and Station WLIB disc jockey, who linked Ellington with all generations and with Beethoven and Debussy. Ellington looked quizzical.

Mr. Taylor introduced Clark Terry, Jerome Richardson, Benny Powell, Ben Tucker, and Grady Tate, who took over from the Sanitation Department band and immediately began "Take the 'A' Train." At the end of the number, Ellington gave them a short standing ovation and sat down and put up his sunshade again. Joe Williams sang "Come Sunday," from Ellington's "Black, Brown and Beige," and was given another standing Ellington ovation. This was followed by "Satin Doll" and still another s.E.o. Dowling took the microphone and said, "You have just heard the sound heard around the world. It makes us proud of our American musicality," and introduced the Reverend John Gensel, a Lutheran missionary to the New York jazz community. The Reverend Mr. Gensel closed some remarks on Ellington by saying, "All of us want him to know that we love him gladly." Dowling read a congratulatory telegram from the president of A.S.C.A.P. and introduced Acting Mayor Screvane, who closed his remarks, addressed to Ellington, by intoning, "Through the years of your eminence, you have avoided being misled by that which was merely popular. You survived the Charleston; you will outlast the Watusi. You have remained unaffected by passing fads and fancies. You built your repute and your work on the deep musical tastes of a people. You captured the spirit of a time and of a whole nation. You were able to do this by demanding of yourself and your associates the highest professional performance. Your standard was perfection." Mr. Screvane then rummaged around in the lectern, found the medal, which was the size of a small pancake, and read the inscription on its back: "Presented in appreciation to Edward Kennedy Ellington, Known as Duke—'Musician of Every Year'—distinguished composer and worldwide Ambassador of Good Will—by Robert F. Wagner, Mayor of the City of New York, by the hand of the Acting Mayor, on this 2nd day of August, 1965." Mr. Screvane handed the medal to Mr. Ellington, shook his hand warmly, and said "God bless you."

Ellington's remarks were brief and gracious. He thanked Screvane and all the others present, explained that he needed a sunshade because he was "a night creature," explained the meaning of the title "The Golden Broom and the Green Apple," brought Billy Strayhorn, his alter ego, onto the platform and announced that Strayhorn —*not* Ellington—was the composer of "Take the 'A' Train" (Strayhorn's response: "Well, all I can say is 'Take the "A" Train' "), embraced Strayhorn, and somewhat hesitantly presented copies of Ellington albums to Screvane and Robert F. Wagner, Jr., apologizing for them as "a sort of understated commercial."

"What a marvellous man!" Mrs. Lomoe said.

1964

# Apple Bobbing

One of the easiest but surest
tests of a jazz performance is whether or not it swings. Deciding this is wholly intuitive, for no one knows exactly
what swinging is. Louis Armstrong and John Lewis and
Buddy Tate swing, but Dave Brubeck and J. J. Johnson
and Jimmy Giuffre don't. Ben Webster and Pee Wee Russell swing, but Lennie Tristano and Shorty Rogers don't.
Fats Waller swung, Jelly Roll Morton didn't. Charlie Christian did, Eddie Lang didn't. Any instrument can swing
(the harp and the tuba included), but a whole group rarely
swings all together. Sometimes the drummer swings, towing
the unleavened after him. Sometimes a trumpeter or a saxophonist swings despite the drummer. Sometimes only half
the rhythm section swings. Sometimes a soloist swings for
an entire solo, and sometimes for just three bars. But this
mysterious process has definite ingredients—sensible
tempo (it is almost impossible to swing at very fast or very
slow speeds, or in plain wrong tempos); keeping good,
but not metronomic, time; an equal mixture of relaxation
and tension and the balancing of form and content (superlative technicians often don't swing, and neither do most
back-country blues singers). Perhaps swinging occurs when
the original is played as if by heart and the familiar is

played as if it were original. Although we still look to the drummer as its chief source, there are a remarkable number of unswinging drummers. Of these, Louis Bellson is probably the most puzzling.

In the early fifties, when such things still mattered, Bellson was reputed to be the fastest drummer alive. He had, his admirers claimed, outstripped Gene Krupa and Buddy Rich. Everything was in his favor. A small, lithe, good-looking man (speedy drummers, like racing-car drivers, are always handsome), he was ambidextrous, he had a light, fresh, sure touch, and he moved quicker than a chameleon's tongue. He studied his instrument constantly, wrote books on drumming, and made innovations in equipment (two bass drums rather than one). He seemed to galvanize the bands he played with (Benny Goodman, Harry James, Duke Ellington, Tommy Dorsey), and his solos were spectacular. Then, in the mid-fifties, the course of jazz drumming moved for good into the channel excavated by Kenny Clarke and Max Roach and Art Blakey, and speed and flashiness gave way to polyrhythms and melodic drumming. At the age of thirty, Bellson—the last of the speed-of-light drummers—was an anachronism. Nonetheless, he has continued to appear regularly, either with Pearl Bailey, his wife, or with his own groups, and his style has not changed. Bellson is a good timekeeper and an assembly-line accompanist. He plays in a monotone, depending on a loud, head-on attack rather than on subtle sorties and sallies. He uses one large ride cymbal constantly, spreading predictable offbeat strokes around his tomtom, snare, and bass drums. He accompanies pianists and trumpeters in the same way. He smiles steadily while he plays, and is an almost apologetic showman. His solos are long, overbearing, and just about as fast as they look. He is apt to start with riffling strokes on his high hat, broken by occasional offbeats on his other cymbals or on his snare. He switches to his snare, and he flies through a flurry of rimshots (he keeps his snare tightly muffled, so they sound like an axe on live wood), interspersed with rolls and one-two, one-two-three tomtom strokes. He will prolong this pattern (his approach depends on momentum rather than on the unexpected punch), gradually easing in more and more complex rolls, which he distributes very quickly between the snare and one tomtom, as if they were one drum. Suddenly he launches trip-hammer left-hand strokes on the snare (few drummers can match his left hand), while his right hand floats in a lackadaisical half-time fashion from tomtom to tomtom, from tomtom to cymbals, from tomtom to snare. But his right hand soon catches up with his left, and, his volume rising, he moves into a steady backandforth, backandforth roar on the snare and the tomtoms. His smile turns to a grimace, he grits his teeth, a vein in his neck bulges, and he begins a fast roll on his bass drums with his feet, stops, starts, stops, and then looses a gusherlike bass-drum thunder, which drowns the cannonading of his hands. Everything vibrates at great speed—hands, feet, head, cymbals, drums. This monolithic noise continues for a minute (his hands move faster and faster), and then, with the listener long since prepared for the summit, Bellson pauses, smiles dazedly, and indefatigably retraces his steps, in hot pursuit of infinity.

The Bellson excursions that I heard at the Metropole, with a fifteen-piece pickup group, didn't swing, and neither did his backing up, most of it read from drum parts and done—even the slow tempos—with sticks. His band consisted largely of New York musicians—among others, Bill Berry and Ray Copeland (trumpets), Jimmy Cleve-

123

land and Quentin Jackson (trombones), and Gene Quill and Seldon Powell (saxophones). The arrangements, by such as Neal Hefti, Bill Holman, Marty Paich, Quill, Ernie Wilkins, and Bellson himself, were mechanical and resembled those now favored by Count Basie and Woody Herman. Although Bellson is a static performer, his personality is apparently catching, for the band frequently swung, pulling him along after it. Powell, Cleveland, Jackson, and Copeland soloed enthusiastically and well, but Bellson's solos were nearly endless and unnerving to watch. At their outset, the house lights dimmed and a large spotlight was rolled up just below him, where it peered up through his cymbals like a bird watcher peering through leaves. The eerie effect was like holding a flashlight below the chin in a dark room, and one had the feeling that the next number might include apple bobbing or blindman's buff.

# Trial Run

Having tried a while ago to untangle the genealogy of the tenor-saxophone dynasty founded by Coleman Hawkins, and—according to fresh research—failed, I shall try again. Hawkins' immediate and most important descendants were Herschel Evans, Chu Berry, and Ben Webster. Out of Evans and Berry came Dick Wilson, who had no progeny. From Evans came Buddy Tate, and from Berry and Webster came Don Byas. Webster alone invented Paul Gonsalves. Byas, in turn, produced—with the help of Webster—Lucky Thompson, and Byas and Thompson produced Benny Golson, and there the line rests. (Sonny Rollins, skipping backward a generation, is a direct offshoot of Hawkins and Charlie Parker, the last of whom founded his own dynasty.) Of the survivors of this table (Berry, Evans, and Wilson are dead), Thompson and Byas, by virtue of deerlike styles and long residence in Europe, are the most elusive. Thompson, though, has recently returned, and was on view in a concert at the Little Theatre.

In many ways, Thompson's style is the best possible distillation of the styles of Webster and Byas. Webster, harnessed to a big tone and a relentless legato melodic gift, has never been particularly agile, while Byas, an extraordinary technician, has frequently allowed his fluidity to flood his emotions. Thompson's notes and accents are more sparing that Byas's, and his fluidity is calculated. He is a drier performer—an attack that is heightened by his occasional trumpetlike statements. In contrast to Webster, his tone is middling, and moves easily between a thin softness and the hardness found in Rollins and John Coltrane, both of whom listened to him. All his work is tinted by the blues. A steady, gentle intelligence also lights it, preventing it from slipping into the romantic or the elliptical.

The concert I attended (a second one was held later) was beset with minor troubles. Thompson's drummer dragged fast tempos and raced medium ones; the event was apparently being recorded, which caused chills and hesitations; and Thompson—away so long from the big swim—seemed apprehensive and even apologetic. At the same time, the rest of his colleagues—Dave Burns (trumpet), Benny Powell (bass trombone), Danny Turner (alto saxophone), Cecil Payne (baritone saxophone), Hank Jones, and Richard Davis—provided at nearly every point a yea-team support generally absent in pickup groups. The dozen selections were by Thompson, who also did the nicely turned arrangements, and they alternated between the blues and carefully constructed ballads. His composing is original and thoughtful, and, like that of Benny Carter, reflects his improvisations. During the evening, Thompson switched back and forth between the soprano saxophone, which he first tried in Europe, and the tenor. His soprano is a piping, small-toned copy of his tenor playing, and at times had an almost beseeching sound, which may have been the result of nerves or pitch troubles. His tenor saxophone was most effective in a slow ballad, " 'Twas Yesterday," in which he used long vibratos and a buzzing tone, and in a medium blues, "Mr. Carefully," in which he came closest to the exquisite balancing of opposites that marked his work in the forties and fifties. Jones is distinguished by his beautiful touch and by delicate, introverted single-note figures that give the impression of being stated in parentheses. Davis broke through his brilliant technique in "Mr. Carefully," playing a dozen choruses full of double-stops, scalar leaps, guitarlike slurs, and those twanging notes peculiar to Charlie Mingus. Powell's solos were witty but glossy (how long will it be before modern trombonists find their way past the anti-trombone style of J. J. Johnson?), and Burns and Payne were adequate. Thompson, making his first appearance in New York in six or seven years, may well have settled down at the later concert. If so, delights surely abounded.

# Triumph

The curse of the originator is adulation. His inventions, diffused and sullied by admiring hands, disappear behind a skein of imitations. But some originators, through sheer inventiveness, outwit their apostles; no matter how often their work is emulated, it remains indestructible. One such figure is the pianist Earl Hines, who, visible in New York just once in the past decade, recently held forth with stunning results at the Little Theatre.

Hines founded one of the three schools of jazz piano playing. The earliest, made up mainly of blues pianists, flourished under Jimmy Yancey and his disciples Meade Lux Lewis and Albert Ammons. The second, an outgrowth of ragtime, was established by James P. Johnson and others. Hines, drawing in small part from these traditions and in large part from himself, came to prominence in 1928. The effect was startling; no one had ever before played the piano that way. Like Bix Beiderbecke and Jack Teagarden and Louis Armstrong, Hines seemed to spring up unique and fully grown. Before Hines, jazz pianists had been orchestral and baroque (the stride men), or one-track primitive (the blues men). The ground between was bare. Hines retained the orchestral quality and skimmed the

128

cream from the blues, but he subordinated these to remarkable innovations. His style, which has changed little, is
marked by enormous rhythmic impetus, rich harmonies,
total unpredictability, and a singular joyousness. Hines did
not—despite the critical cliché—invent the single-note
melodic line in the right hand. He did, however, compound
usually incidental methods of earlier pianists with knifelike
arpeggios, on-time and double-time runs that disregarded
bar measures, and octave doublings. He frequently added
tremolos to the last in an attempt to shake a vibrato from
a vibratoless instrument. (He is celebrated for his hornlike
approach, and in this sense he should be.) At the same time,
he set off his single-note patterns with chords played a little
behind the beat or in rapid staccato ladders. In his equally
important left hand, he occasionally commemorates the
stride pianists' oompah bass, but more frequently he uses
tenths, trills, isolated chords placed everywhere around
the beat, and percussive single notes. His hands seem at
war. A right-hand run races ahead of a fragment of stride
bass; a left-hand trill rumbles while the right hand rallies
irregular octave doublings; staccato right-hand chords are
poised, like an inverted pyramid, on a simple legato left-
hand melody; sustained right-hand tremolos cascade toward ascending left-hand block chords. These devices constantly advance and retreat, and now and then dissolve into
brief arhythmic interludes in which the beat gives way to
a whirling, suspended mass of chords and single notes.
(This exciting, treading-water invention was carried to
Cloud Cuckoo lengths by Art Tatum, and, possibly as a result, has been abandoned by modern pianists, which is too
bad.) Hines was the first pianist to make full use of dynamics. With an infallible sense of emphasis, his volume may
swell in mid-phrase or at the outset of a new idea and then

fall away, before cresting again a few measures later. He makes sound flash. The epitome of the solo pianist, Hines is freest without a rhythm section. He is, though, a masterly accompanist who, with a discreet tremolo or seemingly wandering melodic figure, immeasurably heightens the greatest and the meanest soloists. Hines has sporadically let down in the past decade or so, and in slow tempos he may even turn rhapsodic, as if all that muscle were going to fat.

Hines—tall and quick-moving, with a square, noble face—is a hypnotic performer. His almost steady smile is an unconscious, transparent mask. When he is most affected, the smile freezes—indeed, his whole face clenches. Then the smile falters, revealing a desolate, piercing expression, which melts into another smile. He tosses his head back and opens his mouth, hunches over, sways from side to side, and, rumbling to himself, clenches his face again, tears of sweat pouring down his cheeks. His face and his manner are his music—the sort of perfect, non-showman showmanship that stops the heart. And time and again at the Little Theatre, Hines did just that. Each of his thirty-odd numbers—about half were medleys devoted to such as Fats Waller and Duke Ellington—was done as if nothing had come before and nothing would come after. Brilliance topped brilliance. He exhibited arpeggios that made Tatum sound electronic and Monk scraggly; shocking dynamic shifts; melancholy, turned-in chords; an unbelievable rhythmic drive; lyricism upon lyricism; and a juxtaposition of moods that made one laugh with delight. "Love Is Just Around the Corner," "I Ain't Got Nobody," and "Rosetta" were done without his fine but expendable accompanists—Ahmed Abdul-Malik (bass) and Oliver Jackson (drums)—and they were awash with stride passages, staccato chords, hide-and-seek runs, quick double-time accelerations, and arhythmic interludes, one of them (in "Love Is Just") done in the upper registers, and giving the impression of tremors chiming crystal. "Tea for Two," a tune surely beyond rescue, was converted into an impressionistic lullaby, as well as an extraordinary display of dynamics; after several measures of floating half-time chords that appeared to be leading up to a brassy stride or block-chords passage, Hines, pausing a split second, slid into an even softer roundabout, on-the-beat run. Its timing and taste and delicacy took the breath away. Similar wonders occurred in "Stealin' Apples"; "Sweet Lorraine," in which he sang in a way reminiscent of Jelly Roll Morton; and "St. Louis Blues," a bravura performance topped with a right-hand, two-note tremolo that he held for six choruses while his left hand played casual middle-register melodies and accompaniment for bass and drum solos. Poised on the lip of melodrama, he never slipped. He was joined in three numbers by Budd Johnson, a tenor saxophonist, former colleague, and sturdy eclectic who admires Coleman Hawkins, Lester Young, and Stan Getz. Hines, whose face was a study in pleased concentration, provided backing that unwittingly shaded Johnson at nearly every turn. Early in the evening, Hines suggested that he was not giving a concert but was simply playing in his living room for friends. Concert or musical soirée, its likes won't happen again.

# Interregnum

Two recent records—
"Miles Davis: Seven Steps to Heaven" (Columbia) and
"Interaction: The Art Farmer Quartet" (Atlantic)—dem-
onstrate that the kingly succession of trumpeters that has
dominated jazz instrumentalists for forty years has at last
broken down. This dynasty began with King Oliver and,
at roughly ten-year intervals, was carried forward by Louis
Armstrong and Bix Beiderbecke, then Red Allen, Roy Eldridge, and Dizzy Gillespie. (Coleman Hawkins, Lester
Young, and Charlie Parker are the only non-trumpeters of
equal eminence.) When Gillespie's time was up (fashion
generally dictates any change), he relinquished the sceptre
to Miles Davis, and for a time Davis had a good grasp on it.
Then it became evident that Davis was suffering from certain inadequacies; despite occasional marvellous bursts,
his style was too monochromatic and too oblique, and his
technique faltered. In the meantime, Art Farmer, a trumpeter who is two years younger than Davis, was quietly coming along. His tone and attack, out of Gillespie by way of
Kenny Dorham and Clifford Brown, resembled Davis's, but
he had more technique. He also had less confidence and
more perseverance. Now, through sheer accumulating ex-
cellence, Farmer is neck and neck with Davis, and we have,

in place of the traditional champion trumpeter, a pair of co-ruling first-rate second-rate trumpeters. And they form a comely pair, for they complement one another perfectly.

Davis's style is autocratic, and it has become so highly stylized that it often appears to have little connection with what he plays. Medium-tempo tunes are handled with one set of mannerisms and slow tunes with another. (He rarely visits up tempos.) As a result, the fascination of his work lies not in what he does with a specific number but in what a specific number does, if anything, to him. Davis's tone, which slips steadily in and out of focus, is largest at slow tempos—or at least it was before it disappeared behind the mute he now perpetually affects at such speeds. This mute lends his playing a bemused air, and it helps mask the fluffs that dog him. But it also soft-pedals his extremely adroit rhythmic manipulations. He is frequently called a "melodic" soloist, possibly because he chooses his notes carefully and sparingly, possibly because he spatters occasional phrases with dabs of melody. However, he is more concerned with the time value of these notes than with what notes they are. In a slow solo, he tricks his listeners by issuing two or three connected, on-the-beat notes, abruptly and unexpectedly pausing for a beat or so, and then landing on a single note, which he will quickly smear, restate briefly, and smear again. Or he will slide into a peculiar double time in which he plays ahead of the original beat but behind actual double time, or he will plant a row of vibratoless notes, each held for a different length of time —on the beat, in front of it, or in that area between the off-beat and the beat that was first discovered by Gillespie and Parker. (No matter how many times one hears the celebrated recording of "Ko-Ko" by Parker and Gillespie, it is impossible to predict the exact instant when the two horns come in at the end of Max Roach's solo; they split a split second.) Davis's slow playing is a calculated lisping, an attack of hesitancy and discreet forward rushes; at its best it is striking, at its worst it is messy. Davis is more bullish in the middle tempos, which he usually plays open-horn. Stridency creeps into his tone, clams proliferate, and one senses that he has difficulty translating into sound what he hears in his head. Again the rhythmic placements are most important, and arresting melodic ideas appear incidental. The excitements in Davis's work are small and intense and enduring. One no longer looks for perfect solos but for spots and passages that stand as miniature perfections.

Farmer's aplomb and subtlety and precision have often led listeners into dismissing him as slick. But Farmer is a rare musician; instead of using technique to project emotion, he uses emotion to project technique. He cares a great deal about tone and timbre and the notes he uses and how they are arranged. And the urgency of this pursuit, which has lyricism and melodic content of a high order, is its own reward. However, one must *listen*, for Farmer's style is totally self-sufficient; it never leans on the listener. His tone has become increasingly gentle and generous since his recent switch from the trumpet to the flugelhorn, which, when properly played, sounds like a trumpet with a felt hat over its bell. He has no vibrato, and he eases out of his notes exactly as he eases into them. For a time, Farmer was under the sway of the late, mellifluous Clifford Brown, but his attack has since become more and more spare. Within this spareness, Farmer is rather daring. He employs many of the patterns invented by the bebop trumpeters—fast runs, off-notes, sudden tempo shifts—but he omits half the notes. Instead of riding up the scale from the middle range on the backs of a dozen notes, he will sound the middle note and then the top one, and sometimes he will leave out the middle note and make a perfect big-interval leap. Tempo does not affect his playing. He brings an equal assurance and balance to slow ballads and middle-speed blues. Farmer is a one-volume player (this explains, more than anything else, the seeming sameness of his playing), and he stays in the middle register. A conservative who exercises his gifts fully, he is often more winning than those revolutionaries who pedal empty air.

"Interaction" is an altogether successful recording. Farmer's quartet, formed a year ago, includes Jim Hall on guitar, Steve Swallow on bass, and Walter Perkins on drums. There are four standards, a Charlie Parker tune, and a Brazilian *bossa-nova* number. Farmer is especially admirable in "Days of Wine and Roses" and "By Myself," in both of which he offers the sort of polite melodic improvisation patented years ago by Bobby Hackett, and in the searching and graceful "Embraceable You," which he treats with a welcome firmness. The quiet tension he sustains throughout this number is remarkable. Hall echoes Farmer or indulges in little unison or contrapuntal passages, and always solos well. Swallow is one of the new school of bassists who are attempting to transpose the rhythmic freedom and quavering tonal qualities of the Indian ragas and Django Reinhardt to the bass. In fact, he is so strong tonally (possibly he is overrecorded; many bassists now are) and uses such a variety of rhythms and sliding tones that he sometimes upsets the delicate balance of the group. Perkins, though, attempts to forestall this, and in "My Little Suède Shoes" he takes an excellent solo, using tom-tom rim shots and a long series of irregular strokes sounded on a cymbal held tightly in one hand.

The Davis recording is erratic. The six numbers are

played by two groups. Davis is joined in one by George Coleman (tenor saxophone), Herbie Hancock (piano), Ron Carter (bass), and Tony Williams (drums), and in the other by Vic Feldman (piano), Carter, and Frank Butler (drums). The first group offers standard Davis quintet fare, with loosely arranged ensembles based on broken rhythms and breaks and framing long solos. However, two of the quartet performances are notable. These are oblique reworkings of "Basin Street Blues" and "Baby, Won't You Please Come Home." Davis uses a mute in both (the first is very slow and the second a little faster), and generally follows this routine: remote obeisance to the melody, done with flat off-notes, well spaced, and little, drifting smears; a slight improvisational bearing down and a gradual shift into that odd Davis semi-double time; full double time; and a sudden return to the original tempo and more bows to the melody. The results are fresh structures, with typical unaligned jambs and warped shingles, and they suggest that the old Dixieland repertory contains many tunes far more challenging than those fashionable among modern musicians. Davis's only striking accompanist is the eighteen-year-old Williams; he should be watched.

# Out Here

The house of jazz is full of ghosts. Harried by the winds of economics, the nomad demands of their work, a swiftly changing music, and public fickleness, jazz musicians appear and disappear with bewildering frequency. Probably the most celebrated of these elusive spirits is Mary Lou Williams, the unique pianist, arranger, and composer. Some weeks ago, when, after a decade and a half of semi-obscurity, she miraculously materialized at Hickory House, on West Fifty-second Street, I went to hear her. It was soon after her opening, and when I arrived she was at a grand piano, with a bassist and a drummer behind her, and was playing "My Blue Heaven." Dressed in a black sleeveless gown, cut low in the back, she looked even prettier than the last time I had seen her, many years before. Her black hair was arranged in a loose helmet, and on her right arm she had a watch with a wide gold strap. She sat very straight, her body motionless and her elbows brushing her sides, as if she were pouring tea. Her head and her face, however, were in steady, graceful motion. Sometimes she shut her eyes and tilted her chin up, so that the light from a spot bounced off her high, prominent cheekbones, giving her a regal appearance. Sometimes, her eyes still shut, she moved her head counterclockwise in an intense, halting manner, punctuated with rhythmic downward jabs. When she was pleased by something her bassist or her drummer did, she rocked gently back and forth, partly opened her eyes, and smiled. She never looked at her long, thin fingers, which lay almost flat on the keys. Various blues and such numbers as "Caravan," "It Ain't Necessarily So," and "The Man I Love" sailed effortlessly by; she sounded marvellous.

The triumph of Miss Williams' style, I realized as I listened, is that she has no style. She is not an eclectic or an anthologist or a copyist; she is a gifted and delicate appreciator who distills what affects her in the work of other pianists into clear, cool, highly individual synopses. The grapes are others', the wine is her own. In the late twenties and early thirties, echoes of Jelly Roll Morton and Fats Waller and Earl Hines hurried through her work. The mountainous shadow of Art Tatum passed over around 1940, and by 1945 she had become an expert bebop pianist. Since jazz piano—the otherwordly convolutions of Cecil Taylor aside—has not moved very far since then, she is now a post-bebop performer, her chords and single-note melodic lines applauding such juniors as Bill Evans and Red Garland. But while discreetly judging her peers she often scoops them. In the forties, she advanced certain dissonant chords that became part of Thelonious Monk's permanent furniture. She also outlined the sort of Debussy impressionism that no modern pianist confronted by a number like "Polka Dots and Moonbeams" would be caught without. In the thirties, she perfected an airy, slightly joshing form of boogie-woogie that pointed a way out of the mechanized morass that that singular music had sunk into. Miss Williams' present work, I discovered at Hickory House, is an instructive history of jazz piano—a kind of one-woman retrospective of an entire movement. Her technique is faultless, and she has Art Tatum's touch. Fragments of boogie-woogie basses—in six-eight, rather than four-four or four-eight, time—frequently appear in her introductions. These are relieved by muted left-hand figures and right-hand chords that abstract the melody. Spare single-note lines surface in the right hand; their arpeggios are mere serifs, and they include generous rests. These melodic lines, strung between the chords of the tune like telephone wire, soon thicken, and she moves on to intense chords, often in double time or placed off the beat. Things begin to rock insistently and lightly, and after a few cloudlike melodic statements she returns to the six-eight introduction. Along the way, a Waller stride bass or an Ellington dissonance drifts by; a Basie aphorism is struck; big-interval Hines chords leap up and down the keyboard; a serpentine Bud Powell figure is carefully unspooled. But uppermost are a delicacy and wit and lofty invention that imply absolute knowledge.

At this point in my ruminations, the music stopped. Miss Williams, having announced the intermission pianist, got down from the stand, which is enclosed in a long, ovaloid bar, and, after speaking a few words to a group of well-wishers, retired to an empty booth at the rear of the room. I went over and introduced myself, and she asked me to sit down. A waiter brought her some coffee.

"I never could drink," she said. "When I was with the Andy Kirk band, back in the thirties, the boys had what they called the Hot Corn Club—named for the corn liquor they bought—and they were always trying to get me to drink. Backstage during a tonk game, somebody would make me a drink and I'd take one sip, and when I wasn't looking they would refill the glass, so I always thought I hadn't had but a taste. Once I was back at the piano, it would go right to my head, and I'd almost faint, and sit there woozy, saying 'Oh, my heart! Oh, my heart!,' and that broke the boys up." Miss Williams laughed—a low, tumbling, girlish chuckle in the quick flow of her talk—and lit a cigarette. The smoke closed her eyes, which are brown and slanted and heavy-lidded.

I told her how much I had enjoyed her playing.

"I was off yesterday and I'm as stiff as a board," she said. "My fingers get stuck in the cracks. And that bass player of mine—if he'd only play jazz! He plays the bass like a guitar, with all those slurs, and he runs high notes when I'm trying to play funk. He's not with me, and it makes me mad. I'm going to call him tomorrow and nail his foot right to the floor and tell him he should go with the symphony." She shook her head, and laughed again.

I said she looked anything but unhappy on the stand.

"The madder I am, the more I smile," she assured me. "And when I stomp my foot on the beat, it means nothing is happening. I'm dry. When I stop, it's like Erroll Garner said—'When Mary keeps her leg still, look out. Something is starting to *build*.' But all I've been doing tonight is bang my foot. Sometimes you get cold, you freeze up, but you just play until the inspiration comes. You play what you know, and play it as well as you can, and then the feeling starts. A bad audience or a waiter dropping a tray can take your inspiration. If you have a dead rhythm section, you shut it out of your mind, and you learn this the hard way. If you make a mistake, you work something good out of that mistake. We were doing 'How High the Moon' a while ago, and I hit a wrong note in a chord, and what I did was go off immediately on a different tack and work that wrong note into a pattern that fitted. It sounded way out, but it was all right. You have to be on your tiptoes every minute. No one can put a style on me. I've learned from many people. I change all the time. I experiment to keep up with what is going on, to hear what everybody else is doing. I even keep a little ahead of them, like a mirror that shows what will happen next. One reason I came out here again is the sounds I hear in modern jazz. They're disturbed and crazy. They're neurotic, as if the Negro was pulling away from his heritage in music. You have to love when you play. Lord, I've talked talked talked music to young musicians, but they don't listen. So I've decided to show them, make them *hear* the soul." Miss Williams ground out her cigarette and took a sip of coffee. "Young musicians—and old ones, too—are coming in every night, and they're listening," she said.

With flawless timing, Thad Jones, Bobby Brookmeyer, and Mel Lewis walked in and stood at the bar. They were members of Gerry Mulligan's band, which was appearing around the corner at Birdland.

"Too many young musicians learn from records, and copy wrong chords and wrong notes and don't know it," she continued. "I can hear them, because I have perfect pitch. I'm going to stay out here and teach them."

Miss Williams looked at her watch and rose, and I asked her to join me during the next intermission.

"I've got to talk to my stepbrother," she said. "He's due now. But why don't you come with me to Elmsford tomorrow to my dressmaker? She moved up there recently from New York. I've grown fat since I last played, and I have to have all my dresses let out. Joe Wells—he owns Wells' Restaurant, up on Seventh Avenue—is going to drive me. You be at my house about ten o'clock."

When I left, several sets later, Miss Williams' bassist

was running high notes, she was smiling, and I could see from the posting motions of her skirt that she was banging her foot.

Mary Lou Williams is the only first-rate female musician in an unsentimental and peculiarly male music. There is little about the life of a jazz musician to attract women. The hours are long and topsy-turvy, the living conditions on the road are strikingly uncongenial for the traditional feminine pursuits, and most women lack the physical equipment—to say nothing of the poise—for blowing trumpets and trombones, slapping bass fiddles, or beating drums. Those female instrumentalists who have cropped up in jazz in the past thirty or forty years have decorated pianos, harps, guitars, or vibraphones, and, in the main, they have dropped quickly out of sight. (Since jazz is predominantly an instrumental music, the great female jazz singers, like Bessie Smith and Billie Holiday, form a separate conclave.) But Miss Williams has survived. She is also one of the few jazz musicians, male or female, who have survived the swing era, which she graced as a pianist, arranger, and composer with the Andy Kirk band.

Taken together, the big swing bands resembled an iceberg. In plain view were the Goodmans, Shaws, Jameses, and Hermans; partly above water were the Basies and Ellingtons and Luncefords; and below were countless unknown, though often excellent, groups. A considerable number of these sub-surface bands came from the Midwest and the Southwest, including, among others, those of Kirk, Jay McShann, Harlan Leonard, Jap Allen, Troy Floyd, and Jeter-Pillars. They formed, along with Count Basie's band, the so-called Kansas City school of jazz, playing a loose, easy, blues-based music that, through such graduates as Lester Young and Charlie Christian, assisted at the birth of bebop in New York in the early forties. In some ways, the Kirk band was better than the Basie band; its personnel remained almost unchanged throughout the twelve years Miss Williams was with it, and it had a casual precision that Basie's band, with its stellar iconoclasts, often lacked. Moreover, the Kirk band had a calmness and obliqueness that set it apart from the Kansas City bands; it implied what its peers shouted. Part of this was due to its best soloists— Miss Williams, Dick Wilson, Shorty Baker, and Ted Donnelly—and to its drummer, Ben Thigpen. Donnelly was a serene, thoughtful trombonist in the style of Benny Morton, and Wilson was a subtle, big-toned tenor saxophonist who had the fleetness of Chu Berry but none of his garrulity, and who also shared Lester Young's adventurous harmonies and rhythms. Baker was an economical and legato trumpeter whose solos had a lyric slow-motion quality. Miss Williams' own solos—she was distilling Hines and Tatum much of the time—were graceful and meditative. Ben Thigpen (the father of drummer Ed Thigpen) had a light, flexible touch and perfect time, and certain of his methods presaged modern drumming. Part of the Kirk band's unforced assurance also came from Miss Williams' arrangements, which were uncluttered and advanced. She used clarinet trios to spell out her attractive blues melodies; she opened and closed numbers simply, with a soloist and the rhythm section; her improvised-sounding saxophone passages suggested the creamy writing of Benny Carter; and there were odd, beautifully constructed background harmonies, often played by the saxophones and trombones. Her best arrangements had a small-band compactness. They also had an almost schoolmarm purpose, and unfailingly pointed up both the tunes and the frequent solos.

Miss Williams left Kirk in 1942 (the band petered

out several years later) and joined the remarkable collection of singers, instrumentalists, dancers, and comedians that travelled back and forth between Café Society Downtown and Café Society Uptown during the Second World War. This informal repertory company was brought together by Barney Josephson, who owned both night clubs, and at various times it consisted of the bands of Teddy Wilson, James P. Johnson, Frankie Newton, Edmond Hall, Red Allen, and Eddie Heywood; comedians like Imogene Coca, Zero Mostel, and Jimmy Savo; the Kraft Sisters, who were dancers; such singers as the Golden Gate Quartet, Joe Turner, Mildred Bailey, Billie Holiday, and Josh White; and pianists such as Mary Lou Williams, Meade Lux Lewis, Albert Ammons, Pete Johnson, and Hazel Scott. Miss Williams worked this attractive circuit until 1947, and then, having been visible for the greater part of seventeen years, abruptly became a ghost. Jazz itself had turned transparent. The big bands had been replaced by esoteric small groups that played bebop or cool jazz. Dancing—and the musicians who played for it—had been obliterated by a thirty-per-cent wartime cabaret tax. Fifty-second Street, which had cradled jazz since the thirties, was being taken over by office buildings. Jazz musicians—particularly those weaned on swing—had not felt so put upon since the early days of the depression. Miss Williams played at occasional concerts and in night clubs, and in 1952 she went to Europe for two years. She found things pretty much the same on her return, and, with the exception of a recording date, she lay low. Then, in 1957, the reasons for her disappearance changed; she was received into the Catholic Church, and entered a period of religious fervor. Rumor had it that she had quit music for good. Her admirers, long accustomed to her jack-in-the-box ways, mourned but waited.

Miss Williams lives alone in a two-and-a-half-room apartment on the second floor of a yellow brick building on Sugar Hill, near 144th Street and St. Nicholas Avenue. When I rang her doorbell, a minute or two past ten, I was greeted by a short, solid, nattily dressed man wearing horn-rimmed glasses and smoking a cigar.

"*Entrez*," he said. "Joe Wells. I been hurrying Mary along, and she's about ready."

I found myself in a narrow hall facing a small, cheerful kitchen. To my right, the hall ended in a living room, crowded with an upright piano, a sofa, a couple of cabinets, a portable phonograph, an aluminum worktable, and a glass-topped coffee table. The top of the piano was covered with religious statues. There were three bright windows. Miss Williams appeared from the darkness at the other end of the hall, carrying a shopping bag filled with clothes. She had on a brown nutria coat, a brown woollen dress, and tan leather boots. Her hair was in mild disarray, and her eyes were puffy with sleep.

"Mornin'," she said.

"My, my. You ready?" Wells asked.

She opened the front door, and Wells and I trooped downstairs after her. "We used to have a doorman years ago," she said to me as we passed through the foyer. "But he wouldn't let *anybody* in, so we got rid of him."

It was raining outside, and Wells' car, a new Buick, was pebbled with water. "You two get in back," Wells ordered. "No sense us all jamming the front. Now, where's this Elmisford, Mary?"

"Elmsford," Miss Williams said. "Elmsford, New York." She pulled a slip of paper out of her pocket. "Get on the Major Deegan and the Thruway, and get off at Exit 8. Then I'll tell you where."

Wells crossed the 149th Street bridge and worked his way onto the Deegan through the Bronx Terminal Market.

"How far is this Elmisford?" he asked.

"She said about twenty-five miles. A half hour."

"Lord! I've got a twelve-o'clock appointment—with a lady. And I make it a rule never to keep a lady waiting."

"You kept me waiting plenty of times. Get over in the middle lane, Mr. Wells."

"Cool and easy. I've never had an accident in my life."

"Well, I've had two. It's the people who have had the accidents are the good drivers. It gives them mother wit on the road."

Rain, wiping at us from all sides, erased conversation, and no one spoke for several minutes.

"I've been driving since I was twelve," Miss Williams said eventually. "When I was eighteen, I was driving one of the cars the Kirk band travelled in. My first husband, John Williams, who played the alto and baritone, had been with Kirk about six months—the band was still led by T. Holder then—and I'd been jobbing around Memphis waiting for him to send for me. I wasn't playing regularly with the band yet. I'd wait outside ballrooms in the car, and if things went bad and people weren't dancing, they would send somebody to get me and I'd go in and play 'Froggy Bottom,' or some other boogie-woogie number, and things would jump. The regular pianist, Marion Jackson, was a wanderer, and I replaced him around 1930. My, what a band that was! It was a happy band, a good-looking band, an educated band. We had love for each other. There was a lot of love among musicians in the thirties—not like it is now, with everyone for himself. We had the type of boys that even if a woman they met didn't respect herself, they did. I was never allowed to go around by myself. My husband or two or three of the boys were always with me. I was well sheltered. But we had a hard, hard time at first. We were stranded all over—in Buffalo and Chicago and Cincinnati and Greeley, Colorado. When Kirk came backstage after a job with his head down, we'd know he hadn't been paid, and one of the trumpet players would take out his horn and play the 'Worried Blues,' and we'd all laugh. I made a little extra money by manicuring the boys' nails. They paid me a nickel, and I'd take it out of the money they made from cards, which I held for them. In Greeley, we stayed next to a cornfield, and I ate corn right up to the farmer's back door. The boys played a little semi-professional baseball there. It was hot summertime, and I carried water for them. Stumpy Brady, the trombonist, nearly got himself killed chasing balls he couldn't see. It seems you've got to starve a little before you can get on. Else you get that swelled head. My husband never let me get one. He trained me. Once, I developed an introduction I liked so much that I played it and played it until he finally knocked me right off the piano stool: 'You don't play the piano that way. Just because you did that "Twinklin'"'—that was another of my numbers—'you think you're something.' He said unbelievable things to me, but they worked. I was learning to arrange all this time. Don Redman was my model. I could hear my chords in my head but didn't know how to write them. Kirk helped me—he was a good musician—and I learned. I was very high-strung and sensitive. When the boys fooled around at rehearsals with what I wrote, I got mad and snatched the music off their stands and began to cry and went home to bed. I'd discovered I had perfect pitch, and I couldn't stand hearing wrong

147

notes, any more than I can now. But I could expand with that band, and try all sorts of things. We played everything —ballads, jump tunes, novelties, slow blues, fast blues— and they were all different."

I said I had a recording of a 1937 Kirk broadcast from Cleveland in which the saxophone section sounded like Guy Lombardo's.

Miss Williams chuckled and rubbed her nose. "That's right. I extracted things from Lombardo records for ofay college dances. Exit 4, Mr. Wells."

"I see it, Mary."

"When we weren't on the road, we spent most of our time around Kansas City, and there were after-hours sessions every night. They were something else. A good one went right through the next day. Style didn't matter. What mattered was to keep the thing going. I'd stop at a session after work, and they would be doing 'Sweet Georgia Brown.' I'd go home and take a bath and change my dress, and when I got back—an hour or more later—they'd still be on 'Georgia Brown.' Ben Webster came and threw some gravel on the window screen one night and woke me and my husband up and asked my husband if I could come to a session, because they were out of piano players. I went down and Coleman Hawkins was there—Fletcher Henderson was in town—and he was having a bad time. He was down to his undershirt, and sweating and battling for his life against Lester Young and Herschel Evans and Ben, too. But they weren't cutting sessions. I recall Chu Berry sitting out front at a session and listening and not moving. When he got on the stand, he repeated note for note the last chorus the man before him had played—just to show how much he admired it—and then he went into his own bag. Whenever we were in Cleveland, I stayed close to Art

148

Tatum, who worked there—he came from Toledo—when he wasn't in New York. When I had a day or two off, we played pinball in the afternoons, and at night we went to Val's, a little after-hours place, where we sometimes stayed until eleven in the morning. Tatum played, and they gave him fifty dollars. Then I played—usually some boogie—and they gave me five dollars. Tatum taught me how to hit my notes, how to control them without using pedals. And he showed me how to keep my fingers flat on the keys to get that clean tone. Of course, he didn't *show* me anything. He just said, 'Mary, you listen.' But once I showed *him* something. Buck Washington—of Buck and Bubbles—had given me a little run in Pittsburgh, which I used one night at Val's. Tatum said, 'What's that run, Mary? Where'd you get that? Play it for me again, please.' I did, and he developed that run—it covered just about the whole keyboard—and used it until the end of his life. Around 1940, something went wrong between me and the Kirk band. I don't think it was jealousy—or I don't like to think it was, anyway. He had hired several new people, and maybe I wasn't getting as much attention as I used to, and little things upset me—untuned pianos, pianos with nine or ten keys that didn't work. I began to feel my time was up, and one night, in Washington, D.C., I just left. God must have got the ball rolling to move me somewhere else. Exit 6, Mr. Wells."

The rain was heavier, and it had got chilly. Dark escarpments on both sides of the road turned the air gray. Miss Williams shivered, and hunched down in her coat.

"You have a little heat, Mr. Wells? I'm cold. I was so upset when I left Kirk I decided to leave music, and I went home to my mother's, in Pittsburgh. But Art Blakey kept coming over to the house and pestering me to form a group.

So I finally did. We worked a park in Cleveland, and then went into Kelly's Stable, on Fifty-second Street. Shorty Baker—he was my second husband—had left Kirk by this time, and he came with us. Then John Hammond persuaded me to go to Café Society. We were kind of a family there, and Barney Josephson thought of us that way. Josh White was around a lot, and I loved to hear him laugh. He had one of those laughs that come right from the stomach. I was feeling low after work one night, and I didn't want any more of the teasing that was always going around. So I flounced out with some dresses I had to get cleaned. Josh said, 'Where you going, Pussycat?'—which is what they called me. 'We'll take you home.' I said, 'I'm going home by myself. I'm tired of all this mess,' and went and got a cab. About halfway up the West Side Drive, we had a flat tire. It was near zero and blowing hard, and after a while I stepped out and saw another cab coming. It slowed down, and it looked like Josh and some of the others in it. I hollered with all my might, and it must have sounded like '*josSSHHhh*' as they went by. The cab stopped, and somebody got out and walked back. It was Josh. 'Is that *you*, Pussycat?' he said. He started laughing, and he laughed so hard he fell down on the road and lay there, hawing and holding himself. I used to be very quiet in those days—a zombie. When people talked to me, I looked at them and nodded, but in my mind I was writing an arrangement or going over a new tune or thinking about something I had played the last set. And I never smiled while I was playing, so Josh would stick his head out of the curtain backstage and make a face, and that would break me up, and I'd smile. I came closest to getting a swelled head at this time. People would tell me, 'Mary, you're the greatest girl pianist in the world,' and 'Mary, you're the greatest *pianist* in the world,' and for a while I believed it. But I remembered what John Williams used to tell me. So I discarded those compliments, and it's never happened since. After I left Café Society Downtown, I worked on Fifty-second Street with Mildred Bailey. She was a wonderful, big, salty person. She always had dachshunds, and she'd walk from her living room to her kitchen to get a drink, rock, rock, rock"—Miss Williams swung stiffly from side to side and tramped her boots in time—"with these little dogs all around her, and back into the living room, rock, rock, rock, the dogs still there. She joked all the time. People said you couldn't get along with Mildred, but I got along with her fine. All during this time, my house was kind of a headquarters for young musicians. I'd even leave the door open for them if I was out. Tadd Dameron would come to write, when he was out of inspiration, and Monk did several of his pieces there. Bud Powell's brother, Richie, who also played piano, learned how to improvise at my house. And everybody came or called for advice. Charlie Parker would ask what did I think about him putting a group with strings together, or Miles Davis would ask about his group with the tuba—the one that had John Lewis and Gerry Mulligan and Max Roach and J. J. Johnson in it. It was still like the thirties—musicians helped each other, and didn't just think of themselves. Exit 8, Mr. Wells."

Miss Williams fished her instructions from her pocket. "First light, turn left, go past Robert Hall. Turn left on Payne Street. It's the yellow house at the top of the hill."

Robert Hall swung by, and Payne Street appeared, on our right.

"Payne Street, Mary," Wells said.

"She said it was on the left. Maybe that's it down the road by that garage."

Wells obligingly drove down a narrow, winding road through a rubbish-filled field.

"Now, isn't this disappointing?" Miss Williams said. "I was expecting a nice house with a view. That's how she described it."

The road ended in a mountain of old tires, and Wells turned around. "Let's go back and try the other Payne, dollin,' " he said. "Somebody's mixed up."

The other Payne went up a steep hill, and near the top was a small yellow house. A tall woman in a sweatshirt and blue jeans greeted us at the door, with two miniature white poodles dancing around her feet.

Miss Williams apologized for being late.

"That's all right, honey," the dressmaker said. "There's nobody here at the moment. You come in and we'll get right to work. You gentlemen make yourselves comfortable in the living room. We won't be long."

Wells and I sat down on wrought-iron love seats on opposite sides of the living room. A dining alcove with more wrought-iron furniture was at one end of the room and a giant picture window at the other. The walls and ceilings were soft violet. A clump of plastic lilies and a stand containing brass fire irons flanked a raised fireplace. A photograph of a handsome young woman, done in the peekaboo mode of décolleté eighteenth-century portraits, hung over the mantel. A Pollock-type abstraction, full of racing reds and blacks, faced it.

Wells crossed his legs and lit a fresh cigar, and looked out at the rain. "Eleven-fifteen," he said. "I'll never make my twelve-o'clock. And I have an appointment at one, and another at two-twenty. I get very upset when I miss appointments. It tightens my stomach. But I'll do anything for Mary. I've known her since the early forties, and we've

152

had little deals off and on through the years. Right now I'm pushing that record she just made—'St. Martin de Porres,' about the Negro saint. It has a chorus of voices, and she plays. Very lovely. She's the most brilliant woman I know. A little nervous, maybe, but brilliant."

A steady hum of talk came from the next room, and Wells, occasionally jumping up to flick ashes into the fireplace, delivered a discourse on the restaurant business, which he said was very good. Then it was noon, and Miss Williams appeared.

"He talk your head off?" she asked me, and chuckled. She looked wide-awake and pleased, as if she were already in one of her altered dresses.

Wells drove back to the Thruway hunched over, the minutes ticking away almost audibly in his head.

Miss Williams began chanting in time to the windshield wipers: "Watch out. Watch out. Watch out. Da de-da, da de-da," and hummed a little tune, using the same rhythm. "This weather reminds me of the time I got stranded about fifteen miles outside of Pittsburgh. I wasn't more than twelve, and I'd played a job with a union band, and when it was over they wouldn't pay us. We walked all the way home. We moved to Pittsburgh from Atlanta, where I was born, when I was five or six. I've had a lot of names. I was born Mary Elfrieda Scruggs, and later I was Mary Lou Winn and Mary Lou Burley, after stepfathers. I don't know where the Lou came from, but I got the Williams when I was married. I don't remember seeing my father until twelve years ago, when I went to Atlanta. I said to him, 'I bet you don't know who I am,' and all he could say was 'What have you brought me?' I said, 'You have the nerve, after all these years of doing nothing for your children!' But my mother was a good person. She worked most of the time, and my sister, Mamie, and my stepbrother, Willie, took care of me. My mother told my sister she'd kill her if anything happened to me. Of course, things did. I swallowed a pin once, and another time a Great Dane who was rabid bit me and they took me to the hospital for those shots. We had a cousin who could dance, and he and my sister dared me to jump over a box with a lighted candle on top. I did, and I tripped and broke my arm. I was so scared of what my mother would think that I crawled under my bed, with that broken arm, and stayed there for over an hour, until I finally came out crying. People shouldn't say things like 'I'll kill you' to their children. I used to stutter—I still do when I get upset—but I broke myself of the habit. My mother's almost eighty now, and has a heart condition, but she does the Twist, holding her hand over her heart and laughing. She played the organ, and she used to hold me on her lap when I was three, and I'd play. She wouldn't allow for a music teacher to come into the house, but she invited different musicians, and I'd listen. By the time I was six or seven, I was playing the piano in neighbors' houses all afternoon and evening—my cousin or sister taking me—and sometimes I came home with twenty or thirty dollars wrapped in a handkerchief. All I bought was shoes. My mother was a size two and a half, and I was already a five. Up to then, I used to wear her shoes to school, and they hurt so much I had to walk home barefooted. I got to be known all over our part of Pittsburgh. Miss Milholland, the principal of the Lincoln School, took me to afternoon teas at Carnegie Tech, where I played light-classical things. She also took me to the opera, but I guess I was too young, because I still don't like it. I played a home-talent show in an old theatre out in East Liberty, and did all this clowning with my elbows on the keys. One time, the Mellon family sent their chauffeur in a big car into our district looking for a Negro pianist for one of their parties. Somebody told him about me, and that night he drove me and a friend to this mansion, and I played the party. They gave me a check for a hundred dollars. My mother was very upset, and called to see if there was a mistake, but there wasn't. The first pianist who made an impression on me was Jack Howard. He played boogie so heavy he splintered the keys. I also heard a woman pianist in a theatre I went to with my brother-in-law. I can't recall her name. She sat sidewise at the keyboard with her legs crossed and a cigarette in her mouth, and she was wonderful. Earl Hines was a Pittsburgh boy, and, of course, I listened to him every chance I got."

A truck slammed past us, throwing up a curtain of water that landed with a thump on the windshield. Some of it flew in at Wells' window and sprayed Miss Williams.

"That went right on me," she said, and dabbed at her face with a sleeve. "Close your window, please, Mr. Wells, and I'll open mine a crack."

"You open yours a crack and you'll give me a crick," Wells replied.

Miss Williams laughed. "That's what an old man gets for driving around on a day like this," she said.

"Listen, dollin'. I'm just thinking about getting myself engaged. Old man!" said Wells.

Miss Williams laughed again. The rain was letting up, and there was blue sky over a hump of woods. "My first real professional job was with the union band I got stranded with," she said. "My next was with a vaudeville group, The Hottentots. They had a pianist who was an addict, which in those days was about as familiar as going to the moon. He disappeared, and they sent someone to find me. I was

155

playing hopscotch in the yard. When this man saw me, he said, 'Oh, man! Why did they send me all the way out here? This a *baby!*' We went inside, and he hummed a couple of tunes, and I played them back perfectly. I joined the show for the summer. I was about twelve or thirteen, and a friend came with me. We toured carnivals and such, and it was an animal life. The *worst* kinds of people. I was a good student, but I quit high school in my first year and went with another vaudeville group, Seymour and Jeannette. I was in the band, and so was John Williams. They had a trombonist who worked his slide with his foot, or danced the Charleston when he played. After Seymour died, we came to New York, and I sat in for a week with Ellington's Washingtonians in a theatre pit. I remember Sonny Greer and Tricky Sam Nanton. Tricky Sam drank whiskey out of a big jug held over one shoulder. I met Fats Waller at that time—that was about 1926—and I played for him, and he picked me up and threw me in the air. I didn't weigh more than eighty or ninety pounds. He played organ for the movies at Lincoln Theatre, and people screamed, he was so good. Then John Williams formed a group, and we gigged around the Midwest until he joined T. Holder. I took over the band after he left. One of the people I hired was Jimmy Lunceford. I had some rough times with gangsters, and the like, and in a roadhouse I worked near Memphis without the band, this white farmer from Mississippi came in every night and sat out front and stared at me. It shook me. Then the cook told me the farmer said he'd give him fifty dollars if he helped him take me to his farm in Mississippi. When I heard that, I never went back."

We were rolling along beside the Harlem River, and the sun had come out.

"You want to go back to your house, Mary?" Wells asked.

"Take me down to my thrift shop, please, Mr. Wells. I got to pay the rent. It's on Twenty-ninth Street, right near Bellevue."

Wells shook his head. "I'm going to miss my one-o'clock, too."

"I started this thrift shop to help get my Bel Canto Foundation going," Miss Williams said. "The idea for the Bel Canto came to me in 1957. It's a plan to help jazz musicians in trouble with drugs or alcohol. If I ever raise the money, I'll buy a house in the country. I'll only take a small number of patients, and I'll have doctors and nurses and soundproof rooms where the musicians can meditate and play. But they'll work, too—hard physical work. I'm not an organizer, but I *know* musicians. I've worked with them all through the years. Almost everybody has come to me at one time or another. I put the worst cases in a room down the hall from my place I rent cheap from a neighbor. They stay a couple of weeks, and I talk to them and pray with them and help them get a job. But I can be very hard in my charity, and sometimes I tell them, 'You've got to be a *man*. Stand up and go downtown and get a job. No use lying around Harlem and feeling sorry for yourself.' Sometimes they come back in worse shape and ask for money, and sometimes they get on their feet. One boy I've been helping has a job at Gimbels, and he's doing just fine. I've also sent musicians to the Graymoor Monastery, near Garrison. Brother Mario there has been a lot of help to me. I gave a benefit concert at Carnegie Hall to get the Bel Canto started, but it used up more money than it made. Then I tramped all over downtown until I found this place

157

for a thrift shop. I fixed it up, and people in and out of music sent thousand-dollar coats and expensive dresses. I worked twelve hours a day collecting stuff and running the shop. In the evening, I went over to Bellevue to visit with musicians who were there. I raised money, but it went to rent and musicians I was helping. I was living mostly on royalty checks from records and arrangements, and then in 1960 *I* ran out of money and had to go to work at the Embers. I couldn't find anybody I could trust to run the shop. It's been closed off and on almost a year now, but I'm still working on money for the Foundation. Some club ladies in Pittsburgh are very interested."

We turned into Twenty-ninth Street and pulled up in front of a modest store.

"I won't be long, Mr. Wells."

Wells turned around, his eyes wide, and said, "Mary dollin', I've already missed *two* appointments. You take a cab home, please."

"O.K., and thank you," Miss Williams said.

The two of us got out, and the car roared away. Miss Williams unlocked the shop door. "You go in," she said. "I have to give the rent to a man in the next building." On the floor were a couple of Con Edison bills and a letter addressed to Miss Williams. I put them on a table. The walls were covered with paintings by amateurs whose enthusiasms ranged from Grandma Moses to Picasso. Two handsome evening dresses hung in the windows, and around the shop were odd pieces of china, a sewing machine, a butcher's mallet, a rack of clothes covered with a plastic sheet, a cue stick encased in a fancy scabbard, serving trays, a tin lunchbox, rows and rows of shoes, assorted lamps, vases, and pitchers, and a cut-glass bowl. In the back, behind a partition, were piles of books and records, and two

automobile tires in good condition. Everything was pep-
pered with New York grit.

Miss Williams knocked on the door, and I let her in.
"Lord, this place is dirty," she said. "I've got to come down
next Monday and clean." She pointed to a pair of new-look-
ing moccasins. "From Duke Ellington—and this alpine hat,
too. Here's a drawerful of shirts from Louis Armstrong, and
those dresses are from Lorraine Gillespie, Dizzy's wife."

I handed Miss Williams her mail, and she opened the
letter. "It's from a convict upstate—I don't know him," she
said. "He says he's about to get out, and wants to know if I
can help him get a job. He saw a piece in the *Christian
Science Monitor* about Bel Canto. I'll write him and tell
him to pray and call me when he gets here. I receive letters
like this all the time."

Miss Williams put her Con Edison bills in her bag,
and I asked if I could take her out to lunch.

"Thank you, but I'm tired," she said. "I only slept four
or five hours last night. There's a kosher butcher around the
corner who has the best ground beef in New York. I'll cook
us a hamburger at home."

Miss Williams bought the meat and, at a fish market
across the street, picked up a filet of sole for her supper. I
hailed a cab. It was after two-thirty when we reached her
apartment. We ate lunch, which was delicious, at a tiny
kitchen table, and took our coffee into the living room.

"I'm not used to running around like this," Miss Williams said. "If I didn't have my prayers, they'd have to put
me in a straitjacket." She laughed, and lit a cigarette. "My
life turned when I was in Europe. I played in England for
eleven months, and spent money as fast as I made it. I
was distracted and depressed. At a party given by Gerald
Lascelles—he's an English jazz writer and a member of

royalty—I met this G.I. He noticed something was wrong, and he said, 'You should read the Ninety-first Psalm.' I went home and I read *all* the Psalms. They cooled me and made me feel protected. Then I went to France, and played theatres and clubs, and I still didn't feel right. Dave Pochonet, a French musician, asked me to his grandmother's place in the country to rest. I stayed there six months, and I just slept and ate and read the Psalms and prayed."

The living room had settled into twilight. Miss Williams' face was indistinct. She stood up and stretched. Then she knelt on the sofa and, cupping her chin in her hand, looked out the window at St. Nicholas Avenue. It was a little girl's position. "When I came back from Europe, I decided not to play anymore," she said. "I was raised Protestant, but I lost my religion when I was about twelve. I joined Adam Powell's church. I went there on Sunday, and during the week I sat in Our Lady of Lourdes, a Catholic church over on a Hundred and Forty-second Street. I just sat there and meditated. All kinds of people come in—needy ones and cripples—and I brought them here and gave them food and talked to them and gave them money. Music had left my head, and I hardly remembered playing. Then Father Anthony Woods—he's a Jesuit—gave Lorraine Gillespie and me instruction, and we were taken into the Church in May of 1957. I became a kind of fanatic for a while. I'd live on apples and water for nine days at a time. I stopped smoking. I shut myself up here like a monk. Father Woods got worried, and he told me, 'Mary, you're an artist. You belong at the piano and writing music. It's *my* business to help people through the Church and *your* business to help people through music.' He got me playing again. The night before I opened at the Hickory House, I had a dream, and it was filled with dead musicians, all friends of mine. Oscar Pettiford was in it, and Pha Terrell and Dick Wilson from Kirk's band. They were all rejoicing on this kind of stage, and there was a line of showgirls dancing and singing. Oscar was very happy because I was coming out again. It was a good sign."

# Sweet Tedium and
# Crippled Crabs

I invariably feel when I hear the likes of the New Christy Minstrels or Peter, Paul, and Mary or the Serendipity Singers that I'm foundering in milk. Not since the days of the barbershop quartet has a popular music been so bland and cherubic. Its performers exude health and bonhomie. The girls, in flyaway hairdos, are pretty and wholesome and amply constructed, and the boys are handsome and short-haired and flat of stomach. Onstage, all wear crisp, casual clothes and gleaming shoes, and all have wide white smiles. They display the easy presence of good swimmers and tennis players, and were they to appear with snorkels and rackets instead of guitars and banjos nothing would seem amiss. Indeed, this exchange might point up their music. Their "John Henry"'s and "Frankie and Johnny"'s and "Barbara Allen"'s would take on tone and color, and their emotional content would swell to at least that of Doris Day. As it is, they offer sweet tedium (their occasional mouthings of deep-country blues recall children doing a deathbed scene), and it is hard to believe that they are the progeny of Leadbelly and Big Bill Broonzy and Josh White.

Luckily, a large and attentive collection of prospective Peters, Pauls, and Marys were at Hunter College for a concert by such elders and betters as Brownie McGhee and

Sonny Terry, Muddy Waters, and Sister Rosetta Tharpe. Two folk-music fads have been under way in recent years—the Kingston Trio, or white-shoe, fad and the one instigated by John and Alan Lomax and dedicated to finding blues singers who went underground twenty or thirty years ago. This second movement has brought back Roosevelt Sykes, Sunnyland Slim, Lightnin' Hopkins, and Speckled Red, and it was responsible for the presence the other night of Mississippi John Hurt. Most country-blues singers sound like courting seals, but Hurt, dressed in work clothes and a wide-brimmed brown derby, sang with a singular softness and un-self-consciousness. (When the audience shouted requests, he would raise his head, make a half-moon with his mouth, look bemused, lower his head, and get on with what he was doing.) Although poor microphone placement made mush of his words, his remarkable guitar playing came through beautifully. His singing was full of open spaces, into which he poured spidery silver figures, many of them made up of *ostinato* basses supporting light, single-note treble lines. The contrast between Hurt and another country singer, the Reverend Gary Davis, was instructive. Davis, a member of the seal persuasion, started each line with a roar, dwindled to a guttural moan, and ended in a mutter. His guitar playing merely lapped at the rocks. Still another totally different singer was Cousin Joe, or Pleasant Joe, a wiry, fox-faced man from New Orleans, who in the course of five numbers (he accompanied himself on the piano) managed to parody most schools of blues singing—genuine and imitative. His sad blues were so sad they dissolved, his up-tempo blues had a mischievous Stepin Fetchit air, and he sang a blues that began with this champion verse:

> I wouldn't give a blind sow an
>   acorn, a crippled crab a crutch,

No, wouldn't give a blind sow an
   acorn, a crippled crab a crutch,
'Cause I found out that the woman
   I love, she ain't so such a much.

The better-known singers at the concert were surprisingly uneven. They tended to cavort nervously and to Uncle Tom, as if such theatrics would help them match the wild success of their juniors. Sister Rosetta Tharpe, who is reminiscent of Mahalia Jackson and Julia Lee, strutted and bounced and drowned herself out with a roaring electric guitar, and Sonny Terry (harmonica) and Brownie McGhee (guitar) issued a combination of arch jokes and barnyard sounds that occasionally made way for Terry's eerie harmonica. Unfortunately, the last and best performers on an overcrowded program were Muddy Waters and his first-rate pianist-accompanist, Otis Spann. Caught between the clock and a sated audience, they simply never got a chance.

# Drummin' Man

Jazz is not inclined to the corporate form, yet the ripples made by its few institutions often travel on long after the greatest non-joiners are forgotten. This is true of the ripples set off in the late thirties by the Benny Goodman band, which was the best-equipped, best-run, and best-lighted institution the music has known. They take the form of recordings (more than a million copies of the Goodman Carnegie Hall concert album have been bought—a figure unmatched among jazz L.P. albums), a nostalgia aging like a good soft cheese, and the continued renown of such Goodman alumni as Harry James, Teddy Wilson, Lionel Hampton, and Gene Krupa. Krupa, who is fifty-five, is possibly the steadiest Goodman wavelet. He is one of the handful of universally known jazz musicians, and he remains the most famous jazz drummer. He records frequently, and he draws sizable crowds wherever he plays. And he is credited with putting jazz drumming on the map and with showing the public the way to such lesser-known drummers as Baby Dodds, Jo Jones, and Sidney Catlett.

Krupa came to prominence in 1935, after being hired away from Buddy Rogers by Goodman. Not much later, Goodman boomed, and Krupa boomed with him. In the seven or eight years before that, Krupa had recorded frequently with such jazz groups as the McKenzie-Condon Chicagoans and the Mound City Blue Blowers, and with Adrian Rollini, Goodman, Red Nichols, and Bix Beiderbecke; he had made his living, though, with the dance bands of Russ Columbo, Irving Aaronson, Mal Hallett, and Rogers. He stayed with Goodman until 1938 and then, shooting out of the Goodman canon, formed his own band, which was a commercial success. He gave it up for a time in the early forties, re-formed it, and abandoned it for good in 1951. He has since toured with Jazz at the Philharmonic and with small groups. His big band offered a fare consisting largely of novelties, ballads, and showcases for the leader's drumming. His small groups, which have included the likes of Charlie Ventura, Eddie Shu, and Teddy Napoleon, are his big groups in miniature.

Krupa the drummer is difficult to isolate from Krupa the showman. Short, handsome, dark-haired, and smiling, he established the image of the drummer as madman. It was an image—calculated or not—that hypnotized the eye and stopped the ears. When he played, his hair fell over his eyes; he chewed gum; he hunched over his drums or reared back, arms straight in the air, like a politician at a rally; he sweated; in his climactic moments he converted his arms and hands and drumsticks into sculptured blurs. The mania for speed had begun to take hold by the late thirties, and Krupa was its epitome. Sorting out the components of the thunder underlying this spectacle was not easy at the time, because it was a new thunder. Before Krupa, drummers had largely been timekeepers. Their rare solos were limited by their technique, and their showmanship was homely. Krupa, however, was the first book-learned drummer. He started, in the twenties, as an admirer of Baby Dodds and Zutty Singleton, and slowly expanded their

styles by keeping a four-four beat on the bass drum, by re-
lying on cymbals rather than on wood blocks and temple
blocks, and by instituting the crackling rimshot. He tended
to rush the tempo, and he was heavy. Then he began studying his instrument and, before he joined Goodman, fell
under the sway of Chick Webb.

When all this had settled, Krupa's style—or better,
manner, for he had and has little style—went something
like this: As an accompanist, he was busy and unselective.
He got a low-thyroid sound from his drums, and he depended a good deal on the high-hat, on which he achieved
a fair imitation of Webb's clean, imperious *shoo shi-shah.*
His ride-cymbal work was straightforward and largely inaudible (light, small cymbals were in vogue until the mid-
fifties), and he sometimes punctuated breaks with a sock
cymbal the size of a cookie. He occasionally marked the
afterbeat on the partly closed high-hat or on the tom-toms.
He used rimshots continually—on afterbeats and offbeats,
and for double on-the-beat blams. His time was still uneven,
and he now rushed fast tempos and dragged slow ones. The
total effect was predictable and mechanical, for much of his
energy went into his solos. These had a good deal in common with Singleton and Webb, but they were more academic. He might start with rapidly swelling and subsiding
rolls on the snare (accented here and there on the rims),
break into an irregular pattern of rimshots mixed with tomtom beats, press into an even, multi-stroked roll, pass his
way with greater and greater speed through half a dozen
drum rudiments, and close with staccato rimshots. He didn't
bother to adjust his volume, and he rarely paused, not realiz-
ing that unexpected silences in drum solos are twice as
stunning as a mounting roar. His brush solos were fast and
crowded. Through the years, Krupa has grafted a few of

the innovations of modern drumming onto his approach, but in the main his playing has not changed. What he started has been carried forward, in different ways, by Buddy Rich and Louis Bellson.

These reflections have been caused by "Drummin' Man: Gene Krupa" (Columbia), which consists of thirty-one reissues and one unissued number made between 1938 and 1949. Thirty are by Krupa's big band and two by his trio. Aside from several decent semi-bop numbers from the late forties (Gerry Mulligan arranged one) and a fine 1939 Leo Watson scat vocal ("Tutti Frutti"), the album is valuable only for eight selections done between late 1941 and early 1942, when Roy Eldridge was with the band. (In many ways, these recall the Paul Whiteman-Bix Beiderbecke recordings.) Indeed, "After You've Gone," "Rockin' Chair," and "Let Me Off Uptown" are almost all Eldridge, and, despite their occasional grandstanding, they are magnificent. "After You've Gone," which Eldridge had recorded several years before with his own band, is taken at a machine-gun tempo, and it includes three Eldridge breaks that have been matched on records only by Dizzy Gillespie. In the slow "Rockin' Chair," Eldridge is at the height of his powers. His tone is brilliant and edgy, but he plays softly, alternating dancing middle-range notes with high, surreptitious jabs, and he closes many of his phrases with a loose vibrato. The opening of his solo in "Let Me Off Uptown," which includes cheering-crowd sounds from the rest of the band, is an idiotic and priceless moment. He solos briefly and well on the other sides, and in "Knock Me a Kiss" he delivers a classic, funny, lowdown vocal. Krupa's backing up in the album is instructive, and his solos are short and restrained. But his drumming is no better and no worse than that of such forgotten contemporaries as Frankie Carlson (Woody

Herman's band), Mickey Scrima (Harry James), and Moe Purtill (Glenn Miller). Nor does it have much in common with the groundbreaking that was being done elsewhere—with no one but musicians looking—by Sidney Catlett and Jo Jones and Dave Tough. The booklet accompanying the album has good photographs and an exclamatory appreciation by George Simon.

# Mingus Regained

Even more dismaying than the mediocre artist who spreads himself thin is the gifted artist who compresses his abilities into one area, stuffing his particular sausage to the bursting point. Charlie Mingus, the incomparable bassist, is of the latter bent. Indeed, because of his awesome energy and the limitations of his instrument, his sausage has long since burst. The explosion multiplied Mingus, first producing Mingus the exhorter. This Mingus lectures audiences on their inattentiveness or rudeness and writes steaming notes for record liners and letters to music-magazine editors. Another Mingus is Mingus the organizer. In 1960, this Mingus, along with Max Roach, put together, ran, and played in a successful rump jazz festival at Newport that survived Big Brother itself when Big Brother was closed down by the Newport Riot. He next presented himself at Town Hall with a superlative thirty-odd-piece band, but the evening was devoted largely to vicious-circle explanations by Mingus to the audience of why he wasn't playing more and talking less. Not long after, still another Mingus appeared—Mingus the autobiographer. The newspapers noted that this Mingus had completed a long and controversial autobiography, which would be published soon. Its author, the papers added, had decided to leave music and live in Europe. (The book is unpublished and Mingus is here.) All the while, Mingus, in addition to growing a beard, had been steadily swelling in size, as if he needed more room to house his many selves. Then it became clear that the inevitable struggle was at last shaping up between Mingus the bassist and his offshoots. For a time, it looked dark for Mingus the bassist; he quit the instrument altogether and tried the piano, on which he resembled a watery Thelonious Monk. But the balance of power abruptly and mysteriously shifted, and Mingus the bassist floored his usurpers. He took up his instrument again, lost seventy or eighty pounds, cut off his whiskers, shackled his extraneous selves, and opened at the Five Spot with a brand-new quartet. I had forgotten, I discovered a night or two after his return, what a marvel the old Mingus is.

Mingus's music is ruthlessly honest. He is incapable of giving a performance for the sake of a performance. When he feels right, his music is exhilarating; when he is angry, his music is angry; when he is dispirited, his music is dispirited. (During his piano period, his music seemed wholly indifferent.) The other night, Mingus was reportedly in a fury, and his music showed it. (The day before his opening at the Five Spot, an acquaintance of his told me, he had wound up an engagement on the West Coast and hadn't been paid what he had hoped.) It was raw and loud and exhausting. Each of the five numbers I heard lasted upward of half an hour, and had the tone of a brilliant, galloping harangue. No rhythm or tempo appeared to satisfy him. In rapid succession, he used waltz time, four-four, six-eight, and Oriental rhythms. He doubled and tripled tempos, used curved tempos (slowly accelerating and decelerating), and played without tempo of any sort. He used stop-time and shuffle rhythms. There were some noble moments. In "Meditations," he played a long bowed solo that was beautiful despite its sounding flat throughout. (He had complained to the management at the outset of the number that the piano was out of tune and had apparently then perversely tuned his bass to match the piano.) In "The Fables of Faubus," which has a sly, sarcastic melody, he took the subtlest bass solo I've ever heard. No note was accented beyond its time value; there were runs of bewildering speed and precision; there were ringing pauses and dense sprays of notes that dissolved when they hit the air. Best of all, in an untitled medium-tempo blues, was a series of four-bar exchanges with Danny Richmond, his drummer. Mingus was all over Richmond, parodying his breaks, suggesting new ones, and capping Richmond's answers. Richmond's ensuing solo reflected the fervor that his leader had worked him into. The rest of the quartet was swept along by the tide. Jane Getz, a new pianist, and no relation to the tenor saxophonist, kept her head above water, and Clifford Jordan, an easygoing hard-bop tenor saxophonist, did even better. At one point in the evening, Mingus the exhorter appeared briefly, trading insults with a heckler in the audience. The exchange went no further than that (at its conclusion Mingus, in the manner of a pitcher disgusted with an umpire's call, turned his back squarely on his antagonist and went on with his work), but it suggested that Mingus the bassist must remain on guard.

# Slow Motion

The oddest thing about the sudden and brilliant vortex of bebop was that it seemed to engulf not only the musical styles that preceded it but its inventors themselves. Within a decade after its arrival, in 1945, it had swallowed most of its founders and early adherents. Charlie Parker and Fats Navarro were dead. Max Roach and J. J. Johnson were musically dry, and Kenny Clarke, also treading old glories, was soon to go abroad for good. Howard McGhee and Al Haig had simply disappeared, as had Dodo Marmarosa. Thelonious Monk appeared to be permanently in the wings. And Bud Powell had begun the unsettling pattern of stays in hospitals that continues to dog him. Only Dizzy Gillespie and the late Oscar Pettiford remained afloat. Powell has been the most painful of these casualties, for he was perhaps even more revolutionary than Parker and Gillespie.

Art Tatum prepared the way for Powell. Tatum's style hinged on breathtaking arpeggios and on a discursive harmonic play that became massive and dictatorial in the arhythmic interludes he increasingly favored. But his virtuosity eventually took on a strained, dandyish quality that suggested his style had reached a narcissistic dead end. Powell simply started where Tatum stopped. He first trimmed away the fat, by converting the left hand, which had been a timekeeper since the days of ragtime, into a levering, pushing agent for the right hand. (The bass and drums quickly filled the ensuing rhythmic vacuum.) He then fashioned in the right hand long and lean single-note melodic lines that were apt to start and break off in odd places and that followed one another so rapidly they sometimes appeared to overlap. The jaggedness, rhythmic complexity, and plethora of flatted notes in these melodic lines gave them a sharp, dry, hard aspect; they seemed, in contrast to Tatum's thunderheads, to be all bone and metal. Powell and Monk had started off in the same direction in the mid-forties, but Monk went Gothic, while Powell remained spare and classical. Such a style as his, with its delicate balance of speed and melodic originality, moves on a tightrope, and in the early fifties Powell slipped. The melodic lines blurred and grew introverted, he slowed down, and many of his pieces had an incomplete, bewildered air. His health, it was soon clear, was hobbling him. Nonetheless, he has continued to play between his withdrawals from music— sometimes inchoately, sometimes with all his early invention.

With this sad chronicle in mind, I stopped in at Birdland to hear Powell, who had just returned from six years in Paris. It was a strange and affecting evening. He has gained weight, which adds to his impassive Oriental look, and between numbers and during his accompanists' solos he sat large and still, eyes hooded, slowly twiddling his thumbs. It was a stony inertia, and his playing reflected it. The old mastery was there, but it was caught in an eerie slow-motion embrace. The long, barbed melodic lines hung together, but they flowed somewhere below the beat, like the delayed-action timing in a dream. Occasionally he caught up and held tight, only to fall below again, with a flurry of missed notes. Entire passages went by in a monotone, but they were relieved by abrupt, articulate, flashing figures. These good moments cropped up in the blues—three of the twelve numbers I heard—and in "Shaw-Nuff," "I Know That You Know," and "52nd Street Theme," all taken at high tempos that seemed to sustain rather than outdistance him. Most important, Powell invariably gave the impression of being wholly confident about his ideas; one could almost *see* them start bright and bold from his mind and then, more often than not, twist away before reaching his fingers. His accompanists—John Ore on bass and Horace Arnold on drums—were models of steadiness.

# Basie

D e c c a,
starting up from its prolonged accidie, has released "The
Best of Count Basie," which reissues twenty-four recordings made between 1937 and 1939, and which contains as
much original, subtle, and poetic music as any jazz album
that comes to mind. Basie should not be mentioned without
Duke Ellington, and vice versa; in the late thirties the two
bands, though they were never popular, ruled the spectrum
of big jazz bands. Because of surface dissimilarities, they
were often considered direct opposites, but they were really
kissing cousins, and it is surprising that they eventually
diverged as much as they did. Both leaders were from the
East and were tutored by James P. Johnson and Fats Waller. Both attracted sidemen influenced by Louis Armstrong
and Coleman Hawkins and New Orleans jazz, and both had
absorbed the early experiments of Don Redman and
Fletcher Henderson. Both bands had superlative soloists
(who were sometimes stylistically similar), superlative-
sounding sections, and the ability to swing. (Basie, though,
learned first.) Despite their size—fourteen or so men—both
groups achieved a unified, small-band sound; their sections
were never used for display but were strictly melody or
riff-carrying vehicles or marvellously colored backdrops for

176

the soloists, all of whom seemed to drift out of and melt back into their sections like ghosts. (Some soloists war constantly with the bands they work in.) But Basie and Ellington were totally original, and this virtue finally sent them down their separate pikes. Ellington was primarily a composer, who used his band to explore and exhibit his ideas, and after a time it became inextricably linked with him; neither could have existed without the other. Basie was first and last a *jazz* musician who early in his career became fascinated by the blues, the rhythmic possibilities of stride piano, and the value of true improvisation. All his efforts were bent toward raising these aspects of jazz to their highest denominations. He became an expert borrower and distiller of the best that was around him. He shaped the blues of the Southwest—where he spent seven years before forming his own band, in 1935—into a sporting, cheerful form that made all other blues sound mulish. Even his slow blues, though often elegiac, were invariably relieved by the Oxford accents of Jimmy Rushing or the mocking obbligatos of Dickie Wells. He thinned his stride piano by rationing the oom-pah left hand and reducing the right hand to widely spaced beginner's chords and single notes. He did this for lightening purposes and to allow his champion rhythm section (Freddie Green, Walter Page, Jo Jones) to shine through. This rhythm section has, of course, never been equalled (its only serious rival worked together for just one night, at a concert in the Metropolitan Opera House, in 1944—Art Tatum, Al Casey, Oscar Pettiford, and Sidney Catlett—and it's a wonder the house still stands), and it diverted jazz rhythms into lighter-than-air channels that are still being explored. He had such a rhythm section, as well as soloists who were fresh improvisers, because of his uncanny knack for hiring original musicians. His soloists, in addition to possessing varied styles, rarely repeated themselves and often surpassed themselves. Only Ellington and Fletcher Henderson made equally homogeneous collections out of such iconoclasts. (This was not always so with Henderson, a laissez-faire man.) Basie's reed and brass sections found that pleasant middle ground between the slapdash and the immaculate. The results were suppleness and clarity. Beyond that, his sidemen handled their section parts with affection and even excitement; some of the riffs and melodic passages, particularly among the trombones, assumed a personal sololike quality.

At least eight first-rate soloists passed through the Basie band in the late thirties. The most notable, because of the space they were given, were the tenor saxophonists Lester Young and Herschel Evans. Their styles were in most ways antithetical. Young had a dry Boston tone, he often played behind the beat, and he based his variations on melodic rather than harmonic ideas. His solos represented spare *new* melodies and were frequently witty. His relation to the band in a solo was that of a migrating bird to a tree: he circled, perched briefly, preened, and moved on; he enhanced the band, but it did not alter him. He was unique, and founded a new school of tenor-saxophone playing. Evans grew directly out of Coleman Hawkins. He had a rich tone, a pronounced vibrato, hovered on or near the beat, and was unstinting with his emotions. For some reason, most saxophonists have tended to avoid blue notes, leaving those illegitimate notes to trumpeters and trombonists. Evans used them continually, and they gave his style an urgency and appeal that were in striking contrast to Lester Young's casual aloofness. He seemed, especially in those fast numbers in which he was allowed a full chorus, to engage in hand-to-hand combat with the rest of the band;

sometimes he disappeared in the sound of the accompanying sections, and sometimes he rode triumphantly over them. Basie's brass soloists were equally imposing. Buck Clayton was liquid and lyrical, in the manner of Bill Coleman and the Louis Armstrong of the middle thirties, while the younger Harry Edison was staccato and pushing. Until the arrival of Benny Morton and Vic Dickenson, Dickie Wells *was* the trombone section. He had been a great trombonist for almost a decade before he joined Basie, and his high notes, smears, off notes, complex introversions, and rambunctiousness offset the sweetness of Clayton and Evans and the detachment of Young. Dickenson learned something from Wells, but his fine wit was always his own, and Morton had been a polished, stately performer since his Fletcher Henderson days. Perhaps the most remarkable thing about Basie's stable was that it won so often so soon; Ellington's magnificent 1940 band had taken well over a decade to find its stride.

Basie, born in Red Bank, New Jersey, is a medium-sized, solidly set-up man who affects a mustache and a quiet, smiling manner. He leads the band from and with his piano, and has been known to drop his hands from the keyboard in admiration for the band's finest feats. His band grew out of one that had been led by Bennie Moten in the Southwest in the mid-twenties. From time to time, Moten's band swapped personnel with Walter Page's Blue Devils, an equally renowned Southwest group that included Buster Smith, Eddie Durham, Lips Page, Lester Young, and Basie himself. Basie took over after Moten's death. When the band was discovered by John Hammond in a small Kansas City night club, it had just nine pieces and was, from all reports, perfectly proportioned. Its bookers thought it advisable to add four or five men—a bit of meddling that was for a time disastrous. It was as if a trim man had suddenly gained twenty-five pounds. By 1937, when the band did its first recording, the extra weight had been converted to muscle, and it remained that way. Toward the end of the forties, the intuition and homegrown inspiration that had sustained the group had hardened, and this, together with the departure of his best soloists and dwindling business, forced Basie to disband. From 1949 to 1952 he led a bright small group, and then he formed his present band—a smooth, heavyset machine that never falters and never surprises.

With the exception of occasional ballads and up-tempo standards, the old Basie band played just three kinds of numbers—slow, medium, and fast blues. Its slow blues were generally distinguished by a delicate, muted Buck Clayton solo, backed by dreaming organ chords or distant wa-wa brass figures; a Jimmy Rushing vocal, with Dickie Wells or Lester Young obbligatos; and a brief full-band climax. Sometimes Basie soloed, using perhaps six or eight notes, which only deepened the misterioso atmosphere. The medium-tempo numbers had rich trombone figures, casual riffs that were lobbed back and forth between the sections, and solos that seemed extensions of or inspirations for these riffs. At this speed, the band suggested that it was barely tapping its reserves. It generously dipped into them at fast tempos, achieving a drive and exuberance matched only by Ellington and Jimmy Lunceford. The soloists blew themselves red, the riffs took on an irresistible momentum, and Basie himself often fell back on his stride piano. In Leadbelly's words, the band rocked church.

The Decca set reveals all these delights. "Swinging at the Daisy Chain" has that eerie quality, and it is also notable for Basie's sidestepping stride solo, a muted, far-away Clayton, and a mourning Evans. "Panassie Stomp" and "Every Tub" are monuments of heat and power, as is "Doggin' Around," in which Evans battles his peers with classic results. "Swinging the Blues" is possibly the most attractive riff number ever recorded, and it has an Edison solo that shoots like a branch from the main trunk. "Topsy," "Sent for You Yesterday," and "Jive at Five" are medium-tempo swims and have peerless Young and Evans solos. Evans is at the center of "Blue and Sentimental," which explains once and for all how a big jazz band should handle pretty material. (Listen to the perfect, freakish contrast between Evans' billowing periods and Young's lemony clarinet.) Basie himself is everywhere in the album—introducing numbers with plunging left-hand chords or helium right-hand notes, pushing and pushing his soloists, and coasting through those moment-for-meditation bridges in the last chorus. Nostalgia feeds on the dated; this Basie band is still brand-new.

# A Creative Thing

The flute, one of the most ancient and most lyrical of instruments, has long occupied a second-best, decorative position in jazz. This injustice, however, may soon be righted singlehanded by an extraordinary twenty-two-year-old flutist named Jeremy Steig. I began to suspect this after hearing Steig's first recording, a Columbia offering called "Flute Fever," in which he demonstrates —on a notably fragile instrument—a technique and tone and fervency as bold and easy as those of Sonny Rollins and Ornette Coleman. Steig's talents are displayed on the record cover as well as inside it. The front of the cover is taken up by a Steig painting of a green-clad flutist dancing his way across a riotous jungle under a Van Gogh sun, and on its back are four funny Steig caricatures of the musicians on the record, including a self-portrait that shows the artist, flute in mouth, sitting cross-legged atop a grand piano.

I recently called on Steig at his small Greenwich Village apartment, and found a slim, brown-haired man with a gentle face and a gentle voice. He led me into a room looking out on a garden and containing a low bed, books, a tape recorder, and a work-table on which two flutes stood like rockets at the ready. I asked him if he was pleased with the record. "Yes, I am," he said. "I wanted to do 'Lover Man' over, and on 'Willow Weep for Me' I mixed up the last two notes on the bridge. But 'Oleo' and 'So What' are pretty much what I had in mind. The session was tough. I didn't sleep for two days, I was so nervous, and the studio was this great big dully lit room that made me feel like a dot. Then the a.-and-r. man and Denny Zeitlin, the pianist he brought in for the record, got this thing going, and it was Denny this and Denny that between the studio floor and the control room until I began to wonder whose session it was. I was on the verge of tears a couple of times. But I'm seeing Columbia next week about another recording. I want to do one of children's songs— 'Go Tell Aunt Rhodie' and 'Dark as a Dungeon' and 'What Shall We Do with the Drunken Sailor?' and a great Greek song my mother just brought back on a record from Greece. I play every chance I get, but when I'm out of work, my father, who's the artist William Steig, helps me. Last week, I sat in for a set with Bill Evans at the Café au Go Go. I didn't ask him. I wouldn't have dared. He asked me, and he even paid me. He just reached in his pocket and said he had some old money and gave it to me. Bill Evans can do everything, including play a good game of golf. But he can't play the flute. He kept asking me how I did this or did that. It really boosted me up playing with him. What a great thing to happen!

"I took up the flute when I was eleven. My mother suggested it. I knew I could play it, just from blowing on Coke bottles. I've been improvising ever since I started, but I studied three years with Page Brook, of the Philharmonic. I went to the High School of Music and Art, and I started playing jazz when I was sixteen, and started that humming I do when I'm playing—parallel fifths or holding a single note—the next year. The best things about my playing I learned by myself or from records by Thelonious Monk and Rollins and Gerry Mulligan and Miles Davis. I used to sit in at jam sessions around town, but the other horns drowned me out, and who wants a five-foot-two kid with a flute hanging around anyway? Then two years ago I busted my head in a motor-bike accident down in Bermuda. It paralyzed the left side of my face, and my left ear is deaf. I had to learn how to talk and walk again. I had to *start* again. The doctors said I'd never be able to play, but I re-learned, and a funny thing happened. Before the accident, I played very melodic, very strict flute, and afterward it all came out atonal and wild. I couldn't understand Ornette Coleman before, and afterward I understood him perfectly. I can control only half my mouth, so I invented this gadget." Steig held up a two-inch square of what appeared to be matted adhesive tape. "It goes inside my left cheek and it keeps the air from escaping. The tendency is for the right half of my mouth to get stronger and stronger, and I have to keep pushing my food over to the other side, where there's no taste anymore, to try and keep things even."

Steig paused and rubbed the left side of his face. "Would you like some tea? I'll fix it, and you go in the bathroom—just there around the corner—and look at my murals."

I obliged, and was confronted by two large murals painted on adjacent walls and lit by a high skylight. Both are in the spirit of Steig's album cover, depicting tropical scenes awash with flutists, naked women, big, heavy birds, palm trees, and shouting colors. "When I'm painting or drawing," Steig said, coming up behind me, "my playing is better, and the other way around. I think of my flute as a kind of sound track for my art and my art as an illustration of my flute. I take a sketchbook to clubs with me and draw before I start to play. It's as good as a warmup set. And I draw between sets. Everything works together. You should keep your whole life that way—improvising. Improvise all the time, no matter what you're doing—lighting a pipe, washing your face. It makes a creative thing out of life."

Steig took me back to his living room and handed me a mug of tea. He picked up a flute and began fingering it. "I can take a flute and sit in with Greek musicians and Oriental musicians and Indian musicians and jazz musicians. It fills a gap among the instruments. It can make every sort of sound. Here's how a Villa-Lobos flute piece ends." He slipped his adhesive square inside his cheek, put the flute to his mouth, squinted his left eye, and stared balefully at me with his right one. Out came two startling banshee wails. Then, pulling the flute apart, he blew across the top of the lower section, producing heavy, bumping moans, which gradually melted into a melody. "That's good for a certain kind of accompaniment," he said as he reassembled the instrument. Then he played a fast blues, and suddenly began humming what he was playing. He hummed a single note, held it, and worked out a succession of trills on the instrument that hovered around the hum like a bee around a flower. He stopped and smiled. "It's a fantasy thing," he said. "But it's got to mean something. I try to get the wind or colors or the motion of a swing moving through the air into my playing. I used to do a piece called 'Tantrum'—all screams and moans and groans. I want to play way-out flute that's not so way out it gives somebody a headache. I'm long after Charlie Parker. I get a bigger kick from John Coltrane and Rollins and Bill Evans. But I like Leadbelly and Robert Johnson, the old blues singer, and Mitchell's Christian Singers. I've studied those falsetto notes and wails of Johnson's, but I didn't realize how great he was until I

185

tried to *play* him. I want to experiment with an echo chamber, a reverberator that's attached to the microphone. It will help me hear myself, and if I'm fast enough I'll get a double vibrato. And it would work fine with a bass flute, which is so soft it's hard to hear. I'd use this electronic stuff with a really good rock-'n'-roll group I have in mind—two guitars, an electric bass, and drums, with the drummer using a maraca on a tambourine fastened to his big tomtom. I want to do a Happening, but with *good* painters, my music, and maybe people climbing a tree and playing instruments—all on a big stage and so that everything works together. And I want a modern group, but I'm not up to it yet. There are things—Coltrane's 'Giant Steps' is one—that I just can't do yet. Every year, people stop expanding and drop off and are gone. You have to stay with it, and I will, because I can do anything."

# Chicago, Chicago

Some of Chicago's finest musical moments occurred between 1920 and 1930, when it was a way station (Kansas City was another) on the grand twenty-five-year peregrination of jazz from the South to New York, where it settled for good in the early thirties. Advance guards had been arriving in Chicago from New Orleans and elsewhere since before the First World War, and by 1925 one could find there such eminences as King Oliver, the Dodds brothers, Jelly Roll Morton, Kid Ory, and Louis Armstrong. These men, who represented the second generation of New Orleans jazz, were playing a highly stylized form of their forebears' invention, and Armstrong's Hot Five and Morton's Red Hot Peppers recordings caught its last, superb gasps. But astonishing things grew out of the ruins. Armstrong and Earl Hines, who worked together for a time, became the first great jazz soloists, abandoning the constricting New Orleans ensemble. At the same time, a number of young white musicians from the Chicago area suddenly coalesced and produced a new ensemble-solo music that is generally known as Chicago jazz. (A third kind of jazz in Chicago, fostered by a host of Negro blues pianists and singers, continued its homespun ways, and exists to this day.) These men worshipped Oliver and Arm-

187

strong and Hines, and they had listened to an earlier white band, the New Orleans Rhythm Kings, but their music was their own. It seemed, next to the tattered New Orleans banners, very snappy and very modern. Much of the small-band Negro jazz in Chicago in the twenties had a legato manner; the trumpeters used trembling vibratos, the clarinettists were baroque, the trombonists lumbered, and the drummers slid along on endless snare-drum rolls. It was a patient, lyrical music whose fires were hot but low. The white Chicagoans had the new-broom quality that bebop offered fifteen years later. They used charging four-four rhythms, rapid shuffle rhythms, and unexpected breaks and stops. The drummers experimented with rimshots and afterbeats, and for the first time the bass drum became a fixture in recording studios. The horn men, who had no time for vibratos, adopted—in contrast to Armstrong's barn-swallow motions—short, quickly turning phrases that had a throwaway sound. The staccato gallop replaced the legato glide. And fresh ensemble devices were constructed. The collective passages were distinguished by odd harmonic interludes and by end-of-the-chorus explosions that were approached sotto-voce or abruptly dropped in, like a burst of applause. Since the soloists were not at first distinguished, it was the total impression of crackle and hurry that counted.

The nucleus of Chicago jazz came out of Austin High School as the Blue Friars—the brothers Jimmy and Dick McPartland (trumpet and guitar), Bud Freeman (saxophone), Frank Teschemacher (clarinet), Dave North (piano), Jim Lannigan (bass), and Dave Tough (drums); Floyd O'Brien (trombone) was a ringer. They were soon joined by Eddie Condon, Mezz Mezzrow, Joe Sullivan, George Wettling, Muggsy Spanier, and Gene Krupa. The godly Bix Beiderbecke visited with them, and so did Benny Goodman. By 1930, the depression had driven most of the Chicagoans hopefully on to New York, where, continuing to starve, they were exposed to the wonders of Fletcher Henderson and Chick Webb and Duke Ellington. New recruits appeared—Brad Gowans, George Brunies, Pee Wee Russell, Jess Stacy, Wild Bill Davison, the Marsala brothers, Bobby Hackett, and Jack Teagarden, the last of whom remained only a visiting fireman. It was less a school now than a free-floating group of individuals who made their livings from recordings, with hotel and society bands, and with the early swing bands. Indeed, men like Krupa, Goodman, Stacy, and Tough never formally returned to the fold. Then, in 1938, Commodore Records began recording the survivors, and they had a renaissance—or, better, they reached the fruition the depression had blocked. For the next six or seven years, a steering committee made up of Max Kaminsky, Davison, Hackett, Russell, Brunis and Gowans, Sullivan and Stacy, Wettling and Tough and Condon, and assisted now and then by Teagarden, Fats Waller, and the Marsalas, produced countless records that were often superior to the pioneer 1927 Chicago sessions. Russell, Gowans, Teagarden, Hackett, Stacy, and Davison were first-rate soloists, and the ensembles retained their fire-brigade quality. Then bebop, the Joyce of jazz, arrived, and the Chicago school, which had mysteriously never become more than a highly proficient mutual-admiration society, went under. A remarkable number of its charter members are still active, but they are usually heard as soloists backed by rhythm sections or as members of hybrid groups. (Not long ago, a band at the Metropole consisted of Buck Clayton, Russell, Kaminsky, J. C. Higginbotham, Freeman, and Ben Webster; the music was Babelian.) On the few occasions when

189

the Chicagoans have been brought together for "reunion" recordings and the like, the results have been fitful.

By and large, the best numbers in Columbia's recently released "The Sound of Chicago (1923-1940)" are by 1927 and 1928 Austin High School groups. Their efforts include the celebrated "Liza," "Nobody's Sweetheart," and "China Boy," by Red McKenzie's and Condon's Chicagoans, two Condon quartet numbers, and two Freeman small-band selections. There is a lickety-split atmosphere and a general authority that sweeps over the sporadic raggedness. The most interesting soloist is Jimmy McPartland, an assiduous Beiderbecke admirer. Frank Teschemacher, whose early death called forth a small cult, now seems only a juiceless Russell. The jazz genealogists notwithstanding, Freeman *does* suggest the Lester Young of a decade later, and all of Gene Krupa is there, including the razzle-dazzle.

The rest of the forty-eight numbers in the album are often academic, for Columbia long ago reissued the Armstrong Hot Five and Hot Seven records, Victor owns the Jelly Roll Morton Red Hot Peppers, and Decca the weird 1929 Jabbo Smith sessions. But the atmosphere is lightened by several Armstrong offerings, by some fair blues and piano selections, and by scattered after-the-fact records made in the thirties—among them a couple of Earl Hines big-band numbers, two first-rate Jimmy Noones, and three superlative 1937 Roy Eldridge small-band efforts, the best of which, "Heckler's Hop," has a classic trumpet solo. The lavish booklet has the customary good photographs and a text by John Steiner, who appears to know more gossip about Chicago jazz than the musicians themselves could possibly have caused.

# Ground Hog

Marshall Stearns, the jazz historian, is writing a pioneering study of American dancing, and the other day he called up to say: "You should know about the tap exhibition at the Village Gate tonight. I've organized it with the help of Art D'Lugoff, the owner of the Gate, and it's a one-shot affair. It will be built around Ground Hog, a legendary dancer from Cincinnati whom I've been trying to locate for the past ten or eleven years. Charlie Atkins, who has danced at the Newport Jazz Festival, says that Ground Hog is better than Baby Laurence. Then I heard, a week ago, that Ground Hog was in New York. He's been here only twice—in 1938, with Count Basie, and in 1951. And briefly both times." Ground Hog, Stearns went on, began dancing in 1928, when he was six, with four dancers named the Whitman Sisters. He was a "pic," the term for small Negro children hired off the streets of Southern towns on the Theatre Owners' Booking Association circuit by entertainers and incorporated into their acts. "Rhythm Red, Ground Hog's sidekick, will be at the Gate, too," Stearns said. "He claims that Ground Hog has avoided New York because he is disdainful of it, but Ground Hog says he has been waiting for tonight for twenty years. Lon Chaney and Chuck Green will be there. Green is a disciple of John W. Bubbles. Jo Jones will head up the backing. We'll kick off at ten-thirty, and we'll only have about half an hour, so don't be late. Ground Hog may disappear tomorrow."

When I arrived at the Village Gate, I was greeted by Stearns, who is tall and large-headed and bespectacled. "There are now six dancers instead of four," he said. "Gentleman Pepe and Tommy Powell have been added. Nipsey Russell, a comedian who is a fine dancer himself, is here. I'm trying to persuade Max Roach, who's coming, to accompany Ground Hog on drums in one number. He's told me he has learned more from tap dancers than he can say. There's Roach now." Stearns deposited me at a table under the brow of the bandstand and excused himself.

A pianist and a bassist appeared above me, followed by Jo Jones, who was wearing a dark suit and white socks, and by Stearns, who sat on a stool beside Jones at the back of the bandstand. Stearns pulled a microphone over to him, cleared his throat, and made some remarks about tap dancing as a "lost art" and about Ground Hog as a "lost dancer."

Suddenly, five of the six dancers bounded onto the bandstand, accompanied by a medium-tempo "Tea for Two," the tap dancers' national anthem. Tapping and spinning and bowing in unison, they worked one chorus and departed, eyes right and smiles fixed.

Stearns introduced Gentleman Pepe, formerly of the team of Brown & Beige. Pepe, thin and fox-faced, was wearing a dark suit and a red vest, and he began with a medium-tempo "Lullaby of Birdland." Swinging his arms, he slipped from on-the-beat to double-time steps, walked backward tapping, stopped, leaned forward, and, his hands flat and low over the floor, rattled his way to the front of the stage.

192

He straightened up, caught his breath, and announced, "This will be a little impromptu thing, a Sunday punch of music." Turning to the musicians, he said, "Give me a chorus of 'Laura' after my solo thirty-two-bar tap." Pepe's feet moved so fast they almost buzzed, and when the music started, he loosed some thundering steps.

The next dancer, Tommy Powell, was described as the sparkplug of the Hi-De-Ho Boys. The musicians played "Fly Me to the Moon," and Powell, in a gray suit and a matching hat, started a Raggedy Andy dance, his arms floppy, his legs bent, his head lolling from side to side. Then he tightened up and spun around, releasing a spray of serious steps, and at the last minute became a doll again. Powell went into a fast "How High the Moon," tapped half a chorus or so, executed a couple of admirable splits and broke into rapid steps on one leg, his other leg held above the floor at a forty-five-degree angle. Then he took off his hat, tossed it onto the toe of his lifted foot, tapped in a one-legged circle, kicked the hat in the air, and caught it on his head.

Powell almost collided with the next entry, a heavy man dressed in a blue suit and identified as Lon Chaney, a one-time prizefighter. Chaney announced a dance called the Paddle and Roll, which was full of slow, gliding, jumping-rope steps. Despite his relaxed air, he was clearly working harder than his predecessors, and Nipsey Russell, seated by the bandstand, shouted "Ha-ah!" Chaney returned the compliment with intricate, nibbling steps and ricocheting handclaps, which made him sound like several dancers instead of one, and after a stop-time chorus, marked every four beats by Jones on the bass drum, he bowed to Russell, his face streaming.

Chaney was followed by Rhythm Red, an equally

large man, in white shoes and a pearl-gray suit. Rhythm Red looked shy and, standing near the rear of the stage, said, "It's a pleasure to be here this afternoon. I don't have anything to say about myself. I do the best I can and get off." He edged into floating, almost pottering patterns, which caused Russell to shout, "You're a race horse on the curve! Go now!" Rhythm Red obliged, urging himself on with a string of soft "Yeh"s. "Get it proper!" Russell shouted. Rhythm Red responded with a long sequence of sliding-tapping steps, and at the end of it Russell was graced with another bow.

A tall, flat cardboard figure in a baggy suit—Chuck Green, of Chuck & Chuckles—appeared. He began *a cappella,* shifting quickly back and forth between medium and fast tempos. His concentration was complete and his steps were offhandedly perfect, and the room seemed to sit up and lean forward. Jones broke in on the drums, and Green worked out an astonishing series of counter-rhythms, which flowed in and out of Jones's beat. Stearns reared back in amazement. Russell shouted unintelligibly. Green's patterns, now on the beat, grew increasingly fervent, and when he suddenly finished, he was swamped with cries of "One more!"

Stearns said, "And now the Lochinvar from the West —Ground Hog!" Nothing happened. Then a short, mischievous-faced man with a gap-toothed smile and new patent-leather shoes appeared. He was already dancing, and he was talking, too: "Let's do it à la Charlie Parker. [Machinegun steps.] Now watch this one. [Heels clicking rapidly together and on the floor.] Chuck, Chuck Green was up here. That's the challenge. [More heelwork.] Now, I wonder where *these* belong. [Triple-time steps at the front of the stage.]" Ground Hog flung open his arms, made pigeon toes, and scraped his feet toward each other, ending each scrape with a flutter of beats. Max Roach, who had slipped onto the bandstand, sat down at Jones's drums and began a furious tempo. Ground Hog jumped, assumed a mock expression of surprise, and began dancing in a jiggling half time. Chuck Green reappeared and joined him. Roach cut the tempo in half and relinquished his seat to Jones. Ground Hog nodded at Jones, smiled, and said, "He's an oldster, he's an oldster." Ground Hog and Green exchanged steps, alternately copying and parodying each other. Roach, standing near Jones, tapped two drumsticks together, and Ground Hog, his head forward, looked hard at Green and said, "I'm going to *put* something on you." Ground Hog's lightning taps were flawlessly returned by Green. Ground Hog improvised on the same pattern, and said, "I *know* you can do better than that." Green came back with a new pattern and Ground Hog, aping it, shouted "Oh, you want to play show biz!" and, flying into the air, landed smack on his knees, his legs crossed behind. Then he sprang up and into a bewildering, straight-faced volley of fast steps, and, abruptly laughing, threw his arms around Green. The two men rocked back and forth together. Ground Hog pushed Green away and raised his arms over his head. "Finale! Finale!" he cried. "Let these guys dance!" The remaining dancers poured onto the bandstand and into an easy "Lady Be Good." Ground Hog danced apart from them and, at the sound of an ear-splitting rimshot from Jones, froze to attention, then slowly bowed. The lights went out.

1965

# Sunshine Always Opens Out

Late last winter, Earl "Father" Hines, the consummate pianist, gave a concert at the Little Theatre, on West Forty-fourth Street, that is still mentioned with excitement and awe by those fortunate enough to have been there. The obstacles Hines faced that night were formidable. He was fifty-nine, an age when most jazz musicians have become slow-gaited; he had, except for a brief night-club appearance, been absent from New York for ten years, and the occasional recordings that had floated east from Oakland, where he had settled, had done little to provoke demands for his return; and he had never before attempted a full-length solo recital—a feat that few jazz pianists, of whatever bent, have carried off. He met these hindrances by first announcing, when he walked onstage, that he was not giving a concert but was simply playing in his living room for friends, and by then performing with a brilliance that touched at least a part of each of his thirty-odd numbers. Not only was his celebrated style intact but it had taken on a subtlety and unpredictability that continually pleased and startled the audience. Even Hines' face, which has the nobility often imparted by a wide mouth, a strong nose, and high cheekbones, was hypnotic. His steady smile kept turning to the glassy grimace presaging tears. His eyes—when they were open—were bright and pained, and his lower lip, pushed by a steady flow of grunts and hums, surged heavily back and forth. He made quick feints to the right and left with his shoulders, or rocked easily back and forth, his legs wide and supporting him like outriggers. Between numbers, that smile—one of the renowned lamps of show business—made his face look transparent. It was exemplary showmanship—not wrappings and tinsel but the gift itself, freely offered.

I found Hines' fervency and grace indelible, and when he appeared with a small band for a week at Birdland not long ago, I called him at the mid-town hotel where he was staying and asked if I could visit him. His voice was heavy, but he spoke quickly and clearly: "Man, that's a hard job at Birdland. It's ten to four, which I'm not used to anymore, and it wears me out. I got to bed at seven yesterday, but I had to be up and downtown for my cabaret card, then to a booking agency, then to a rehearsal for the Johnny Carson show. I didn't get to bed until six-thirty this morning, and then some damn fool called me at nine and said [his voice went falsetto], 'Is this Earl Hines, and did you write "Rosetta"?' I won't say what I said. So I'm a little stupid. I'm *breathing*, but I don't feel like jumping rope. You come tomorrow around one. It's my last day at Birdland, and maybe I'll feel better because of it."

When I arrived, Hines was stretched out on his bed watching an old Edward G. Robinson movie on television. He had on white pajamas, a silver bathrobe, and brown slippers. A silk stocking hid the top of his head. The room was small and hot and cluttered with suitcases, and its single window faced a black air shaft. Hines' eyes were half shut and there were deep circles under them. He motioned me to a chair at the foot of his bed and asked me to turn down the television. "I haven't eaten yet, so I just ordered up some chicken-gumbo soup and a Western omelette and plenty of coffee and cream. It'll probably come by suppertime, the way room service goes here. Yesterday, I asked for ham and eggs for breakfast and they sent a ham steak and candied sweets and stringbeans and rolls, and when I called down, the man said he was two blocks from the kitchen and how could he help what the chef did?" Hines laughed —or, rather, barked—and rubbed a hand slowly back and forth across his brow. "I mean, I don't know what has caused New York to tighten up so. All the hotels—including this one—want musicians to pay in advance. My goodness, it's almost dog-eat-dog. Pittsburgh, where I'm from, is a country town compared to New York, where it takes every bit of energy to keep that front up. The streets are all littered, and last night I go in the back door at Birdland and three guys are laying there, sick all over theirselves. Next time, I go in the front door, and two guys want a dime, a quarter. I've been all over this country and Canada and Europe, and how clean and nice they are. I'd be ashamed to tell people I was from New York. Maybe I been away from home too long. It's three months now. I finish this recording date I have with Victor tomorrow and the next day and—boom— I'm off. Stanley Dance—he's the jazz writer and an old friend from England—set up the Victor date. He's coming by around now with tapes of some records I made with my big band in the late thirties that Victor is bringing out again. He wants me to identify a couple of the soloists. My man Stanley."

There was a knock, and a portly mustached man walked briskly in. He was carrying a small tape recorder. "Hey, Stanley," Hines said, and sat up straight.

"Did you get a good sleep?" Dance asked, in a pleasant Essex accent.

"Oh, people start calling at eight or nine again, but

I'll sleep later, I'll rest later. I'm not doing *nothing* for a month when I get home."

"If it's all right, I'll play the tapes now, Earl." Dance put the machine on a luggage stand and plugged it in.

Hines stood up, stretched, and pummelled his stomach, which was flat and hard. "I haven't been sick since I was twelve years old. In the thirties, when we were on tour in the East, I'd work out with Joe Louis at Pompton Lakes. We'd sit on a fence awhile and talk, and then we'd throw that medicine ball back and forth. That's why my stomach is so hard today." He sat down next to the tape recorder, crossed his ankles, clasped his hands in his lap, and stared at the machine. Dance handed me a list of the titles on the Victor reissue and started the tape. The first number, "Piano Man," was fast and was built around Hines' piano.

Hines listened attentively, his head cocked. "I haven't heard that in I don't know *how* long," he said. "That was a big production number in the show at the Grand Terrace, in Chicago, where I had my band from 1928 to 1940. I played it on a white grand piano and all the lights would go down, except for a spot on me and on each of the chorus girls, who were at tiny white baby grands all around me on the dance floor. When I played, they played with me—selected notes I taught them. Just now at the end I could picture the girls going off. Gene Krupa came in a lot, and he used that number for *his* show number—'Drummin' Man.' He just changed the piano parts to drum parts. I told him he was a Tom Mix without a gun." Hines laughed. "What's that?" he asked when the next number began.

" 'Father Steps In,' " Dance said.

Hines hummed the melody with the band. A trumpet soloed. "That's Walter Fuller. He was my work horse." An alto saxophone came in. "That's Budd Johnson, my

Budd. He'll be down at Victor tomorrow. He usually played tenor." Hines scat-sang Johnson's solo note for note. "He sounds like Benny Carter there."

"G. T. Stomp," "Ridin' and Jivin'," and " 'Gator Swing" went by. "The only trouble with this record, Earl, is there are so many fast tempos," Dance said.

"It was a very hot band. That's why the people were all so happy in those days. Nobody slept at the Grand Terrace. When we went on the road, the only band we had trouble with in all the cutting contests there used to be was the Savoy Sultans, the house group at the Savoy Ballroom, in Harlem. They only had eight pieces, but they could swing you into bad health. They'd sit there and listen and watch, and when you finished they'd pick up right where you'd left off and play it back twice as hard. We had a chance, we ducked them. *Everybody* did."

A waiter rolled in a table and placed it beside the bed. "Am I glad to see you, even if it is almost suppertime!" Hines barked, and he sat down on the bed. "Stanley, could we finish that after I've had something to eat? I only eat twice a day, and never between meals, and I get hungry. Take some coffee. Did they bring enough sugar? I like a lot of sugar and cream." He opened a suitcase beside the night table and took out a two-pound box of sugar. He put it on the table and barked again, "I never travel without my sugar bag. I learned that long ago." Hines filled a soup bowl from a tureen and buried the soup under croutons. Dance sipped a cup of coffee and watched Hines. "Earl, you were talking a bit the other day about what it was like to be the leader of a big band."

Hines looked up from his soup and put his spoon down. He wiped his mouth with a napkin. Then he picked up his spoon again. "An organization is no bigger than its leader, Stanley. You have to set an example—let them know *you* know what you're doing. An animal will fear you if you're leading, but you let down and he'll get you. Same thing with handling a big band. For that reason, I used to stay a little apart from the band, so there wouldn't be too much familiarity. But I had to be an understanding guy, a psychologist. I had to study each man, I had to know each man's ability. I'd be serious with one, joke with another, maybe take another out for a game of pool. Once in a while I'd give a little dinner for the band. But I was very strict about one thing. The band had to be on time, particularly on the road. There was a twenty-five-dollar fine if you missed the curtain in a theatre, and a dollar a minute after that. It cost five dollars if you were late for the bus, and a dollar a minute after that. We even fined the bus driver if he was late. The fines worked so well, after a while I could take them off. As I said before, I've always stayed physically in condition. The band knew I'd fight at the drop of a hat, even though I had an even disposition. I believe the only time I lost my temper was on the road when a trombonist I had was bugging me and I picked him up and had him over my head and would have thrown him off the bus if the boys hadn't stopped me.

"The Grand Terrace was very beautifully done—a big ballroom with a bar in the back and mirrors on the walls, with blue lights fixed here and there on the glass. Those mirrors were like looking at the sky with stars in it. The bandstand was raised and had stairs coming down and around both sides for the chorus girls and the show. The dance floor was also elevated. The Grand Terrace was the Cotton Club of Chicago, and we were a show band as much as a dance band and a jazz band. We worked seven days a week, and how we did it I don't know. There were three shows a night during the week and four on Saturday. The hours were nine-thirty to three-thirty, except on Saturday, when we worked ten to five. The chorus girls—we had fourteen or sixteen of them—were very important. They were ponies—middle-sized girls who were not overweight and could dance. Or they were parade girls, who were taller and more for just show. The chorus line, coming down the stairways, opened the show. Then there was a vocalist, he or she. A soft-shoe dancer or ballroom team came next. Then maybe a picture number, with fake African huts and a big fire and such. The highlight of the show was a special act, like the four Step Brothers or Ethel Waters or Bojangles, and then everyone on for the finale. Sometimes a comedian like Billy Mitchell took the dancers' spot. He had a trick of turning one foot all the way around, so that that foot pointed one way and the other the other way, and he'd walk along like it was nothing and bring down the house. It was always a good hot show, with everything jumping. The girls were its heart, and they really danced. They'd come off the floor wringing wet. They spent a lot of money on their costumes, and we always had two women backstage to put on buttons and fasten snaps and adjust new costumes that sometimes didn't arrive until half an hour before show time. I was a stickler for the boys in the band dressing, too, and we had a costume fund. One cause of my feeling for clothes was George Raft. I'd visit him in his hotel room when he was in town and he'd have three trunks of clothes. He'd tell me not to buy expensive suits—just suits that looked good—and to have plenty of them and change them all the time and that way they'd last. I had shoes made to fit my suits from the Chicago Theatrical Shoe store. They were dancers' shoes—sharp-looking, with round toes, and soft, so that they fitted like a glove.

Wherever I went, they'd send a new pair if I needed them, because they had my measurements. A valet took care of my clothes, and there was another valet—a band valet—for the boys."

Hines emptied the tureen into his soup bowl. "The Grand Terrace was always an orderly place. The audiences were mixed. Segregation never crossed anyone's mind. Friday nights we had college kids and we had to learn the college songs. Saturdays we got the office and shop people. Sunday was seventy-five per cent colored, and Mondays were tourists. On Wednesdays we got elderly people and played waltzes. The racketeers owned twenty-five per cent of the Grand Terrace, and they always had four or five men there—floating men. They never bothered us. 'We're here for your protection, boys,' they'd say. If they were going to run some beer from Detroit to Chicago, they'd figure the job out right in the kitchen. I'd be sitting there, but it was hear nothing, see nothing, say nothing if the cops came around. There was pistol play every night during prohibition. No shooting; just waving guns around. I was heading for the kitchen one night and this guy went pounding past and another guy came up behind me and told me to stand still and rested a pistol on my shoulder and aimed at the first guy and would have fired if the kitchen door hadn't swung shut in time. Some of the waiters even had pistols. The racketeers weren't any credit to Chicago, but they kept the money flowing. My girl vocalist might make fifteen hundred a week in tips for requests, and she'd split it with the boys, and they'd put it in the costume fund. The racketeers owned me, too, and so did the man who controlled the other seventy-five per cent of the Grand Terrace. This was something I didn't fully realize until late in the thirties. We were always paid in cash—one hundred and fifty a week for me and ninety apiece for the boys in the band. I couldn't complain. The Grand Terrace was our seat nine months of every year, and we had a nightly coast-to-coast radio hookup, which gave us solid bookings for the two or three months we were on the road. I couldn't afford to hire stars for the band, so I had to *make* my stars. In this way, I brought along Ivie Anderson, the singer, and Ray Nance, the trumpet player. Duke Ellington took both of them from me. And I developed other singers, like Ida James and Herb Jeffries and Billy Eckstine and Sarah Vaughn, and I had musicians like Trummy Young and Budd Johnson and Dizzy Gillespie and Charlie Parker."

Hines exchanged his soup bowl for the Western omelette and poured more coffee. He chewed carefully. "We had a doctor at home, Dr. Martin, and he always said all your sickness derives from your stomach. I've never forgotten that. I was a wild kid in the twenties and thirties and I drank a lot, but what saved me was I always ate when I was drinking. The music publishers had something to do with my drinking. After we had our radio hookup, they'd come around every night, trying to get me to play this tune or that." Hines shifted into falsetto again: "'I got a little tune here, Earl, and I wish you'd play it and blah blah blah,' and then he'd buy me a drink and another publisher would buy me a couple of more drinks and I'd end up drinking all night and then I'd have to drink some more, if we had a record session early the next day, to keep going. I'd forget where I left my car, and I got so tired sometimes I'd put on shades and play whole shows asleep, with George Dixon, my sax man, nudging me when I was supposed to come in. I never considered myself a piano soloist anyway, so I was happy to just take my little eight bars and get off. It's the public that's pushed me out and made me a soloist. Then one night the owner of the Grand Terrace said, 'Earl, you're drinking yourself to death.' I thought about that and I decided he was right. When we went on the road soon after, I quit. I was all skin and bones. I bought a camera and took a picture of every pretty girl I saw to pass the time, and when I came back to Chicago I weighed one hundred and eighty-five. I only drink now after I'm finished work. But people *still* are after me to buy me drinks, and you hate to keep saying no. It almost agitates you."

Hines pushed his plate away and lit a big cigar. He arranged a couple of pillows against the headboard, leaned back, and swung his feet onto the bed. He puffed quietly, his eyes shut. "The excitement of the Grand Terrace days was something you couldn't realize unless you were there," he said, in a low voice. "It was a thrill when that curtain went up and us in white suits and playing and you knew you'd caught your audience. I bought my way out of the Grand Terrace in 1940 after I finally learned about all the money I was making and wasn't seeing. I kept the band together until 1948. By then it had twenty-four musicians and strings. But things were changing, with the entertainment tax and higher prices and fewer and fewer bookings in the theatres and ballrooms. I saw the handwriting on the wall, and I disbanded and went with Louis Armstrong's All Stars, which had Jack Teagarden and Sid Catlett. I didn't care for being a sideman again after all the years I'd spent building up my reputation. Play some more of that tape, Stanley. Let me hear that band again."

Midway in the fourth or fifth number, I looked at Hines. His cigar was in an ashtray on the night table, his eyes were shut, and his mouth was open. He was asleep.

I had told Hines I would stop in at Birdland that night, and during dinner I mulled over his view of himself

as reluctant soloist. The remark was surprising, for although
Hines has spent a good part of his forty-year career as an
influential leader of big and small bands, he is valued
chiefly by musicians and listeners as a pianist. When he
came to the fore in Louis Armstrong's celebrated 1928 recordings, the effect he created was stunning. Most jazz
pianists were either blues performers whose techniques
were shaped by their materials, or stride pianists whose
overgrown basses and purplish right hands reflected the
old-fashioned hot-house luxury of ragtime. Hines rushed
into the space between these approaches with a unique,
almost hornlike style. He fashioned complex, irregular
single-note patterns in the right hand, octave chords with
brief tremolos that suggested a vibrato, stark single notes,
and advanced harmonic chords. His left hand, ignoring the
stride pianists' catapult action, cushioned his right hand.
He used polished tenths and offsetting, offbeat single notes,
and he sometimes played counter-melodies. Now and then
he slipped into urgent, shimmying arhythmic passages full
of broken melodic lines, heavy offbeat chords, and jagged
let's-play-tag melodies. Hines and Louis Armstrong became the first jazz soloists to sustain the tension that is the
secret of improvisation. Each of Hines' solos—particularly
any that lasted several choruses—had a unity that was
heightened by his pioneering use of dynamics. He itali-
cized his most felicitous phrases by quickly and gracefully
increasing his volume and then as quickly and gracefully
letting it fall off. In this way, he gave the impression of a
dancer repeatedly moving toward and receding from the
listener. At the same time, he retained the emotional sub-
stance of the blues pianists and the head-on ryhthms of the
stride men. His earliest recordings still sound modern,
and they must have been as shocking then as the atonal
musings of Ornette Coleman are now. In time, his followers

included Mary Lou Williams, Teddy Wilson, Billy Kyle, Jess Stacy, Nat Cole, Eddie Heywood, Erroll Garner, and Art Tatum, the last of whom became the founder of present-day jazz piano. Hines' style has changed little. In the forties, he revealed a startling fondness for candles-and-wine music, but during the fifties and early sixties, when he spent dogged years on the West Coast with both semi-modern and Dixieland groups, he demonstrated that he could play any kind of jazz piano and keep his basic style unblemished.

Hines was at the piano when I got to Birdland. The bandstand was dark and he was alone, unreeling a progression of soft, Debussy chords. A couple of spotlights went on, but the illumination seemed to come from Hines himself. He was immaculate; his smile, permanently in place for the evening, gleamed, and he was wearing a dark suit and a white shirt and dark shoes. His jet-black hair was flat and combed straight back, and he appeared as limber as a long-distance swimmer. I had heard from a friend who had visited Birdland a night or two before that the group Hines happened to have at the moment was the sort of ingenuous, good-time, doubling-in-brass outfit that used to be found at the Apollo Theatre, in Harlem. It was, my friend had said, a surprising group—for Hines and for Birdland. It had a drummer and an organist, a male vocal trio, and a female alto saxophonist who sounded like Charlie Parker and who also sang. My friend was right. The next forty-five minutes were totally unpredictable, and Hines' assemblage soon seemed twice its actual size. The vocal trio sang together and separately; the organist soloed and sang a couple of numbers; the lady saxophonist not only emulated Charlie Parker but sang by herself or with the trio; the drummer took over for a long spell; and Hines, after eight-bar sips here and there, played a fifteen-minute solo medley. All this was executed with the precision of a Grand Terrace show, and when it was over, Hines, who stopped by my table, was soaking wet. "I'm trying something nobody else is," he said, mopping himself. "I've had this group six months and I want to reach young and old. You play Dixieland, you get the old and drive away the young. You play modern, you get the young and keep away the old. A girl asked me last night, 'Are you Earl Hines' son? My mother used to listen to your dad at the Grand Terrace in 1930.' The young don't believe I'm me and the old are too tired to come and see. But I want both, and the manager has told me he's seen types of people in here all week he's never seen before. People have also said I'm crazy to have such a group, that the public wants to hear my piano, and that's why I put that medley in every show. This band is a kind of variation of what I was trying to do in my own club in Oakland, which opened last December. It had an international tinge. I had Irish and Chinese dancers and Italian and Japanese vocalists. I had Negro and Chinese and white waiters. I had Jewish musicians. I had Mexican and Chinese comedians. Then I found out one of my partners wasn't international and that the other didn't know much about show business, and I got out."

Hines ordered coffee, finished mopping himself, and lit a cigar. "I have a photographic memory for chords, and when I'm playing, the right chords appear in my mind like photographs long before I get to them. That gives me a little time to alter them, to get a little clash or make coloring or get in harmony chords. It may flash on me that I can change an F chord to a D-flat ninth. But I might find the altering isn't working the way it should, so I stop and clarify myself with an offbeat passage, a broken-rhythm thing.

I always challenge myself. I get out in deep water and I always try to get back. But I get hung up. The audience never knows, but that's when I smile the most, when I show the most ivory. I've even had to tell my bass player I'm going into the last eight bars of a tune because he wouldn't know where the hell I was. I play however I feel. If I'm working a pretty melody, I'll just slip into waltz time or cut the tempo in half. My mind is going a mile a minute, and it goes even better when I have a good piano and the audience doesn't distract me. I'm like a race horse. I've been taught by the old masters—put everything out of your mind except what you have to do. I've been through every sort of disturbance before I go on the stand, but I never get so upset that it makes the audience uneasy. If one of my musicians is late, I may tell the audience when he arrives that I *kept* him off the stand because he needed a little rest. I always use the assistance of the man upstairs before I go on. I ask for that and it gives me courage and strength and personality. It causes me to blank everything else out, and the mood comes right down on me no matter how I feel. I don't go to church regularly, because I'm generally too tired from the hours I have to keep. I'd only fall asleep, and I don't believe in going just to say, yes, I go to church every Sunday. One Easter Sunday, I played in the Reverend Cobbs' church in Chicago—a standing-room-only church, he's so popular with his parishioners. I played 'Roses of Picardy.' They had three hundred voices in the choir. I played the first chorus; the choir hummed the second behind me and sang the lyrics on the third. Good God, it shook me up, the sound of those voices. I had nothing but goosepimples, and I stood right up off the piano stool. It was almost angelic." Hines paused and listened as the leader of the alternate group announced him onstage. He turned to me before he got up. "Why don't you come to the Victor session tomorrow? Stanley Dance is picking me up at the hotel about one and we can all jump a cab down there together."

Hines looked fresh and eager the next day. He was smoking a pipe and watching television, and he was wearing a black silk suit, a striped tan sports shirt, and pointed shoes trimmed with alligator leather. He had on a dark porkpie hat and dark glasses. Stanley Dance was telephoning. "He's checking Budd Johnson to make sure he's left for the studio," Hines said. He pointed to his glasses. "I wear these to shut out those photographers who turn up at every record session and seem like they're popping pictures of you from right inside the piano."

"Budd's on his way," Dance said. "And Jimmy Crawford and Aaron Bell are definite for drums and bass."

"Fine, fine. Stanley, bring that fake book, please, in case they ask me to play something I recorded forty years ago. Everybody but me remembers those tunes."

When we were settled in a cab, Hines leaned back and tilted his hat over his eyes. It was drizzling and the traffic was heavy. "Coming down in that elevator puts me in mind of Jack Hylton, the English bandleader, and the time he came to Chicago in the thirties. He was staying at the Blackstone and asked me if I'd come and see him. When I got there, the elevator man told me to take the freight elevator around back. Like a delivery boy. That upset me and I refused and pretty soon the assistant manager and the manager and Hylton's secretary and Hylton himself were all there and it ended in my going up in the front elevator. I don't say much about race, but it's always in the back of my head. I've tried to handle it by thinking things out up front and avoiding trouble if it can be avoided—like when I bought my house in Oakland four or five years ago. It has four bedrooms, a maid's room, family room, kitchen, parlor, and a fifty-foot patio in back. It's almost too much house. It was a white neighborhood before my wife and I and our two girls came, and I knew there might be trouble. The house belonged to a guy down on his luck and it was a mess inside and out. It's in an area where people keep their lawns nice, so before we moved in I painted the outside and installed a watering system and hired a Japanese gardener. I painted the inside and put in wall-to-wall carpets and drapes. When it was the best-looking place around, we moved in. We haven't had any trouble. But I've learned those precautions the long, hard way, beginning when we were the first big Negro band to travel extensively through the South. I think you could call us the first Freedom Riders. We stayed mostly with the Negro population and only came in contact with the Caucasian race if we needed something in a drug or drygoods way. On our first tour, in 1931, we had a booker named Harry D. Squires. He booked us out of his hat, calling the next town from the one we'd just played and generally using his wits, like once when we got stopped for speeding. Squires told us before the cop came up, 'Now, we'll just tell him we're a young group and haven't had any work. So get out all your change and put it in a hat to show him what we're worth.' And that's just what we did. The cop got on the bus and we all sat there looking forlorn and half starved, and he looked in the hat, which had ten or twelve dollars in it, and he let us go. That was our first acting duty. Going South was an invasion for us. We weren't accustomed to the system, being from the North, and it put a damper on us. Things happened all the time. They made us walk in the street off the sidewalk in

Fort Lauderdale, and at a white dance in Valdosta, Georgia, some hecklers in the crowd turned off the lights and exploded a bomb under the bandstand. We didn't none of us get hurt, but we didn't play so well after that, either. Sometimes when we came into a town that had a bad reputation, the driver would tell us—and here we were in our own chartered bus—to move to the back of the bus just to make it look all right and not get anyone riled up. We pulled into a gas station early one morning and a trombonist named Stevens got out to stretch his legs. He asked the gas-station attendant was it O.K., and he said, 'Go ahead, but I just killed one nigger. He's layin' over there in the weeds. You don't believe me, take a look for yourself.' Stevens got back on the bus quick, and the next day we read about the killing in the papers. They had a diner at another gas station, and my guitarist, who was new and very, very light-skinned, ducked off the bus and went right into the diner. He didn't know any better and we didn't see him go in. When we'd gassed up, I asked our road manager, a Jewish fellow who was swarthy and very dark, to get us some sandwiches. The counterman took one look at him and wouldn't serve him, and my road manager glanced up and there was my guitarist at the counter, stuffing down ham and eggs. We never let that manager forget. It was a happening we kept him in line with the rest of the trip."

Hines laughed quietly and looked out of the window. It was raining heavily and we were crawling through Twenty-eighth Street. "We played a colored dance somewhere in Alabama and it worked out there was a gang of white people sitting back of us on the stage because there wasn't any more room on the floor. They'd been invited by the Negro who was giving the dance, since he worked for one of the whites. We'd only been playing fifteen min-

215

utes when along came this old captain, this sheriff man, and told me, 'You can't have those white people up there. You get them off that stage.' I said I didn't know anything about it. Fifteen minutes more and that cap'n was back. 'You and these niggers get out of here and out of this town. You have half an hour.' He escorted us personally to the town line. I found out later he knew all those white people, but they were the cream of the town and he was afraid to say anything to them, except to tell them after we'd gone that one of my boys had been looking at a white woman and that was why he drove us out. But I had me a victory in Tennessee. I went into a drygoods store to buy some shirts. The clerk said, 'You want something, boy?' I told him. He took me to the cheapest section. I told him I wanted to see the best shirts he had. 'Where you from, boy, to ask for things like that?' I pointed at some ten-dollar silk shirts. 'Give me five of those,' I said. 'You want five of *those?*' He started to laugh and I showed him a fifty-dollar bill. After that, that man couldn't get enough of me. Money changed his whole attitude. Money shamed him. I spent close to eighty-five dollars, and when I came out all these local colored boys were looking in the front window, noses on the glass. They said, 'You go in *there?* Don't *no one* go in there!' Well, those were the days when if you were a Negro and wanted to buy a hat and tried it on it was *your* hat whether it fitted or not.

"But there were good times, too. We were always seeing new territory, new beauty. In those days the country was a lot more open and sometimes we'd run into another band and just park the buses by the road and get out and play baseball in a field. We travelled by train, also, but buses were only twenty-eight cents a mile and you kept the same bus and driver throughout a whole tour. There was always a little tonk game on the bus at night. The boys put some-

thing for a table across the aisle and sat on Coke boxes and
hung a flashlight from the luggage rack on a coat hanger.
I generally sat on the right side about four seats back of
the driver, where I kept an eye on things. They played
most of the night, and it was amusing and something to
keep you interested if you couldn't sleep. Our radio broad-
casts made us well known after a while and sometimes
we felt like a Presidential party. People would gather
around the bus and say, 'Where's Father Hines? Where's
Father Hines?' Father was a nickname given to me by a
radio announcer we had at the Grand Terrace, and one I'd
just as soon be shut of now. I had a kiddish face then and
they expected an *old* man from my nickname, so I'd just
slip into the hotel and maybe go into the coffee shop, but
when these people found out who and where I was they'd
come in and stand around and stare at me. Just stand and
stare and not say anything, and if I looked up they'd pre-
tend to be looking away in the distance."

*Hines is greeted at the R.C.A. Victor recording
studio, which is on East Twenty-fourth Street, by Brad
McCuen, an a.-and-r. man of Sydney Greenstreet proportions. Hines goes immediately into the studio, which is
bright and chilly and thicketed with microphones. Jimmy
Crawford is setting up his drums and Aaron Bell is putting
rosin on his bow.*

HINES (*in a loud, happy voice*): O solo mio, o solo
mio. Hey, Craw, man. And Aaron. A *long* time, *a long* time.
(*All shake hands warmly.*) We're going to do something
today. But just leave all the doors open so we can git out if
everything goes wrong.

CRAWFORD: You look wonderful, Earl. Just wonderful.

HINES: I feel like a million dollars. (*He takes off his*

217

coat and sits down at a grand piano and rubs his hands together and blows on them. McCuen leaves a list of prospective tunes and a large gold ashtray beside Hines, who
lights a cigar. McCuen is followed into the control room
by Dance, still carrying the fake book. A round, genial
man enters the studio. He is dressed all in brown and has an
Oriental face.) My Budd. Budd Johnson. (The two men
embrace and laugh and pound one another. Hines returns
to the piano and plays ad-lib chords, which gradually crys-
tallize into a slow "It Had to Be You." Crawford and Bell
join in. Hines has already vanished into what he is doing.
His mouth is open slightly and his lower lip moves in and
out. His face, disguised by his hat and glasses, looks closed
and secret. A photographer comes out of the control room,
lies down on the floor near Hines, and starts shooting pictures. Hines finishes two choruses and stops.) Hey, Mr.
Camera Man, would you mind waiting on that? You're
getting me all nervous. (The photographer gets up, mumbles, and retreats into the control room.) You ready, Budd?
Tenor would be nice for this. Rich and slow and warm.
Pretty tenor. I'll take the first two choruses and you come
in for one. I'll come back and you come in again for the last
sixteen bars.

McCUEN (in a booming voice over the control-
room microphone): Ready to roll one, Earl?

HINES: Let's do one right away. (After the last note
dies away, Hines jumps up, laughs, snaps his fingers, and
spins around.) Ooooo-wee. Budd, how'd you like that ad-
lib ending? I couldn't do that again to save my life. I didn't
know if I was going to get out alive or not. Shoo, man.

McCUEN: We'll play it back.

HINES: No, let's do another real quick. I feel it.
Here we go. (The second take is faster and the ending more

*precise.*) All right, let's hear that. (*The music comes crashing out of two enormous loudspeakers. Hines gets up and moves over beside the nearest wall. His hands hang loose at his sides. He throws back his head, opens his mouth, and listens. He is even more concentrated than when he plays. He doesn't move until the number ends. Then he does a little dance and laughs.*) I'll buy it. I'll buy it. Beautiful, Budd. Just beautiful. You can shut those doors now.

(*During the next couple of hours, the group does* "I've Got the World on a String," "A Cottage for Sale," "Linger Awhile," *and a fast original by Hines. Two or three takes suffice for each tune. Hines wastes no time, and after each playback he starts playing again.*)

HINES: "Wrap Your Troubles in Dreams." Budd, you rest on this one. We'll do about four choruses. (*The first take is indifferent, but on the second one Hines suddenly catches fire, moving with extraordinary intensity into the upper register in the third chorus and shaping the fourth chorus into a perfect climax.*)

McCUEN: Let's try another, Earl. That opening wasn't quite right. (*Hines looks surprised, but immediately makes another take. After the playback, he shakes his head.*)

HINES: I don't know. Let's go again. (*In all, twelve takes, including false starts, are made. Each is slightly faster, and each time Hines appears less satisfied. The last take is replayed. Hines is leaning on an upright piano in the center of the studio, Bell and Johnson flanking him.*) You know, I don't *feel* it, I'm not *inside* that tune. I'm not bringing it *out*.

BELL: Earl, you know it's getting faster and faster?
HINES: Yeh? I didn't notice.
JOHNSON: Earl, you were *cookin'*, man, way back

there on that second take, and they never did play it back for you.

HINES (*looking puzzled*): That right? Hey, Brad, can you play that *second* take for me. You never did, and I can't recall it. (*It is played, and slowly Hines' face relaxes. Johnson snaps his fingers and Bell nods his head.*) Budd, you got it, man. You were right. *That's* it, and we wasting all that time when the *good* one is just sitting there waiting to be heard. Man, I feel *young* again.

(*It is now almost six o'clock, and McCuen suggests that they meet again the next day. He thanks the musicians. Hines moves to the center of the studio, lights a fresh cigar, and stretches his arms wide. Crawford and Bell and Johnson fall into a loose semicircle before him.*)

HINES: Thank you, Craw, and Aaron. Just fine, man. Just fine. Budd, I haven't heard that baritone of yours in I don't know how long. You take Harry Carney's job away he doesn't look out. (*Johnson beams.*) The piano they got here makes it feel good, too. You play on a bad instrument and you want to take just eight bars and get out. *So* many clubs now have cheap pianos. It's the last thing the owners think of. They wouldn't put a well behind their bars and dip water out of it, instead of having faucets, so why do they have pianos that are cheap and out of tune?

JOHNSON: That's right, Earl.

BELL: Yeah, Earl.

HINES: In the forties, we played a place in Texas and they had a *miserable* piano. It was even full of water from a leak in the roof first night we were there. When the job was finished, Billy Eckstine and some of the boys decided to take that piano apart. Man, they clipped the strings and loosened the hammers and pulled off the keyboard and left it laying all over the floor. (*All laugh.*) I just finished

220

four weeks in Canada, and the owner of that club must have had a hundred-dollar piano, it was so bad. And he had this fancy bandstand with a great big Buddha sitting on each side of it and they must have cost a *thousand* dollars apiece. I asked him, "Man, why do you spend all that money on Buddhas and decorations and not on a piano?," and he answered blah blah blah, and got mad. Now, that's crazy.

CRAWFORD: Well, you told him, Earl.

HINES: It's the same thing nowadays with dressing rooms. No place to put on your makeup or rest and change your clothes between sets. (*Hines' voice has slowly grown louder and he is almost chanting. His listeners intensify their responses.*) They got one room down at Birdland, one small room, man, and we can't use it when Vi Redd—she's my saxophonist—goes in there, and when she's finished there's no time left anyway. I have to go back to the hotel between every set and change clothes. It's only a couple of blocks and I don't mind, but what if it's snowing or raining and I catch my death?

JOHNSON: Earl, I was down to the Copa a while ago and it's the same there. You got to go out and walk the sidewalk.

HINES: That's what I mean. That's what I mean. You remember the old days all the theatres had good dressing rooms and places to sit down? Of course, these young musicians don't dress anyway, so maybe it doesn't matter. The band opposite me at Birdland, led by that young trumpet player—what's his name?

BELL: Byrd? Donald Byrd?

HINES: Yeh. Well, the first night they all dressed in different clothes and have scuffy shoes and no neckties. We come on, all spruced and neat—ties, of course—and you watch, the next night they got on ties and suits and their hair combed and they look *human*. And those young musicians don't know how to handle themselves before an audience. Never look at the audience or tell it what they're playing or smile or bow or be at all gracious. Just toot-toot-a-toot and look dead while the other guy is playing and get off. No wonder everybody having such a hard time all over. No one—not even Duke or Basie—raising any hell anymore. They just scuffling to keep that payroll going. That's why I have this different group, to reach the young people and teach them the old ways, the right ways, not the rock-and-roll ways. I've always helped the young people along, developed them, showed them how to dress and act and carry themselves properly. I've been at it so long I couldn't stop. Well, man, all we can do is be examples. A man can't do no more than that.

JOHNSON: Amen, Earl. Amen.

After Johnson and Crawford and Bell had left, Hines suggested that Dance and I come back to his hotel for a drink. The rain had stopped, and we found a cab on Third Avenue. Hines, still wound up from his oration and the recording session, sat on the edge of his seat, puffing at his cigar. "Why didn't somebody tell me I still had these dark glasses on? I wondered why I couldn't see anything when I came out of that building. The reason I've always looked out for the young people, I guess, is because my dad always looked out for me. I don't think there was anyone else in the world who brought up their children better than my mother and dad. We lived in Duquesne, where I was born, and my mother was a housewife. My dad started on a hoisting machine—or histing machine, as they called it—on the coal docks and worked his way up to foreman. He was a loosely type fellow. He never chastised me for the medium things, and I didn't have over four solid whippings from him. I never was brought in at night at the time the average kid in my neighborhood was, and it looked like I was let run helter-skelter and my dad was criticized for that, but he defended himself by saying if you don't chastise your child continually he will confide in you. When I was twelve, he sat down with me one night at evening table after my mother had gone out and told me I was too old to whip anymore and how to conduct myself. 'I'm not a wealthy man,' he told me. 'So I can't get you out of serious trouble.' He told me *everything* that night—about the different kinds of women and men I'd come up against, and how to tell the good from the bad, about thinking you're outsmarting someone else when he's probably outsmarting *you*, about staying on lighted streets at night, and such as that. It gave me the confidence that's always guided me. A lot of the children of strict parents where I grew up ended in jail. The exceptions were far and few.

"My family was very musical. My mother was an organist and my dad played cornet. My uncle knew all the brass instruments and my auntie was in light opera. My dad was also the leader of the Eureka Brass Band, which played for picnics and dances and outings. I was nine or ten when I was taken on my first outing. We travelled from McKeesport about twelve miles in four open trolleys, which were chartered. The band rode the first trolley and played as we went. After the picnic there was dancing in a hall and the children who were allowed to stay were sent up to a balcony, where they had a matron to watch us. Some of the kids roughhoused, but I just leaned over the rail and listened and watched. It was such a pretty thing to see all those people dancing and flowing in one direction. The

men seemed so pleasant to the women and the women back
to the men. My mother started teaching me the piano when
I was very young. I also tried the cornet, after my dad, but
it hurt me behind the ears to blow, so I gave it up. I had
my first outside piano lessons when I was nine, from a
teacher named Emma D. Young, of McKeesport. My next
teacher, Von Holz, was German and pretty well advanced.
I was studying to be a classical artist. I loved the piano and
I was always three or four lessons ahead in my book. My
auntie lived in Pittsburgh, and when I went to Schenley
High School, where I majored in music, I lived with her.
I was interested in conducting and watched the directors
of pit orchestras every chance I got. And I memorized all
the music I heard, some of it even before the sheet music
came out. When I was about thirteen, my life changed. I
had a cousin and an uncle who were playtime boys and
they used to take me downtown to the tenderloin section
with them. I was tall and they fitted me out in long trousers.
The first time they took me to the Leader House, which
had dancing upstairs, I heard this strange music and I
heard the feet and the beat and so much laughter and happiness I asked my uncle and cousin could I go upstairs and
listen. They put a Coca-Cola in my hand and I did. Pittsburgh was a wide-open town and there wasn't such a ban
then on children going into clubs. A hunchback fellow
named Toadlo was playing the piano. He was playing
'Squeeze Me,' and singing. His playing turned me around
completely. It put rhythm in my mind, and I went home
and told auntie that that was the way I wanted to play. In
the meantime, I was shining shoes and had learned bar-
bering and for the first time I had enough money to get
around. I formed a little trio, with a violinist and a drummer, and then Lois B. Deppe, who was a well-known Pitts-

burgh singer and bandleader, hired me and my drummer for his band at the Leader House. It was summer and I talked to my dad and he said it was all right and I went to work. Fifteen dollars a week and two meals a day. Toadlo still worked there, and so did a pianist named Johnny Watters. He was dynamic. He was more advanced than Toadlo. He could stretch fourteen notes with his right hand and play a melody at the same time with his middle fingers. He liked Camels and gin and in the afternoons I'd buy him a pack of cigarettes and a double shot of gin and we'd go upstairs at the Leader House, and he would show me. Then, at a party, I heard a piano player named Jim Fellman playing tenths with his left hand, instead of the old oompah bass. It was so easy and rhythmic. *He* liked beer and chewed Mail Pouch, so I got him upstairs at the Leader House, too, and he showed me those tenths. I got my rhythmic training from a banjoist named Verchet. He was a musical fanatic. He tried to make his banjo sound like a harp, and he had all these nuts and bolts for tightening and loosening the strings, only the damn thing always fell apart when he played. His instrument case was full of tools and he sounded like a plumber when he picked it up. But he was a heck of a critic of tempo. He'd sit there, strumming like lightning and rocking back and forth in half time, and if I got away from the beat, he'd say, 'Watch-it-boy, watch-it-boy.' So I began to form my little style. I still had the idea of the cornet in my head and I would try things that I might have played on the cornet—single-note figures and runs that were not ordinary then on the piano. And I hit on using octaves in the right hand, when I was with a band, to cut through the music and be heard."

The cab stopped in front of the hotel. When we got upstairs, Hines ordered a bottle of Scotch and ice and glasses. Then he took off his hat, for the first time that afternoon, and flopped down on the bed. He looked tired but pleased. "That Budd Johnson is something, isn't he, Stanley? He was a playing fool today. He was in my big band almost ten years. But I've always been lucky in my musicians. I formed the first band in 1924 and Benny Carter played baritone in it and his cousin Cuban Bennett was on trumpet. He was a *great* trumpet player, but nobody remembers him. We went into the Grape Arbor, in Pittsburgh, and stayed there several months. Eubie Blake, the ragtime pianist, used to come through town once in a while, and the first time I met him he told me. 'Son, you have no business here. You got to leave Pittsburgh.' He came through again while we were at the Grape Arbor, and when he saw me, he said, 'You *still* here? I'm going to take this cane'—he always carried a cane and wore a raccoon coat and a brown derby—'and wear it out all over your head if you're not gone when I come back.' I was. That same year, I went to Chicago to the Elite No. 2 Club, an after-hours place. Teddy Weatherford, the pianist, was *it* in Chicago then, and soon people began telling him, 'There's a tall, skinny kid from Pittsburgh plays piano. You better hear him.' Teddy and I became friends, and we'd go around together and both play and people began to notice me. They even began to lean toward me over Teddy. Louis Armstrong and I first worked together in the Carroll Dickerson orchestra at the Sunset. Louis was the first trumpet player I heard who played what *I* had wanted to play on cornet. I'd steal ideas from him and he'd steal them from me. He'd bend over after a solo and say way down deep in that rumble, 'Thank you, man.' Louis was wild and I was wild, and we were inseparable. He was the most happy-go-lucky guy I ever met. Then Louis and I and Zutty Singleton, who was also with Dickerson, formed our own group, and I don't know what happened, but we like to starve to death, making a dollar or a dollar and a half apiece a night. So we drifted apart, and I worked for Jimmie Noone for a year, and then I went to New York to make some QRS piano rolls. I had a little band rehearsing at the same time, and it was then I got a call to come and open up the Grand Terrace."

The whiskey and ice and glasses arrived. Dance gave Hines a brandy from a bottle on the dresser and poured each of us a Scotch-and-water. Hines lifted his glass in the air. "This is for Stanley. If it hadn't been for him, I'd probably be out of this business now. I was ready to quit about a year ago. In fact, my wife and I were talking about opening a little shop out on the Coast. But Stanley kept after me on that long-distance phone, and persuaded me to come here last winter, and then he set up the record session. I was down low again when I got here last week. But something *good* happened today, and it's going to happen tomorrow. I try never to worry. The greatest thing to draw wrinkles in a man's face is worry. And why should I be unhappy and pull down my face and drag my feet and make everybody around me feel that way too? By being what you are, something always comes up. Sunshine always opens out. I'll leave for the Coast day after tomorrow in my car, and I'll stop and see my mother in Duquesne. My sister, Nancy, and my brother, Boots, still live with her. I'll see my mother-in-law in Philadelphia and she'll give me a whole mess of fried chicken. I'll put that on the seat beside me, along with those cigars and my pipe and pipe tobacco and a map and a gallon jug of water. I'll open the window wide and keep my eye on the road. Stanley, let me have a little more of that brandy, please."

# The New Thing

It is not cricket for the founder of a revolutionary movement to set the engines of rebellion in motion and then disappear. He not only leaves his disciples still recovering from the wounds inflicted by his ideas but leaves them leaning on memory. The ghostly rebel I have in mind is Ornette Coleman, who all but derailed jazz —to say nothing of its admirers—when he first appeared, five years ago. Like the best revolutionists, he was a highbrow disguised as a primitive. He was a largely untutored musician who, with one leap, passed directly from the past (Charlie Parker, country blues, rock 'n' roll) into the unknown. He offered a formless improvisation that ignored melody, chords, keys, and fixed rhythms, and that flowed from the rhythmic patterns or the mood or the sense of pitch and timbre that a particular number inspired in him. He seemed, in effect, to improvise on *himself*. At the same time, he rendered this free music, which has come to be called "the new thing," with an extraordinary force and emotion. Coleman's explorations had chaotic results. Brilliant musicians like John Lewis buried him with praise, while brilliant musicians like Dizzy Gillespie threw their hands in the air. Nonetheless, a group of young and unknown performers began to gather under Coleman's banner—and then, the air still churning, he went underground. No one seemed to know why he had turned his back. Rumor had it that he felt he was underpaid, that he couldn't find satisfactory accompanists, that he had quit to learn the trumpet and the violin. Then, not long ago, he abruptly materialized at the Village Vanguard.

One batch of rumors was right: Coleman, looking leaner and more unassailable than ever, appeared with a couple of alto saxophones, a trumpet, and a violin. His accompanists were Dave Izenzohn on bass and Charles Moffett on drums. Coleman played the saxophone in his first number, a beseeching dirge whose melodic line moved in huge atonal steps, and he proved that he has compressed his style even more since his 1963 Town Hall concert. His phrases, though still wrapped around off-notes and off-rhythms, are shorter, and his tone is more controlled. He has largely abandoned the animal shrieks that characterized his early work for soft, almost honeyed passages. At one point, he even unrolled a straight melody, with Izenzohn bowing in unison, that recalled Schubert lieder. Coleman's second number—I heard three, each of them close to half an hour in length—was "fast." (Actually, there are no fast or slow or medium tempos in Coleman's music; the beat, or suggested beat, changes from measure to measure and sometimes from note to note, becoming a cyclical rhythm.) He again played the saxophone and he again employed a quiet tone and short phrases, freshly spiked by freakish but always startlingly *right* notes. The violin suddenly appeared at the outset of the third number. Coleman plays it left-handed, and he is trying to force as much through it as he once jammed through the saxophone. He flattened three and even four strings at once with his bow, achieving weird, steamboat-whistle chords;

he sawed away on off-notes with the speed of a humming-bird's wings; he got unique grinding effects. It was night-marish; the inanimate violin seemed to rise up against the animate Coleman. Midway in the number, Coleman took up his trumpet, which he played in a high-pitched, almost electronic manner. Occasionally, though, he sank into low, tail-switching figures; the instrument instantly stopped rebelling, and the effect was lovely. Coleman's accompanists were magnificent. Moffett went around and around on his circular rhythms, and Izenzohn released a dazzling variety of bowed and pizzicato figures. Indeed, both men worked so closely with Coleman that after a time the trio virtually became one instrument. (At one point, they were meshing in this fashion: Coleman had slipped into a casual riff, Izenzohn was playing rapid offbeat double stops, and Moffett was pushing out broken snare-drum rolls. Each was audible and sovereign, and yet the effect was harmonious.) May the inventor of this instrument again point the way.

The inevitable lag between the start of an artistic revolution and public awareness offers several blessings: it gives the rebels time to test and tighten their dream, it allows disciples to gather and be screened, and it lets the public, without whose support any artistic upheaval is meaningless, absorb the shock and tune in. The waves Louis Armstrong set off around 1925 began lapping at the public ear in the early thirties, and those set off by Charlie Parker and Dizzy Gillespie in the early forties were felt a year or two after the last war. The new thing, the third great revolution in jazz, has suddenly found its audience. This revolution is an attempt to free jazz of its metronomic rhythms and its reliance on chordal or melodic improvisation, set keys, and choruses of specific length. At its loosest, the new thing is semi-atonal and almost wholly free rhythmically. Its audience first appeared last fall, at a series of successful new-thing concerts given by largely unknown musicians in an uptown club called the Cellar. Then, late in December, the Jazz Composers Guild, formed by such Cellar men as Cecil Taylor, and the trumpeter Bill Dixon, the tenor saxophonist Archie Shepp, the trombonist Roswell Rudd, and the alto saxophonist John Tchicai, gave four heavily attended concerts at Judson Hall, and since then it has been putting on a weekly series of concerts in a small dance studio above the Village Vanguard.

Not long ago, I attended a Guild concert given by the New York Art Quartet, one of the Guild's five or six regular groups. The quartet was made up of Tchicai, Rudd, Al Dodson on bass, and Lowell Davison on drums. Dodson and Davison, who is also a pianist, were sitting in for bassist Eddie Gomez and the drummer Milford Graves. The seven long numbers included a Coleman blues, a Parker blues, and pieces by Rudd and Tchicai. For the most part, they recalled the celebrated free-improvisation double-quartet recording made several years ago by Ornette Coleman. Fairly straightforward ensembles bracketed long stretches of collective improvising and long solos that were both supported and interrupted by one or more of the other instruments. Aside from these ensembles, both the collective and the solo improvisations appeared to be completely free. Tonality and measures and choruses were abandoned, and all the while the drummer, who literally convulsed his way around his equipment, maintained the slippery, chattering, beatless rhythm of the new thing. The bassist made complex echoes. Rudd, a former Dixieland trombonist, is the most revolutionary member of the quartet. He is clearly familiar with Dickie Wells and J. C. Higginbotham, but he has reshaped their best-known devices—long, high-register wails, growls, and a pushing emotion—into wild atonal patterns full of staccato runs and wide, off-note smears. He uses the plunger mute effectively, and during a drum solo he vanished behind the backdrop and emitted a series of elephantine roars that toned up the solo considerably. Tchicai, a Dane, lies between Sonny Rollins and Coleman. He was at his best during the Parker blues, which he converted into an atonal, tongue-in-cheek exercise. But the total effect of the quartet was puzzling. Its ease and dedication made Thelonious Monk and even Charlie Mingus sound old hat for the first time, yet within its own free-for-all terms it seemed rather safe and conventional. It drove fast, with seat belts.

The next night, I went to Judson Hall to hear Giuseppi Logan, a Guild sympathizer who plays the alto and tenor saxophones, the trumpet, the trombone, the violin, the vibraphone, and the Pakistani oboe, which looks like a child's tin horn. He was assisted by a pianist (Don Pullen), a bassist (Gomez), two drummers (Graves and Raleigh Sahumba), and a string quartet. Five of the numbers were by Logan, one was by Graves, and one was a collaboration by Logan and Graves. All were of a piece with what I had heard the night before, despite the different instrumentation and the presence of the strings, which were restricted largely to ill-wind sounds or furious pizzicato effects. Atonality reigned, there was a lot of collective improvisation, the rhythmic base went around and around, and everything—solos, collective interplay, ensembles—was self-indulgently long. I suspect, though, that Graves will become the modern counterpart of such pioneering drummers as Sidney Catlett and Max Roach. Even his set of drums was unorthodox, for he used—in addition to the traditional apparatus—a second snare drum (set on a muffling piano stool), a couple of conga drums, a heavy piece of wood shaped like a new moon, and an old bass drum tilted on its side and loosely tuned. Moreover, he had removed the snares on both snare drums, and he used—in place of the customary pair of drumsticks or mallets or wire brushes—a stick and a mallet, a mallet and a wire brush, or a stick and a wire brush. His style is a cascade of strokes placed everywhere in what amounts to a small drum shop. Some were deafening and some were sandpiper snickerings that moved with incredible speed from cymbal to cymbal or from cymbals to drums or from drum to drum. He never sounded a regular beat; instead, he used his ride cymbal for irregular patterns and pumped his high-hat cymbals with such speed and ferocity that he finally turned the top cymbal inside out. Such chaos can make sense in only two ways—tonally, and in relation to what the rest of the musicians are doing. Graves succeeded on the first count, repeatedly developing a welter of booms and rifle shots and clicks and tinklings, but he seemed to have little connection with the horns and strings. His playing needs no one to accompany and no accompaniment; he is a one-man drum corps.

Logan's sheer dexterity masks sly sins. His violin work, made up of a million short, scratchy notes, was demonic; his trombone was equally congested; his trumpet playing was high and strangled; his alto and tenor saxophones—he dangled each instrument from his mouth like a cigarette—were a mockery of Ornette Coleman; his Pakistani oboe was Pakistani oboe; and his vibraphone sounded as if he were pouring loose change into it. Pullen revealed admiration for the ladderlike atonal chords of Cecil Taylor, and Gomez, when audible, was competent.

233

That the string quartet read and played its wan scores with such composure was to its credit. Next to Graves, the most impressive aspect of the evening was its solemnity. The New York Art Quartet had displayed a good deal of humor the night before, but Logan and his associates—to say nothing of the furrowed, rapt audience—had the air of mediums possessed.

Before the arrival of the new thing, jazz offered a soft-sell array of emotions that ranged easily from mourning to exhilaration. It didn't matter much to the musician whether or not the listeners reacted, for he knew when he was good and when he was bad, and he also knew that audiences tend to appreciate or ignore the wrong things; poor drum solos are cheered just as heartily as good ones, which are very rare. But the new thing is hard-sell music. It depends not on mere emotion but on an armored passion. It grits its teeth, seizes the listener, shakes him, and hisses, "Damn you, *listen* to this!" This belligerence is behind most of the movement's confusions and shortcomings. The new-thing musicians play too loudly and appear never to have heard of dynamics (some of the most affecting moments of the likes of Ben Webster and Red Allen have been delivered at a whisper), they play too long (time and again, good solos or good collective passages are ruined by repetition or sheer, wearing length), and they often become so caught up in their own musical gales that they completely forget their compatriots (good jazz rests on collective individualism). At its worst, then, the new thing is long-winded, dull, and almost physically abrasive. At its best—in the hands of Ornette Coleman or Taylor—it howls through the mind and heart, filling them with an honest ferocity that is new in jazz and perhaps in any music.

(Some observers have suggested that the new thing is primarily a social-protest music, that its sledging is still another anti-white Negro shout. If that is so, it will date as quickly as the proletarian novel.) Both the best and the worst of the new thing were in evidence at Town Hall in a concert given by Cecil Taylor, the nominal head of the movement, and four aides.

Taylor is an extraordinary pianist. He is a hammer and the keyboard is an anvil. His single notes and chords and runs ring and clang and thunder. At Town Hall, his exertions forced him to strip down to a sweatshirt, through which one could see his biceps working and bulging. His solos are virtually forged. Part of one might go like this: A legato passage, made up of well-spaced, high-register single notes, struck all around the beat and chosen to form a discordant lyricism, will idle by, and then, after a pause during which one can just about hear Taylor's computer whirring, he will leap to the bottom of the keyboard and let loose a two-handed tremolo, which swells into a volcanic shudder, and then start a series of irregular, pounding left-hand chords while his right hand shoots through a descending-ascending run that may end in a skidding glissando. Abrupt silence. He may then fire a salvo of staccato chords in the middle register, allow his hands to move apart and into different rhythms and dissonant chords, drop his volume, and, after another silence, float back into another legato pool. The intensity in each Taylor solo is unbelievable; it scales peak after peak and then, reaching an impossibly high point, simply passes on to another peak, and to still another. He knocks the wind out of the piano and he knocks the wind out of the listener. This happened at least twice at Town Hall—in his first solo in his fast waltz called "Live," in which his frenzy seemed to freeze, like rapidly spinning spokes, and in his "Soft Shoe," an unaccompanied solo that was notable for its mixture of oblique lyricism and operatic crescendos. The three remaining numbers, also by Taylor, exhibited, at least in their opening and closing sections, the sort of stubborn melodic irregularity that appears in Ornette Coleman's composing. They also included endless solos by Mike Mantler on trumpet and Jimmy Lyons on alto saxophone. Mantler is another adherent of the choked, anti-brass style introduced by Don Cherry, and Lyons, when he was audible, moved around on the plains that stretch between Charlie Parker and Coleman. The rhythm section—Andrew Cyrille on drums and Reggie Workman on bass—assiduously pursued Taylor through his labyrinth. Taylor's own accompanying is, in general, an extension of his solos, and it is puzzling that he uses any other performers at all. He is not merely a pianist but a whole rocketing musical world.

# Headwater

No one needs celebration more than the celebrated. Once renowned, the famous are often shelved, as if the exposure of fame had made them brittle and breakable. One of the fuels the ennobled thrive on is acclaim, and it becomes, like a mirror for a great beauty, one of their very elements. Yet the celebrated must hold up their end; they must, in the manner of a good teacher, stay at least a nose ahead of their students. Coleman Hawkins, who has turned sixty, has done just that for the past thirty years. Indeed, no other jazz instrumentalist has *given* so much for so long. Such peers as Art Tatum and Sidney Catlett and Lester Young kept pace for a while, and then burnt themselves out, while the likes of Louis Armstrong and Dickie Wells have been diluted by time. Hawkins not only invented the tenor saxophone and taught a generation or two how to play it but has steadily breasted fresh methods and fresh schools simply by adapting their best. Most jazz musicians are sentenced to a single style for life, but Hawkins has coined and discarded three distinctive approaches. The first, which lasted until the early thirties, was fluent and aggressive; it sported a lot of notes, a tough tone, and occasional vaudeville effects, and it provided much of the heat for the early Fletcher Henderson band. Hawkins' next attack was rich, serene, and almost unctuous. His tone became massive, his vibrato an easy ground swell. He embraced his materials, warmed them, and released them recharged and resilient. He seemed to add new rooms and new halls to each ballad he played. Chu Berry sprouted from this style, and in 1934 Hawkins recorded a solo in Henderson's "Hocus Pocus" that gave birth to Herschel Evans, who then founded his own seminary. Toward the end of the decade, after a long stay in Europe, Hawkins announced through his flawless recording of "Body and Soul" that he had entered still another period. The romanticism of his preceding attack was turned into muscle, the vibrato was dammed, and his tone took on a full-moon hardness and beauty. This consummate grace was set aside in the early fifties, when Hawkins, having survived bebop and hard bop, began to absorb what appealed to him in those schools. His tone grew thinner and he broke up his solos with silences, rough descending and ascending runs, and feverish wails. He got wilder and wilder, like an aging conservative who dons sneakers and a sports jacket for lunch at the Plaza. For the first time, the emotion beneath the surface of his solos became steadily visible, and once in a while it backed up and burst through.

Such was the case when I listened to Hawkins with a quartet at the Five Spot. In a medium-fast "I Won't Dance," he opened with a high, querulous tone that was at one with his sudden pauses and two-steps-at-a-time runs. In his next chorus his tone ballooned, and he darted through soft, fast figures that were more shadow than sound, and in his third he alternated between legato slides and staccato preaching. It was sweet talk laced with philosophy. A slow "September Song" was even more of a crazy quilt. Quiet runs were followed by staccato stabs, which gave way to slamming pauses, which were broken by furious figures that started and ended in midair. Sometimes he pared his materials to the bone, and sometimes he made them swell and swagger. He did not play much in a long, fast "Caravan," but he was a locomotive when he did. Unfortunately, Hawkins' accompanists—Barry Harris on piano, Major Holley on bass, and Eddie Locke on drums—marched to their own music. Holley pulled the beat in "September Song" almost to a halt, and this depressed Locke. Or perhaps it was the other way around. Harris, a sound post-bop pianist who lets very little air through his notes, worked closely with Hawkins, but it was hard to tell whether his constant echoes of Hawkins' phrases were mocking or admiring. Yet Hawkins, who is now thin and gray and slightly stooped, has long carried his own world with him, and the other night he was busy examining every corner of it, seemingly saying again and again, "You come, too."

# The Lessons of the Masters

The marching-band makeup of the pioneer jazz bands lasted until the early twenties. Then jazz musicians, suddenly aware that they had an art on their hands, began sprucing up their instrumentation. The piano became ubiquitous, and the banjo and the tuba were replaced by the guitar and the string bass. Saxophones—ranging from the soprano to the bass—were adopted, and in time the French horn, the flugelhorn, the flute, the oboe, and even the bassoon appeared. Instruments found wanting were sloughed off. The banjo and the tuba were followed into limbo by the violin and the C-melody and bass saxophones. The unamplified guitar gave way to the electric guitar, and the xylophone to the vibraphone. The electric guitar then fell from favor, and so did the clarinet. And the next casualty, according to the warning signs of the past decade, will probably be the piano. The new-thing musicians, who are well on their way toward dominating modern jazz, have already abandoned the piano because they want chords and rhythms fed to them not by a pianist but by their own imaginations. But even before the eruption of the new thing, the tradition of jazz piano mysteriously began to falter. With the exception of Cecil Taylor, just one original and exciting pianist—Bill Evans—has appeared since Bud Powell. Evans' colleagues, to say nothing of his successors, derive from him, from Powell, or from one another, and they have, moreover, lost the ability to transmit emotion through their instrument. Their technique is high, their content low, and their work has a dwindling, evasive manner. This was made clear at a concert given at Hunter College by eight pianists, three of them of older persuasions and the rest of the modern school. The vitality, originality, subtlety, and sheer pianistic skill of the older players seemed, next to the flaccidness of the younger players, almost ruthless.

The evening was opened by Willie the Lion Smith, the tireless sixty-seven-year-old stride pianist and ham (his heraldic bearings—bowler and cigar over bright-red vest— were in full evidence). Smith is the last of the functioning Harlem pianists, but his attack remains fresh and vigorous. He has two approaches—a pastoral, singing one, reminiscent of Victor Herbert and Debussy, and an eight-wheel drive. In "Love Remembers" and "Echoes of Spring," which are handsome Smith melodies, he moved serenely between ad-lib and oblique rhythmic passages, his left hand implying a steady flow of inner rhythms, which supported the dimity patterns in his right hand. It was a music—sweet yet firm, gentle yet direct—no longer heard in the Western world. Smith's other side appeared in "Hallelujah" (which had a fast waltz passage and some ebullient right-hand figures), in a rocking "I Found a New Baby," and in a sly "Ain't Misbehavin'."

Mary Lou Williams, possibly energized by Smith, was in even better shape. Both her selections were models of understatement, invention, and form. Not a note was superfluous, not an essential was missed. In "Yesterdays," her simple, effortless runs appeared to pour out of her chords, only to form pools of sound that made new chords, and in a boogie-woogie number she at once celebrated and

241

brought up to the minute that majestic discarded form, using a broken-rhythm bass and then a loose four-four beat climaxed by a staccato locked-hands passage. But her performance went by so quickly and quietly that its impact was not felt until the next pianist had begun. He proved to be Thelonious Monk, and *he* appeared galvanized by both Smith and Miss Williams, for the results were three of the finest solos he has ever set down. Everything was right—the parodies of stride piano ("Nice Work If You Can Get It"), the charge-halt-charge runs ("Tea for Two"), the blatted elbow chords, the miraculous rhythmic dives and suspensions, the ad-lib passages that somehow suggested double-time (" 'Round Midnight"), and the over-all Gothic décor, which enhances rather than merely conceals.

Then the modernists took over, and the balloon so nobly inflated in the first half of the concert collapsed. Jaki Byard rendered an opaque tour de force that was meant to be a history of jazz piano but that offered muffled, imitative flashes of the work of such as Jelly Roll Morton, Fats Waller, Earl Hines, Art Tatum, and Cecil Taylor. Toshiko, the Japanese pianist, labored through a long, dull blues based on some Japanese folk songs and then braved a duet with Mary Lou Williams, who was the soul of tact. Wynton Kelly demonstrated his affection for Red Garland, and Herbie Hancock, the youngest of the performers, presented a glib pastiche of Bud Powell and Bill Evans and Garland. Billy Taylor, who served as an extraneous narrator during the evening, played an "All the Things You Are" that had the flavor and texture of angel food, and the evening was closed by a ten-handed round robin on two pianos by Willie the Lion, Toshiko, Hancock, Kelly, and Taylor (Miss Williams, Monk, and Byard had departed). The only steadily audible, steadily unmistakable, and steadily authoritative hands belonged to Smith, whose cigar never even wobbled.

# Northern Lights

Jazz musicians, like all valuable artists, tend to be provincial. The great players often do not know one another or even hear one another. They rarely buy records, even their own, and they generally depend on radio and television for their musical news. They are, by and large, workaday stay-at-homes who avoid all-star get-togethers and who keep the sources of their magic close to their chests. Thus, the recent six-day collaboration of Earl Hines and Coleman Hawkins at the Village Vanguard (they were accompanied by George Tucker on bass and Oliver Jackson on drums) was doubly surprising: It *happened*, and the results were marvellous. Summit meetings, though, tend to start at a shamble. The opening night was reportedly indifferent, and the next night was disastrous. Hines and Hawkins were unavoidably late, and Charlie Mingus, the leader of the alternate group, was asked to begin the evening. But Mingus demurred, telling the audience that he resented being second banana to Hines and Hawkins, that the audience was transparent because it was mostly white, that it didn't know music and would applaud when he purposely played wrong notes, and on and on. During the next hour, he punctuated reluctant bursts of his own music by storming off the stand because the audience, he said, was too noisy, and by firing his pianist,

243

Jaki Byard, when he refused to let a pianist Mingus had invited sit in. By this time, Hines and Hawkins had arrived and witnessed some of Mingus's calisthenics. Hines, an old-school musician who wears a tie when he works, smiles at and speaks kindly to the audience, and obeys show-business codes, apparently was troubled by all this, for he was noticeably uneven during the evening. And this, in turn, upset Hawkins, who turned his back on the audience in his closing number and ambled dispiritedly into the far corner of the bandstand to play to himself.

But two nights later, the planets were miraculously in harmony. Mingus held his tongue and played brilliantly, and Hines and Hawkins worked as one. (They had met just once before their Vanguard stint—at a fine 1944 Keynote recording session.) Their first set was notable for Hines' fast solo version of "But Not for Me," which had a rampaging broken-rhythm passage, and for a Hines-Hawkins "Just One More Chance." Hines' judicious use of the loud pedal and of broad, come-to-me tremolos turned the number into a rolling lullaby, which sent Hawkins into a chorus of soft, dreaming phrases. Between phrases, he seemed to accent his feelings by lightly touching the bell of his horn with the outspread fingers of his left hand; the motion suggested a butterfly landing on a flower. Hines worked even harder behind Hawkins in "Perdido," feeding him offbeat chords, echoing phrases, and monument-building riffs. Hawkins was impassioned in return, and then Hines played a superb solo, full of characteristic hide-and-seek runs and breathtaking broken rhythms. Their second set was even better. Hines did a grab bag of tunes that ranged from "Tangerine" to "Lullaby of Birdland," and then performed a Fats Waller medley that reached its climax in a "Honeysuckle Rose" that sounded—curiously—

as if George Gershwin were playing it. Hines and Hawkins converted "It's the Talk of the Town" into another gorgeous lullaby, and Hawkins complimented Hines with a booming version of Hines' "Rosetta." Hines, with his customary sense of nicety, didn't solo. Both Jackson and Tucker hurried after the masters, whose mutual respect and inspiration seemed to dance in the air like northern lights.

Mingus apparently grasped this vision, for his set was equally exhilarating. A fast "Groovin' High" included a long series of exchanges between Mingus and Danny Richmond (Jaki Byard, rehired, was also on hand, as were a trumpeter and an alto saxophonist), after which they played a volcanic walking-rhythm duet. This was capped by an Ellington medley that ended with a furious "Take the 'A' Train," in which Byard applauded Hines with several measures of flawless 1928 Hines piano, Richmond took a fine solo full of Jo Jones dynamics, and Mingus played some lightning shuffle rhythm. The audience rounded out the evening perfectly by being one of the most cosmopolitan ever assembled; Wilt (The Stilt) Chamberlain was on hand and so was Robert Graves. It wouldn't have seemed odd if they had sat in.

# Zeus

The noble tradition in jazz of the trumpet as a brass instrument began to falter in the early fifties with the rise of such angora-toned performers as Miles Davis, Chet Baker, and Art Farmer. Before that, when a trumpeter stood up to solo one expected the windows to shiver, and they did. But the Davis-Baker-Farmer method now marches on in the persons of the new-thing trumpeters, all of whom heedlessly pinch off their myriad notes—most of them high and most of them barely sounded—and ignore such regimental customs as tone and attack and vibrato. Better indeed if they simply traded in their trumpets for saxophones, their swords for ploughshares, and had done with it. Thus it was a tonic to go down to the Village Vanguard and hear Roy Eldridge, who has been hidden for the past couple of years behind the skirts of Ella Fitzgerald as her accompanist.

Eldridge remains—with his diamond smile, his short, tidy stature, his small, important bay window, and his limitless energy—an irresistible performer. And his style is as of old. His tone at slow tempos still supplicates and enfolds and at fast speeds hums and threatens. In a slow blues chorus, he will begin with two or three long-held notes, shaped into a simple melody and played behind the

246

beat. The last of these notes may end in a whiskey-baritone growl kept low to the ground by a brief, waddling vibrato. He may repeat the phrase, adding several notes, an octave or so higher, that sound almost falsetto because of their suddenness, and then he will pause and—making you hold your breath, since you suspect what may come next—tear into the highest register, seize a high note, hold it briefly, pause again, fall through a wild sotto-voce run, and close the phrase with a mock-pompous growl. High notes are pep pills to Eldridge, and he may shoot back up and blast out two or three more, drop an octave or two for a soughing blue note, and sink peacefully to earth for the end of the chorus. He played four or five such choruses in the slow "Have You Ever Loved a Woman" in his second set; and he sang as many choruses in a voice that was a perfect miniature of his horn playing. (He was accompanied well by Barry Harris on piano and Bob Cranshaw on bass, but Oliver Jackson, his drummer, had time trouble all evening.) "In a Mellotone," which followed, was as exhilarating for its mistakes (a couple of overshot high notes) as for its successes (several more of those Niagara-runs). He began his first set with "I Remember Harlem," in a low, muted mood, abruptly shifted into double time and took out his mute, releasing an engulfing tone and flow of notes (he clearly considers a chorus wasted if he doesn't startle the listener—and himself—at least once), and, after a sunny coda, passed on to an easy "Caravan" type of number that was a welter of high notes, swollen growls, and arching blue notes. This was followed by an extraordinary fast "Undecided." He started with the mute, playing a hundred notes to the measure without a fluff, stepped aside to let Harris and Cranshaw solo, and exchanged eight-bar breaks with Jackson. Then he settled into riff and, suddenly abandoning it for a gorgeous ad-lib passage full of oblique runs and bellying single notes, sauntered into a slow, rocking half time. Lucky Thompson, who preceded him on the soprano and tenor saxophones in both sets, played Mercury, while Charlie Mingus, who led the alternate band, played Zephyr. Eldridge was Zeus.

# Bird

There
are two kinds of apprentices—those who borrow from their
master the bones upon which to hang their own vision, and
those who, fatally mistaking imitation for an art, become
perpetual mimics. The mimics have always outnumbered
the borrowers and this is particularly true in jazz, where
the apprentice faces special problems. His model is almost
schizoid, for it comes in two disparate parts—live and recorded. The live model makes it hard for the student. The
musician may be in bad form, which is confusing, or he may
be brilliant, which is even more trying, since it is nearly
impossible to relish *and* remember more than the brightest
patches in a fine solo. (The excitement induced by first-rate
improvisation also produces interfering static.) And recordings often provide only glimpses of a musician's work,
yet these glimpses tend, simply because they are frozen, to
eventually seem complete and even perfect. One of the
most widely admired jazz musicians was Charlie Parker,
and he made it relatively easy for his emulators. He recorded prolifically and he was on nearly constant view. But
highly gifted jazz musicians have a presence, a mantle of
steady, animating accomplishment, that cannot be trans-
ferred to a record, and when Parker died, ten years ago, at

the age of thirty-four, his students were left with only memories and the tableau of his recordings. Their loss condensed into self-pity and sentimentality (those *graffiti* that appeared all over New York after his death, announcing that "Bird lives"); the mimics, deprived of their sustenance, fed on themselves, and the borrowers wandered into styleless, uncertain meadows. This was plain at a concert given at Carnegie Hall in Parker's memory by his old helpmeet Dizzy Gillespie and by a dozen of their most assiduous students.

Gillespie opened the concert with his quintet, and he was in top form. His style is now governed by a matchless sense of dynamics, by unfailingly swift and subtle rhythmic changes, and by an implied power-in-reserve. His tone has mellowed, his agility increased. In a medium blues, he played several muted choruses that ranged from an easy whisper to excited multi-noted chatter, and as many open-horn choruses that began with an oceanic blast and ended with soft, skipping high notes linked by dodging, Roy Eldridge runs. Of equal merit was a very slow "My Funny Valentine," in which Gillespie used a mute, first playing the melody with offhand delicacy and then employing it as a tail wind for an exultant stream of swoops and climbs and glides.

By and large, second-team men controlled the rest of the evening. The exceptions were Roy Eldridge and Coleman Hawkins, who blew the skin of a Charlie Parker blues very tight, and Bud Powell, whose old self was slowed, in " 'Round Midnight," to a tortured, determined walk that made one both weep and cheer. Another exception was the alto saxophonist Lee Konitz, who now appears to have survived Parker very well. Indeed, he pulled off a remarkable tour de force in a long unaccompanied blues that was a history of jazz saxophone playing from Parker to the present and that was infused with the old-time, hard-knocks emotion Parker released in every solo. The second team at least sweated. J. J. Johnson let loose some blazing choruses of the blues that didn't contain an original phrase, and Benny Green, an occasionally witty trombonist, went on, in another Parker blues, for twenty choruses, three-quarters of them duds. Sonny Stitt, perhaps Parker's most faithful admirer, sounded pale and irresolute, and Kenny Dorham and Howard McGhee, both out of Gillespie, sang their creator's praises. Roy Haynes was on drums throughout, and his accompanying was vigorous hen-party. In the final number, a blues by Billy Taylor, Gillespie reappeared for several more faultless choruses. The evening soared again, and so, for a moment or two, did Bird.

# The Fat and the Lean

The big-band arranger was the most eminent of the middlemen who have fed on jazz for the past forty years. When, in the late twenties, the big band replaced the play-as-you-go New Orleans and Chicago ensembles, its members, in general, had to be told what to do; only one soloist could play at a time, and collective improvisation for more than four or five horns was rabblesome. A tables-of-organization man was needed, and that was what the conventional arranger became. He divided the big band into four platoons—trumpets, trombones, reeds, and rhythm—and assigned three or four men to each. The trumpets were used to decorate, punctuate, or simply make noise; the trombones did comic smears and rumbles; the saxophones toted the melody; and the rhythm section provided wheels. At first, three platoons were subservient to the soloists, but in time the arranger became so powerful that the soloist considered himself fortunate when he was given eight bars. The arranger reached his heart's desire with the sololess score; in a protean, vicarious way, *he* became the chief soloist. The first of the big-band arrangers were Don Redman and Fletcher Henderson, and the last were the tank commanders who kept the Stan Kenton band in dictatorial roar. Not all these arrangers were tabulators. Mary Lou Williams turned the Andy Kirk band into a graceful group, and Benny Carter made his sections sound as if they were improvising. When the big bands went down, in the mid-forties, they took their arrangers with them, and jazz was once again dominated by autonomous small groups.

In the early fifties, a seemingly new breed of arranger—the *composer*-arranger—arrived to meet the increasing need in jazz for new and more flexible forms. (The pioneering arrangers often wrote their own materials, but these were either elementary riff tunes or simple variations on standard tunes or the blues.) The new arrangers generally played in the groups they wrote for, and, more important, they allowed their materials to define their form. The first of them was probably John Lewis, the director of the Modern Jazz Quartet. Lewis, a highly gifted melodist, found his tunes flowing into rondo or fugue forms and even into collective improvisation. Charlie Mingus forced eight or ten pieces through semi-improvised ensembles that paralleled the New Orleans ensemble. George Russell resembled Mingus, but his effects depended on dissonance and atonality. All three of these men restored the soloist to a place of honor. Then, in the late fifties, it became clear that this second generation of arrangers was not wholly original but was simply the late-arriving offspring of Duke Ellington, who for thirty years had been letting every sort of musical form evolve from the content of his compositions. The newest of these Ellington-inspired composer-arrangers are the diametrically opposed Gil Evans and Gary McFarland. Evans grew up during the big-band days, as an arranger for Claude Thornhill, and McFarland is in his early thirties. Evans is a sensualist, McFarland is an ascetic. Evans uses soloists sparingly and only if they suit his writing in tone and style. McFarland favors soloists to the point of allowing two or three to improvise at once.

Evans loves sounds that suggest being smothered in a heavily brocaded bosom. He loves sounds that insinuate and flatter and cozen. He loves the lower regions of the scale. He loves hums and chants and choirs. His passion for these effects has led him to favor woodwinds, French horns, trombones, tubas, and bass violins, most of which can be found in large and luxuriant numbers in his recordings. It has also turned him into an ingenious Berlioz orchestrator who pits muted trumpets against French horns and trombones, working in a muffled shuffle rhythm; a tuba against a heavy reed background; a bass solo against guitar chords, French horns, and muted trumpets. Moreover, these combinations—some of which are unique—change ceaselessly. Evans ignores measures and channels and choruses, and accordingly his music is molten. But it is also impossible to listen to as *music*. It induces metaphors; instead of melody and harmony and rhythm, one is steadily put in mind of colors (russets, mauves, charcoals) and shapes (elephants, hippos) and materials (velvets, satins, silks). Listening to Evans is like eating hallucinatory mushrooms.

Evans' newest effort, "The Individualism of Gil Evans" (Verve), is all plush and Aubusson carpets, and it becomes suffocating in a twelve-minute blues called "Hotel Me." The instrumentation consists of a piano (Evans), two basses, a guitar, drums, a tuba, a French horn, two trombones, and two trumpets. The entire piece is balanced on a ponderous backbeat and is given over to a simple descending figure (strikingly akin to one in a 1941 Joe Marsala recording called "Lower Register") played in heaving tremolos. Not much else happens. Evans appears and disappears and reappears; the rhythm section bulges and subsides; a flute becomes briefly entangled with the piano; the brass rises up and sinks; and then the number, caught in its own tedium, fades away rather than ends—an escapist device used elsewhere on the record.

Evans' scores trap his musicians; McFarland's serve as lubricants. No matter how many instruments McFarland uses, the results are light and economical. There is no stuffing and there is no narcissism. There is, though, plenty of wit and elegance. Just six musicians appear in "Point of Departure" (Impulse!)—Willie Dennis on trombone, Richie Kamuca on tenor saxophone and oboe, Jimmy Raney on guitar, Steve Swallow on bass, Mel Lewis on drums, and McFarland on vibraphone. The McFarland recordings by large groups suggest small bands; this one suggests a big band. His combination of instruments shifts continually. The vibraphone works first in unison with the oboe and is then echoed by the trombone; the vibraphone carries a melody over offbeat guitar chords, and vibraphone and guitar are in turn bolstered by a trombone-tenor saxophone smear; the oboe and the trombone play a theme *a cappella* and ad-lib, and are then pursued by guitar chords and soft wire brushes. Although McFarland's rhythms are full of stop-times, double-time passages, six-eight time, and shuffle rhythms, they form an unbroken flow. There is a good deal of simultaneous improvisation on the record—a welcome idea that arrangers are inexplicably only beginning to experiment with. In "Sandpiper," McFarland and Swallow solo together and are then joined by Lewis. McFarland drops out, leaving Swallow and Lewis to their ruminations. In "I Love to Say Her Name," McFarland and Raney work together, and there are brief ensemble passages throughout that may or may not be improvised. Mc-Farland always ignites his musicians in both ensemble and solo passages, and "Point of Departure" is no exception. Raney, Lewis, and Swallow are in good form, and so is Mc-Farland. Most vibraphonists—possibly because of the tintinnabulous nature of their instrument—sound very much alike. McFarland is unique. He places his notes sparingly and even hesitantly; each solo thinks as it goes along.

"Essence: John Lewis Plays the Compositions and Arrangements of Gary McFarland" (Atlantic) offers six graceful settings for John Lewis's piano. They reveal McFarland as an inventive melodist. His ballads have an elusive, almost fey quality. (This odd strain has appeared before in McFarland's composing.) His blues are fresh and free of the old-timey loam that covers so many contemporary blues pieces. And there is an up-tempo number with a witty flamencan tinge. McFarland uses three groups—an Evanslike ensemble with trumpets, a trombone, French horns, and a tuba; a woodwind-and-saxophone group; and a conventional trumpet-and-saxophone small band. The brass passages—in particular the trumpets—contain the best writing on the record. His trumpets blast discreetly; they play difficult melodic lines with swoop and lightness; they move in behind soloists for sunny organ chords. Moreover, McFarland's brass writing tends here to have a reed-like quality, while his woodwinds and reeds are brassy. Lewis solos at length and is in rare form, especially in the blues "Tillamook Two," for which he produces—at the opening of the fifth chorus of his solo—a descending, at once sure and hesitant single-note figure that carries the sort of emotion that only Bill Evans, among the younger pianists, knows how to convey. Jim Hall solos admirably in a couple of pieces, and Connie Kay appears with all three groups. Kay could make Charles de Gaulle swing.

McFarland's handful of recordings are studio efforts. Would that present conditions allowed him a full-time group. He could then develop what he has so brilliantly begun.

# The Highway

                                        An avant-garde movement can be tested only after it has become passé. It will then have proved itself simply through the changes it has wrought, or it will be forgotten. Consider the first avant-garde in jazz. It emerged in the mid-twenties in Chicago and New York, and consisted of Louis Armstrong, Earl Hines, Bix Beiderbecke, Pee Wee Russell, Zutty Singleton, and Sidney Bechet. Unlike the bebop and new-thing musicians, these men formed no particular school; they were floating iconoclasts who blossomed at about the same time. Armstrong influenced every trumpeter in his generation and many in the succeeding generation, and his effect can still be spotted; echoes of Hines and Singleton are still heard. Beiderbecke immediately attracted a host of white imitators, of whom only Bobby Hackett has cast any shadow, but Negro musicians listen to him, too, and he continues to surface in such odd places as a recent Roy Eldridge record and an occasional Miles Davis phrase. Russell and Bechet, though, became one-man movements. Russell is inimitable, and perhaps only Thelonious Monk has evolved a similarly restless inner vision. Bechet was not quite inimitable—he shaped Johnny Hodges, who taught Ben Webster, who has long had *his* own school—but he was, in a broader fashion, unique. For over thirty-five years (he died in 1959), he compressed more pure, unashamed emotion into his playing than any other musician, past or present. He made it possible for jazz musicians to moan and dance and exult through their instruments, and in his greatest moments he moved the music toward the majesty of opera. But the emotions in jazz have recently—in the hands of the new-thing musicians—become almost savage, and it is a cooling and peaceful experience to return to Bechet. This can be done in a new Victor reissue, "Bechet of New Orleans," which includes sixteen selections made between 1932 and 1941.

Few jazz musicians have been able to avoid the sink of commercialism. Billie Holiday and Lester Young and Sidney Catlett and Frankie Newton are some who did, and Bechet is another. (He spent the last decade of his life as a celebrated vaudeville figure in France, but his playing remained unchanged.) He devoted his life to pursuing those conditions and musicians most congenial to him, and this single-mindedness took him all over the globe. He was born in 1897 in New Orleans, where he studied with the clarinettist George Baquet and heard and worked with Armstrong and King Oliver and Bunk Johnson. In his teens, he travelled through the Southwest, and in 1919 performed in London, where he was applauded by the renowned Swiss conductor Ernest Ansermet, who wrote, with astonishing vision:

There is in the Southern Syncopated Orchestra an extraordinary clarinet virtuoso who is, so it seems, the first of his race to have composed perfectly formed blues on the clarinet. I've heard two of them which he elaborated at great length. They are admirable equally for their richness of invention, their force of accent, and their daring novelty and unexpected turns. These solos already show the germ of a new style. Their form is gripping, abrupt, harsh, with a brusque and pitiless ending like that of Bach's Second Brandenburg Concerto. I wish to set down the name of this artist of genius; as for myself, I shall never forget it—it is Sidney Bechet. When one has tried so often to find in the past one of those figures to whom we owe the creation of our art as we know it today—those men of the 17th and 18th centuries, for example, who wrote the expressive works of dance airs which cleared the way for Haydn and Mozart—what a moving thing it is to meet this black, fat boy with white teeth and narrow forehead, who is very glad one likes what he does, but can say nothing of his art, except that he follows his "own way" —and then one considers that perhaps his "own way" is the highway along which the whole world will swing tomorrow.

Not long after, Bechet was with Bessie Smith in New York, and by the mid-twenties he had recorded with Louis Armstrong and worked with James P. Johnson and Duke Ellington. Then he was off to Paris with Josephine Baker, and in 1925 he went to Moscow with the trumpeter Tommy Ladnier. During the next decade, he was with Noble Sissle in America and Europe, led his own group at the Savoy Ballroom, and for a while (1938) ran a small tailor shop in Harlem. He appeared at Nick's in 1938 and then made a series of celebrated recordings with such men as Red Allen, J. C. Higginbotham, Charlie Shavers, Sandy Williams, Sidney De Paris, and Sid Catlett. In the early forties, he was apt to turn up at the Savoy in Boston, or at one of Eddie Condon's Town Hall concerts, or in an out-of-the-way basement club in Washington, D.C. Three or four years later, he emigrated to France, leaving behind a devout following, which never—perhaps because of his ceaseless skating about—reached the size or fervor of Armstrong's or Beiderbecke's or Hines'.

But this didn't matter, for Bechet's style seemed to celebrate itself. This was particularly true when he used the soprano saxophone, which he favored over the clarinet and which he learned in the early twenties. Bechet was a superb primitive and he had a matronly tone which drowned any ensemble he played in. It was not a big, fake tone, like Chu Berry's or Charlie Shavers', but a solid mass. It was kept in the air by its vibrato, which moved through a series of linked "u"s that gave the effect of being played in an echo chamber. Bechet's solos were highly melodic and largely legato. He would sometimes start a phrase with a couple of staccato notes (a device often used by Charlie Parker, who certainly knew Bechet's work), but it would end in a long-held note that gradually shimmied into a vibrato, or in a descending glissando that might shatter into rooting growls. His playing at fast tempos occasionally gave the impression of a fat man hurrying—and enjoying it—and at slow tempos, where he had the room, he constructed a succession of soaring phrases, large intervals, sudden halts, double-time sprints, and stately, processional, behind-the-beat figures. But no matter what his tempo or materials, his passion never faltered; the meanest blues got the same throne-room treatment as "Summertime." This outflow of emotion was so effortless that at times it appeared almost complacent. It also occasionally came perilously close to the romantic. His clarinet was simply a lesser though equally poignant version of his soprano. The tone was sharper, the vibrato wider, the sweeps and glides closer to the ground. It didn't dominate its surroundings; it sliced through them. Its lyricism matched his soprano's in the way a small Rembrandt matches a large one.

The Victor reissue is needlessly dishevelled. Two of the numbers (one was done with an awful studio Dixieland band, and one is a multiple-tracking one-man-band job) are gimmicks, and three ("I Ain't Gonna Give Nobody None of My Jelly Roll" "Georgia Cabin," and "Twelfth Street Rag") are second-rate. The remaining ones are often marvellous, and are notable for Bechet's easy, mourning clarinet breaks in "Wild Man Blues," for the steady sotto-voce flow of "Egyptian Fantasy," for the gracious ensembles in "Wild Man Blues" and "Shake It and Break It," for Jelly Roll Morton's sad vocal in "I Thought I Heard Buddy Bolden Say," and for Bechet's classic declaiming soprano-saxophone solo—to say nothing of Earl Hines' equally classic statement—in "Save It, Pretty Mama." Victor has promised a second set of Bechet reissues, but the damage has been done. The good selections on the present L.P. are drawn from six memorable sessions, but no more than two of the four sides made at each session are included. Why not reissue such valuable material complete session by complete session? Dark are the ways of a.-and-r. men.

# Frankie ex Machina

The eleventh Newport Jazz Festival was leviathan (seven concerts, thirty groups, forty-five thousand customers), bland, banal, occasionally professional, occasionally original, never exciting, and—a new note this year—unintentionally funny. This comedy provided more than relief; it made the general mediocrity of the weekend bearable. The first burst came on Thursday evening when Pete Seeger, accompanied by his own banjo and by a George Wein group that resembled an amateur *bar-mitzvah* band, sang "Summertime" in spindly shouts. A little later on, Les McCann, a middling West Coast pianist who has grown sleek and plump on a diet of fake blues and gospel music, offered four such imitations, topping them with a Liberace version of "Yours Is My Heart Alone." At the close of the evening, Joe Williams, another melodramatist, began by announcing that both he and McCann, his accompanist, loved "Yours Is My Heart Alone," and then sang it. McCann smiled like someone being told his own joke twenty minutes later. The comic pickings on Friday afternoon came largely from Archie Shepp, a new-thing tenor saxophonist who has been influenced in the worst possible way by Ben Webster and Johnny Hodges and Ornette Coleman: he un-

263

wittingly parodies them. Saturday evening was enlivened by two vocalists—one a Japanese girl who belted out her songs as if she were an electronic machine set for Ella Fitzgerald and Dinah Washington and Judy Garland, and the other a South African girl, tall and Victorian-looking, who sang two numbers in a good voice riddled by a hypnotic effect—each sustained note had a hiccup in it. But Sunday evening was a circus. Frank Sinatra, the celebrated New Jersey Meadows jazz singer, appeared with Count Basie. Sinatra's stint was carried out with Commando precision. Late Sunday afternoon, during a Stan Getz *bossanova* number, a couple of helicopters scouting the area for Sinatra fell out of the sky with a roar and touched down briefly just behind the bandstand. At exactly seven-forty-five, they returned, carrying Sinatra and his entourage, and at nine, after half a dozen desultory Count Basie numbers, Sinatra paraded onstage with his own drummer, his own trumpet player—Harry (One-Note) Edison—and his own arrangements. Basie put on a pair of glasses and started reading his part, and Sinatra sang "Get Me to the Church on Time." Seven or eight vocals later, Sinatra paused, got himself a cup of tea from the piano, and, sipping it stage center, delivered a monologue made up of Bob Hope gags larded with plugs for a Las Vegas hotel that Sinatra has an interest in, recent and forthcoming Sinatra movies, and Dean Martin and Sammy Davis. Then he replaced his teacup, sang ten more songs, and waved goodbye. He was airborne before the Basie band had finished a concluding "One O'Clock Jump." The tab was reportedly thirty-five thousand dollars.

But there was intentional humor, too. Dizzy Gillespie was on hand with his quintet on Thursday and Friday evenings, and although his playing was first-rate, his comportment was even better—particularly on Friday. Working his way through half a dozen south-of-the-border selections, he danced (a series of motions in which his shoulders, hips, and arms became an uninterrupted flow), spent part of a number conducting his drummer, carried on a shoving match with his saxophonist James Moody that ended with a warm embrace, sang a funny calypso tune in a voice a potato would envy, and introduced the members of his band (handshakes all around among the musicians). Earlier on Friday, Thelonious Monk and his quartet strolled through a handful of numbers, each of them full of sly, affectionate pokes at stride piano and of the steady inner pleasure that Monk rests all his music on. Jo Jones aerated Saturday afternoon. Appearing in a so-called drum workshop with Buddy Rich, Elvin Jones, Roy Haynes, Louis Bellson, and Art Blakey, each of whom fired off Judgment Day solos, he restricted himself to brief, toying statements swathed in mischievous grins and eye-poppings. But despite his subtlety and despite Rich's jet stream, Bellson's automation, and an all-nerves Haynes solo, Elvin Jones was the winner. It is his way to manipulate two or three different rhythms at once, and after a time these rhythms seemed to become disembodied and self-sufficient; the fact that they were emerging from a set of drums was almost incidental.

The tedium of the groups led by Carmen McRae and Dave Brubeck and Stan Getz and Billy Taylor and Art Blakey and Oscar Peterson was further relieved by the Modern Jazz Quartet, which on Thursday evening delivered seven numbers, all perfect, all affecting, and all demonstrating that Milt Jackson, with his energy and ululating vibrato, is the Sidney Bechet of the present. On Saturday night, Earl Hines, backed by Earl May and Louis Bellson, played four numbers (one a long medley) that were climaxed, in "Boogie Woogie on the St. Louis Blues," by a couple of brilliant high-register birdsong choruses. Hines was followed by Duke Ellington, whose misdemeanors outshine most men's excellences. The solos were predictable, the bass section was exhilarating but deafening, and Ellington himself seemed preoccupied, both in his manner and in his playing. A young pianist named Denny Zeitlin appeared on Sunday afternoon with a good drummer, Jerry Granelli, and the extraordinary bassist Charlie Haden, who, except in a fine flamencan passage, was largely inaudible. They were followed by the Wynton Kelly trio (Paul Chambers on bass and Jimmy Cobb on drums), which was the best rhythm section of the weekend, and by Wes Montgomery, a guitarist who gets off his clichés with cannonic force.

Friday afternoon, given over to the new thing, was at least original. The Jazz Composers Guild Orchestra, which included Mike Mantler on trumpet, Roswell Rudd on trombone, a reed section (John Tchicai, Charles Davis, and Ken McIntyre), Carla Bley on piano, Steve Swallow on bass, and Milford Graves on drums, moved with shambling precision through two long numbers—one by Mantler and one by Mrs. Bley. They were notable for a slow lyrical interlude in Mantler's piece, in which Mrs. Bley, typing out a solo with one finger, was backed by congested organ chords and some marvellous sleight-of-hand cymbal work from Graves, and for a calypso passage in Mrs. Bley's composition, in which the melody was handled as if the band were on the verge of inventing the fugue. Cecil Taylor finished the afternoon, and, as is his wont, constructed in each solo an immense tower of notes that withstood the great winds his playing generated. There was a lot of *thinking* onstage that afternoon.

The festival was held this year on the side of a gently sloping hill just north of Newport Harbor. The only changes from Freebody Park, which had been the festival site for nine years, were the fine amplifying system and a new, Expressionistic bandstand ringed by myriad multi-colored spotlights and resembling a woman in curlers on a Saturday night. She looked lovely against the stars.

# Perfecto

It has become increasingly difficult to hear Bobby Hackett—the great, no-school cornettist—on the countless mood-music recordings he has restricted himself to in the past ten years. One has, rather, simply been conscious—wherever there is a radio, a jukebox, or Muzak—of a sweet-Leilani flow. These pastoral sounds have provoked myriad critical mutterings to the effect that Hackett has abandoned Jazz for the market place. But he has not; by appearing infrequently in concerts and night clubs and at recordings, he has husbanded his improvisational energies. As a result, each of his jazz outings has been telling and precise and even beautiful—a reminder that he has no peers on his instrument and very few on its twin, the trumpet. This was obvious when Hackett, in company with Pee Wee Russell, Dave Frishberg, George Tucker, and Oliver Jackson, gave the sixth Jazz in the Garden concert at the Museum of Modern Art. It was a superb evening; even the soft rain that persisted throughout the thirteen numbers seemed like applause.

Hackett and Russell have worked together off and on since the late thirties, and they complement one another perfectly. Hackett now plays the way Bix Beiderbecke, his chief model, might if he were alive. He has rounded off

Beiderbecke's celebrated anvil tone, modernized his rhythmic awkwardness, and decorated these alterations with a series of designs that make each solo wholly original and well-nigh flawless. Indeed, it is hard to savor all of a Hackett solo at one hearing, so subtle and trim are his runs (though fully as complex as Dizzy Gillespie's, they are issued in a sotto-voce, almost apologetic fashion), his daring, light-footed intervals, his new-velvet tone, his dynamics (a loud Hackett note would be considered just a stout breath by any other cornettist-trumpeter), his way of accenting unexpected notes and only nodding pleasantly at what precedes and follows them, and his rhythmic agility, which permits him to alter a steady beat into a complex pattern of mazurka advances and retreats. But Hackett is not a miniaturist or a dandy. He matches the emotions of an Armstrong or an Eldridge or a Gillespie through unflagging economy and grace and invention. A *working* jazz soloist is irresistible.

Russell, too, indefatigable, but whereas Hackett is a masterly logician, Russell is an incorruptible idealist-adventurer. This was evident at the Garden in the ensemble passages, in which Hackett quietly prodded and rearranged the melody while Russell swung carelessly back and forth between high pipes and muffled, Holland Tunnel chalumeau sounds. Most collective ensembles are predicated on head-banging, but there was always open space between Hackett and Russell as they moved neck and neck on close and parallel courses through "St. Louis Blues," "Pennies from Heaven," and the opening of "In a Mellotone," in which they played without the rhythm section, giving the impression of two people jogging along slightly above the ground. Their solos were equally complementary. Hackett's seemed already at least a second or third draft, and Russell's were the work of a soldier of fortune. In " 'S Wonderful," he got trapped in a terribly crowded middle-register passage (the notes like bobbing heads) but finally extricated himself with a searching, hopeful off-note wail that found the right concluding note, and in a fast blues he survived a cascade of wild, sliding phrases that were as far out—and twice as funny—as any of the heresies of the new-thing movement. He also got off several heart-turning chalumeau passages that seemed to pass directly from his marrow into the listener's. The rhythm section was exemplary. Frishberg is an odd, centerless pianist who has heard everyone from Luis Russell to Tommy Flanagan, and Tucker, a sound bassist, played a remarkable bowed parody of "Summertime." Jackson took a handful of sensible breaks and a good solo in "Swing That Music." Best of all, the concert was filmed by N.B.C. television; in time, those of us who were on hand can indulge in the old sport of miracle-testing.

# Evans to Tate to . . .

Until recently, jazz has been an unschooled, homemade music. Its inventors have served as its textbooks and teachers, and around each has gathered a host of pupils, the best of whom have attracted their own admirers. (I doubt that the first how-to jazz book—probably a primer on boogie-woogie—appeared before the late thirties.) The effect has occasionally been of a handful of strong voices drowning in their echoes. By and large, though, this neophyte clamor has been beneficial, and when great originators have died young it has been a blessing. Thus we can still hear Bix Beiderbecke in Bobby Hackett and Jimmy McPartland, Jimmy Harrison in Benny Morton, and Herschel Evans in Buddy Tate. The case of Evans and Tate is a little ghostly. When Evans died, in 1939, at the age of thirty, Tate replaced him almost immediately in Count Basie's band. Tate's closeness to his friend was and is uncanny. He resembles him facially (particularly when he wears spectacles) and in his courtly, attractive manner, and his playing is a direct extension. Evans' career was not cut short; it simply changed hands. But Tate, who is fifty, is more than a living memorial. He is one of that small group of generous artists who constantly share with their appreciators the unique emotions generated by creating. Tate invents, moves himself, and in turn moves us—a split-second chain reaction that reveals not so much how he plays as why: to make something utterly new. The results are almost steadily affecting. Tate's solos do not depend simply on improvisation, or even on design, but on burst after burst of emotion. These are shaped into long, falling blue notes, crooning phrases that end in fluttering vibratos, and cries that arch across the upper register. Tate's emotions, which are blue and sorrowing, are invariably honest. There is none of the self-pity and boohooing that leak from the work of some of his contemporaries. He seems to say, Damn, my heart aches; hear it. These outpourings are supported by splendid musicianship. He has a cedar tone, fine rhythmic agility, and a neat harmonic sense. For the past fifteen years, Tate has camped largely at the Celebrity Club in Harlem, and his recent appearance with an eleven-piece band at the Museum of Modern Art was a bracing surprise.

The band was unusual in two respects. Four of its members—Tate himself, Emmett Berry, Dickie Wells, and Eli Robinson (trombone)—constituted a reunion of part of the old Basie band, and six of its members were excellent examples of that inventor-pupil schooling method. In fact, two inventors came with their pupils (Berry with trumpeter Pat Jenkins and Wells with Robinson), while two were represented by them (Evans by Tate and Ben Webster by tenor saxophonist Harold Ashby). One had to look sharp to tell who was soloing. One also had to continually dispel the illusion of hearing the old Basie band, for in "One O'Clock Jump" and a fast "Sent for You Yesterday," the group handled its riffs and swung with the same passionate ease. Tate was in good form throughout and was memorable in a slow ballad, "Born to Be Blue," in which he hung out a series of fat, Japanese-lantern notes, and in

"Every Day," in which he released a descending, terraced wail that caused an outbreak of goose pimples. Berry, possibly dulled by the proximity of Jenkins (they stood side by side), was a slow starter, but in the last couple of numbers he played handsome solos, full of his studied, rocklike notes and muscular legato phrases. At the end of the evening, Jimmy Rushing, another alumnus of the old Basie band, appeared and sang six superb numbers. He shouts the blues as if he were using the wrong end of a megaphone —a big sound perfectly funnelled. And he delights himself, his accompanists, and his listeners. In the next-to-last number, one could almost hear the audience supply the final line of his most celebrated blues couplet. It begins

> Anybody ask you, baby, who was it
>   sang this song,
> Anybody ask you, baby, who was it
>   sang this song,

and ends

> Tell him little Jimmy Rushing, he's
>   been here and gone.

# The Road to Big Sur

In recent years, most of the reports about and the recordings of the annual Monterey Jazz Festival, which began in 1958, have indicated that it has taken up where the lamented Great South Bay Festival (1957-58) left off. Primed with expectation and hope, I attended the eighth edition of the Festival. Like the turtle, most travellers take their houses with them, and I was no exception. The moment I arrived in Monterey, after a three-hour drive down the Coast from San Francisco, the past and present collided. Monterey's houses and buildings seemed a polyglot of Florida Spanish, Long Island motel, and 1910 Frank Lloyd Wright. Its restaurants, I soon found, are vaguely New York "Continental" and are apt to feature Green Goddess salads and sour-cream-loaded baked potatoes that look like galleons under full sail. (Artichokes, which grow in superabundance in nearby Castroville and sell for twenty-five cents a dozen at roadside stands, are not to be had.) Even the air and light in Monterey, loosed now of the dogging summer fogs, rang a bell—the crystalline atmosphere of Maine. But this one-upping traveller's game —professors of comparative literature make a living out of playing a variation of it—suddenly became pointless when, on the morning after I arrived, I drove south through Carmel (an old artists' colony turned genteel tourist trap) to Big Sur. For forty miles, I followed a narrow road strung between imperious hills and precipitous seven-hundred-foot cliffs. Each turn unlocked a more magnificent spectacle than the last. At first, stung by such beauty (sea lions decked the rocks far below, and above me cows, their seaward legs seemingly longer than their landward legs, grazed on steep smooth tan hills), I mentally trotted out the great gorges of upper New York State and the rocky drops on the south shore of Bermuda. But after a few miles none of these props helped. They were oranges and this was a spectacular, brand-new apple; my disbelief was suspended.

It took a little longer to adjust my sights at the Festival, which consisted of two afternoon and three evening concerts. Odd associations kept blurring them. The site, a small, rectangular amphitheatre in the Monterey Fair Grounds, suggested a rodeo corral. The wide, shallow bandstand recalled, with its plush red colors and Pop Art décor, a stage setting for an Off Broadway musical. Oddest of all, the audience tended to behave in the celebrated chattering-guffawing manner of the onlookers in the pit at the Globe Theatre; the most affecting music was overlaid by talk and laughter. Then, as the concerts rolled by, it became plain that the Monterey Festival, which is financially *and* artistically in the black, is what the Great South Bay Festival might have become and what the Newport Festival ought to be. Like the road to Big Sur, it is an original. The Newport Festival enjoys a love-hate relationship with its host town, which abhors it socially and loves it financially; everybody in Monterey—with the chamber of commerce carrying the flag—champions the Festival. Newport seats twelve to fifteen thousand; Monterey seats half as many.

275

An afternoon concert at Newport may include as many as five or six groups that practically jostle one another to gain playing time; there were three groups at the Sunday-afternoon proceedings at Monterey this year. Newport is held in a sprawling arena that precludes any audience-performer intimacy; one could see the musicians' eyes from the back row at Monterey. The ever-increasing bigness and glossiness of Newport reflect a fat-man insecurity; the highly selective, tightly run Monterey Festival exudes confidence. The very size of Newport breeds dullness; the Monterey I attended was never less than professional.

I suspect, though, that the weekend was a couple of notches below those of past years, for there were tedious patches and there was even some out-and-out musical conning. The tedium was contributed largely by the half-dozen vocalists, among them the hipper-than-thou Jon Hendricks, who seemed to appear with every group, and by an ambitious twenty-piece band, which, recruited especially for the Festival and made up of the likes of Harry Edison and Clark Terry, never freed itself of its star-studded specialness, to say nothing of the ironbound arrangements of its leader, Gil Fuller. The not-surprising musical conning was perpetrated by Louis Armstrong, who appeared Friday evening with a group consisting of Buster Bailey, Tyree Glenn, Billy Kyle, and bass and drums. Armstrong restricted himself to interminable vocals of "Hello, Dolly!" and "Mack the Knife" and to a handful of solos, none of them distinguished. (Armstrong is sixty-five, but his recent recordings sporadically prove that he can still play as he did in the thirties. Why, before it is too late, doesn't someone put him in a studio with his peers rather than with his own indifferent band?) Bailey played a couple of good choruses of "Memphis Blues," and then, in

"Night Train," used his clarinet to make vaudeville chuffing noises. Tyree Glenn offered variations on the patent-leather solo he invented twenty-five years ago, larding them with funny-trombone antics. One kept expecting a tiny car to drive onstage and disgorge a dozen clowns. But such mistakes tend to be rapidly forgotten at jazz festivals, and by Saturday evening it was hard to believe that Armstrong had even been there.

Saturday was Local Talent Day at the Fair Grounds. The Festival big band opened the afternoon concert with a fifteen-minute Festival-commissioned composition by Hollywood's Russ Garcia. It belonged in that castle of musical horrors long presided over by another West Coaster, Stan Kenton. Earsplitting brass figures gave way to timpani drums, which paused for Debussy piano passages, which sank into dissonant dying-fall ensemble chords. But things brightened when Denny Zeitlin, a young pianist-psychiatrist resident in San Francisco, appeared with Charlie Haden on bass and Jerry Granelli on drums. Zeitlin has caused a lot of excited chatter in the past year, and it is easy to see why. He is an expert and flashy pianist who draws heavily on Lennie Tristano and Bill Evans, he writes readily identifiable program pieces ("The Carnival," "Mirage"), and he runs a taut trio. Indeed, Haden and Granelli are so good that they outclass their leader. Haden is an alumnus of the original Ornette Coleman quartet as well as a prominent member of the new school of bassists who consider their instrument a Full Orchestra. He took three brilliant solos, one of them spelled out in great, booting single notes and another in luxurious flamencan strumming passages. Granelli is a remarkably prescient accompanist; his accents almost seem to foretell what they are accompanying. He is an equally skilled soloist, and he took an exemplary mallet solo in the slow "Mirage" and a superb solo with sticks in "At Sixes and Sevens," a Zeitlin piece based on 7/4 and 6/4 time signatures. San Francisco was also represented by the alto saxophonist John Handy. Handy has caused—on the West Coast, anyway—as much of a flutter as Zeitlin, and he brought a singular quartet with him, made up of a violin (Mike White), a guitar (Gerry Hahn), and bass and drums. When Handy first appeared, in the late fifties, with Charlie Mingus, he sounded like Benny Carter trying to sound like Charlie Parker. He has since developed a handsome and original style. He plays his instrument perfectly, achieving a tone that is just about the purest ever got by a jazz saxophonist. But Handy puts this conventionality to radical uses, for, ignoring the new thing and John Coltrane's hunt for the lost chord and Sonny Rollins' sarcasm, he concentrates on Melody. His solos are composed of an unfaltering succession of lyrical, few-noted melodies, each set out in long, curving lines, which reach into every register and which are often played at ad-lib or half-time tempos. He is not afraid of a vibrato, and he will enliven these leisurely inventions—his unaccompanied, ad-lib solo in "If We Only Knew" lasted at least ten minutes—by choking his tone and getting a trumpet sound, by fluttering up and down the scales, by growling politely, and by delivering wails that are repeated over and over until they are simon-pure. White, who is an accomplished ensemble foil to Handy, is a well-ordered Ornette Coleman, and Hahn is an amazing guitarist who uses double-stop effects and whose single-note passages have an undersea sound. Handy's ensemble techniques—momentum playing leapfrog with momentum—are derived from Charlie Mingus, and they brought the audience to its feet. And then—stern irony!—who should round out the afternoon but Mingus himself, with a brand-new septet, made up of three trumpets, a trombone, a French horn, a tuba, and drums. When Mingus is upstaged—which is extremely rare—he generally reacts with heroic retaliatory roars or by going comatose. He chose the latter course on Saturday. The only lively number of the four he played was a mock-pomp version of "When the Saints Go Marching In," and even that limped. There were also glimpses of wonderful brass sonorities, a couple of good solos, and occasional stirrings of the extraordinary musical tensions indigenous to Mingus. (The word "indigenous" puts me in mind of the helpful answer I got from a native of Monterey when I asked him the name of a tall, Oriental-looking fir in the Fair Grounds—"It's a fir, indigenous to the region.") But only great teachers are upstaged by their own pupils.

More local talent appeared Saturday night when Earl Hines came onstage with a bassist and a still flawless Jerry Granelli. Since his recent resurgence, Hines has perfected a bill of fare generally made up of whatever he has just recorded, a medley of Ellington or Waller or Erroll Garner tunes, "Memories of You," and a long blues capped by a two-note tremolo that he may hold for a dozen choruses. But he was surprising in "Body and Soul," which was done first as a rhapsody and then in a medium tempo that was notable for a fine, upper-register chorus. Hines was followed by Duke Ellington, who was deep in a three-month Western trip. Ellington was off stride at Newport, but he was in excellent form at Monterey. The reason, I think, was his singular performance, the night before the Festival, at Grace Cathedral, in San Francisco, where he offered a program composed for the occasion. I was lucky enough to be there, and it was a stirring event. Although it was uneven and the acoustics ranged from the inaudible to those of Echo Mountain, the band matched in sound and demeanor the majesty of its surroundings. One extraordinary Ellington number, "David Danced Before the Lord with All His Might," included a passage during which Bunny Briggs, the tap-dancer, executed a series of rapid soft-shoe steps, backed by soft organ chords, a muted trumpet, and a children's choir. The effect was eerie and unique and enchanting. At Monterey, Ellington played upward of twenty tunes, which were climaxed by a repeat of Briggs' "David Danced" and by "The Applejack," in which Briggs both tap-danced and went through a series of feints and slides and bobbings designed to match visually the sounds behind him.

Barring a late and unexpected explosion, Sunday was a day of ease. In the afternoon, Dizzy Gillespie, Rex Stewart, Clark Terry, and Red Allen, backed by a rhythm section, offered five affable exercises that included a lush, virtuoso "Stardust," played by Terry; an aching slow blues, in which Allen played and sang; and a funny "Don't Get Around Much Anymore," played and sung, in a husky beer-barrel voice, by Stewart. Next came "St. Martin de Porres," a short oratorio by Mary Lou Williams that was sung admirably by a local choir and that displayed an almost—so ingenuous and pleasing was it—saintly melody. She then sailed into three first-rate standards. The explosion went off Sunday evening, when Harry James' big band, which, as an observer put it, "resembles Basie's, only it's white," played the "Two O'Clock Jump." Buddy Rich, who has worked with James off and on through the years, was on drums, and his accompanying was the finest I have ever heard from a big-band drummer. He punctuated breaks and shaded melodic passages and underlined crescendos with such pinpointed verve that the musicians were nearly lifted out of their seats, and then he took a breathtaking solo. It had dynamics (a powerful snare-drum roll that sank to a whisper and ended with rapid, clocklike ticking on the snare rims), unbelievable speed (a three-drum section, involving two different rhythms, that was watched with glassy-eyed fascination by the drummers who happened to be in the wings), and a whirling inventiveness. It was a mad, magnificent performance.

The Festival was virtually shepherded by Dizzy Gillespie, who performed at every concert, either with his quintet or as a guest. He also danced, played the piano and the conga drums, sang, and acted as m.c. He was effortless and delightful at every turn. Indeed, without putting his mind to it at all, Gillespie could stage a consummate one-man festival.

I drove back to San Francisco through the olive country, the wine country, the artichoke country, and the prune country. I passed under trees so dense they made little nights on the road, and by hilly green pastures smooth enough to shoot marbles on. It was a perfect coda.

# Zutty

The knell
that is sounded periodically for jazz is ringing again. The
jazz press, which loves to weep over even fancied catastro-
phe, is itself pulling the rope, and there are other signs.
Folk music has seized a considerable chunk of those
listeners who, fifteen years back, might have been studying
jazz. The night-club business, which is probably outmoded
anyhow, is rapidly falling away, and fewer jazz records are
being made. Radio and television have again slammed their
doors. Musicians of every stripe are scratching for work.
But these are, I'm sure, transitory difficulties sown by fad-
dism, and they have little to do with a problem in jazz that
does deserve brooding and even melancholy: the chill that
has crept into the music in the past decade. One feels it in
the glittering younger pianists, in the crushing sarcasm of
Sonny Rollins and the autonomous frenzy of John Coltrane,
in the vapid musings of Miles Davis, and, most depress-
ingly, in the drummers shaped by Max Roach. Sounding
their shrill, high-pitched sets, these drummers create—
with their insistent mono-method of accompaniment—a
hard, false background. They are bric-a-brac performers
who clutter the air. (Max Roach plays with passion?
Rather with a frightening, cold anger. He is the first

*social* drummer.) In an effort to ease these damp humors, I stopped at Jimmy Ryan's to hear Zutty Singleton, the sixty-seven-year-old New Orleans drummer. I confess that I hadn't really listened to Singleton since the days when he was a fixture at the old Ryan's, and hearing him again was a lovely experience. He is, of course, seminal. (So was Baby Dodds, but, with the exception of Dave Tough, his followers never surpassed him.) Sidney Catlett, from whom Roach borrowed all the wrong things, drank of him deeply, and it would profit every drummer under fifty to do the same. The warmth and drive and pleasure that flow out of Singleton and his drums are irresistible. He is a sun.

Singleton's style—to say nothing of his appearance: a gentle, Teddy-bear face, with a high forehead and heavily lidded eyes and a generous mouth, sits easily on a short, solid figure—probably hasn't changed much since 1915. It grew directly out of parade-band drumming, and is centered on the snare and bass drums. Covering these foundations is a steadily changing layer of embellishments, carried out on the cymbals (in addition to a high-hat, which he rarely pedals, he has three cymbals, one shaped like a floppy garden-party hat and sounding like a sharp intake of breath), on three tomtoms, on three cowbells and a wood block, and on the rims of his drums. In the course of an ensemble chorus, Singleton's accompaniment goes like this: He will start with a heavy, accented snare-drum roll, which bulldozes the horns, and a two-beat rhythm on the bass drum. Then he will break the roll, silence the bass drum, and sprinkle his cymbals with fairy beats, shift his sticks to the high-hat, which he leaves agape, and pile into four bass-drum beats to the bar. The high-hat work will be accented with lightly struck eighth notes on the tomtoms, and at the end of the bridge he will circulate between the snare and the cowbells and the wood block and the bass drum, the last of which he smacks with his sticks. Back to the snare for a series of press rolls and rimshots, a couple of tomtom beats and bass-drum accents, and the chorus ends. Singleton's backgrounds are a continually revolving dream of carefully pitched sounds (his drums are tuned to an almost basso-profundo level), which both nourish the horns and move on a private, self-sufficient course. His brief solos are simply extensions of his accompanying, and usually consist of massed rolls topped by a rattling, around-the-set explosion. These solos rear up and burst genially. He exudes delight when he plays. Emotions chase and flicker through him, appearing when he drops his eyelids and hoists his eyebrows, when, abruptly lunging at a cymbal, his stick a truncheon, he clamps his lips shut, and when, delivering a mighty roll, he shakes his head from side to side with a fury that compounds his rhythms. But just his arms and head really move; his trunk is a rigid, stately pivot. Singleton is an elegant primitive. His technique is probably no better than Ringo Starr's. He is apt to speed up or drag the tempo, and he can be punishingly ponderous. But, oddly, his wayward cymbal work, his constant broken rushes around his set, and his always surprising rhythmic deviations are not in the least old-fashioned. In fact, they are strikingly similar to the heretic experiments of Milford Graves, the best of the new-thing drummers. Singleton, who has surely never even heard of Graves, would shock him.

# Dauntless

Of all the arts, music is the most difficult to transmit humor through. It abounds with such first cousins as gaiety and whimsey and sweetness, but most of its rare straight laughs are parodic (the "Classical Symphony" and Thelonious Monk's twittings of stride piano), verbal (librettos and lyrics), or simply slapstick (the gallows episode in the "Symphonie Fantastique" and the farmyard effects of the Original Dixieland Jazz Band). In jazz, though, there is a small group of instrumentalists and singers who, free to roam their own emotions as well as the timbres of their horns and voices, have perfected an often sardonic wittiness that they express through freakish notes and timbres (Pee Wee Russell), through oddly shaped or even surrealistic melodies (Sonny Rollins), and through comic juxtapositions (a couple of bars of "Yankee Doodle" tossed into the bridge of "Body and Soul"). The results are both musical and funny. These wits share several basic characteristics. All are inimitable or the founders of schools, all can move within the space of a bar or so from humor to pathos or vice versa, all are consummate improvisers, and all are daredevils. The most adventuresome was probably Dickie Wells. His playing has subsided in recent years, but he was as bold and in-

ventive and funny during his great period (1935-50) as any
jazz musician past or present. Indeed, it is surprising that
his glory lasted as long as it did; the trombone is a high-
fuel-consumption instrument, and in every solo Wells fed
it heart, mind, and soul.

Certain instruments tend to dominate jazz at certain
times, and the turn of the trombone came in the early thirties. Jack Teagarden and Jimmy Harrison had just converted it from a hod carrier into a graceful miler, and they
were followed by a host of fluent and original men, such as
Sandy Williams, Claude Jones, Lawrence Brown, J. C.
Higginbotham, Benny Morton, Vic Dickenson, and Wells.
They plumbed the instrument, exploring its almost illim-
itable tonal properties (from a husky lullaby to a shriek),
releasing its warmth and lyricism, and developing astonishing techniques. The venerable image of the trombone as
a *Weltschmerz* clown was destroyed. Wells swam along
easily with his peers for a time, but in the mid-thirties, not
long before he joined Count Basie, he suddenly shot off on
his own, perfecting an attack whose imaginativeness and
assurance placed him beside Louis Armstrong and Coleman Hawkins.

The best way to keep a beautiful style from becoming a bore is to rough it up a little. Wells was a master of
the purposeful blemish. In one solo, he might play with a
legs-on-the-table insolence. In another, he might affect a
blurred, almost drunken attack, and in another he would
construct a mass of shrieks and dense, middle-register
phrases that alternately forced one to rear back in surprise
and hunch forward in concentration. He finagled with his
tone as well. He could, particularly when playing obbligatos behind Jimmy Rushing, make it clear and hallooing.
At middle tempos, he often used huskiness that seemed to

buzz the listener. And at high speeds, his sound became imperious and rough; there was no time for niceties. His command of vibrato, which generally governs its users, was flawless. He used a vibrato to make notes sing that *should* sing and he abandoned it on notes that should come to a dead stop. His sense of rhythm and harmony was intricate and exciting. He was at home before, on, and after the beat, placing his notes to create a system of rhythmic checks and balances. His choice of notes was always daring; it resembled the rummaging in odd corners practiced by Red Allen and Lester Young. He used a lot of blue notes (which tended to slide off and end abruptly), large intervals that sometimes covered several registers, and strange off-notes, sounded in a disconnected, isolated manner, for emphasis. Each solo seemed a search for notes that had never been used before. At the same time, the construction of his solos was almost geometric, and it was illuminated by dynamics that occasionally placed roars beside whispers. One of Wells' middle-tempo blues solos might go like this: He would start with a six-note phrase, employing just two or three different notes, group the first five together and isolate the sixth, pause, repeat this phrase (dropping slightly less than a whole tone), pause again, press the two phrases together (changing a few of the notes), and unroll still another phrase, as a variation on the originals. All this would be played in a soft growl. Then he would slope into a long legato phrase, full of blue notes and off-notes, leap into the upper register and emit a shriek, which would be quickly followed by a soft echo an octave or so lower, and end with a whispered *pathétique* phrase. Only when the solo was over did the listener realize that Wells had made him think, laugh, exult, and feel melancholy. Few actors could pull so many stops so fast.

Contact Records has made it possible to hear Wells at the height of his powers by reissuing, in "Classic Tenors: Coleman Hawkins and Lester Young," four matchless sides made in 1943 by Wells, Bill Coleman, Young, Ellis Larkins, Freddie Green, Al Hall, and Jo Jones. (The entire L.P. is superb, for the remaining eight selections are by two Hawkins groups, one including Shelly Manne, Oscar Pettiford, and Eddie Heywood, and the other Coleman, Larkins, and Manne, among others. The quartet's recordings of "The Man I Love" and "Sweet Lorraine" are among the best of all jazz records.) The Wells group is drawn in part from the old Basie band, and it has the same wit, precision, and drive. The rhythm section pedals as easily through a walking blues as it does through a hammers-of-hell "I Got Rhythm," and the horns react brilliantly. Wells turns all the faces of his style to the light. In a relaxed "Linger Awhile," he uses his husky tone, several high-register swoops, and a curving legato bridge. He is seventy-six trombones in "I Got Rhythm," and climaxes a wild, roaring solo with a series of hand-over-hand climbs, each of them reaching a higher note than the one before, and each of them shouting with laughter and high spirits. "I'm Fer It Too," a take not used for the original, 78-r.p.m issue, starts as a slow blues, with Wells doing two eloquent anti-*Weltschmerz* choruses, in which he growls, uses odd, deep off-notes and a couple of shouts, and closes with one of his grimacing, disconsolate phrases. Coleman and Young keep pace with him throughout, and in "I Got Rhythm" Young delivers several blinding choruses that match anything he recorded. This is magic, permanent music.

Wells drifted out of the Basie band in the late forties, and since then he has made only sporadic appearances. Somewhere along the line, the surf and wind went out of his playing, but his ideas are still occasionally original and winsome, and his use of the sly and unexpected is undiminished. He is a gentle dream of his old self. But one need only turn to his recordings of the thirties and forties to hear the beat of his unique comic heart.

1966

# Hide and Seek

How remarkable that those two great phenomena of American music—Duke Ellington, who is sixty-six, and Louis Armstrong, who is a year younger—are still inescapably with us. Despite advancing age and the public apathy that long careers ironically induce, both men continue to roam the world with their bands, appearing at concerts and festivals, in movies, on radio and television, in night clubs, and on recordings, all the while producing a great deal of original and eventful music. They are, as founders and makers, the poles of this music. Ellington, the composer-bandleader-pianist, runs a matchless musical continuum that steadily instructs and delights, while Armstrong, the trumpeter-vocalist, defines and redefines the lyrical heart of jazz. But they have done this in utterly different ways. Ellington is the quintessence of grace and graciousness; Armstrong, long concealed behind a vaudeville mask, suggests an "evil" roughness and readiness. (New Orleans musicians are celebrated among their Northern colleagues for their "evil" quality; that is, they are said to possess an inborn suspicion and even a resentment not only of one another but of all comers.) Ellington does much of the listener's work for him; Armstrong, operating from within his self-caricature, demands patience and even fortitude.

Now and then, Armstrong pays off. One remembers a late, wet night at Newport in the fifties when, after rolling through his customary nonsense with his own group, he appeared with a big band made up of high-school students and played with an ease and magnificence that carried over into the concluding "Star-Spangled Banner." The same thing has happened with recordings he has made in the past ten years. His refashionings for Columbia of W. C. Handy and Fats Waller songs are invaluable, and, more recently, his rendition of Ellington's "It Don't Mean a Thing (If You Ain't Got That Swing)," with the composer himself at the piano, is fresh and beautiful. There is even a golden moment on his own tiresome "Hello, Dolly!," when he injects that surprising pause of a beat and a third between his singing of the words "This is Louis" and "Dolly." What a masterly rhythmic hitch! There are, as well, superlative moments in "The Best of Louis Armstrong" (Decca), a set of twenty-four reissues made between 1949 and 1957, and in "Louis Armstrong in the Thirties/in the Forties" (Victor), twelve numbers done in 1933 and in 1946 and 1947.

In his way, Armstrong has wielded even more power in jazz than Ellington, whose music is self-contained and largely inimitable. He began laying about him in 1924 when, joining Fletcher Henderson, he converted the Henderson band from an imitation white dance orchestra with New Orleans overtones into the first big jazz band. He did this by demonstrating an unheard-of improvisatory power and a brand-new rhythmic freedom. He was the first jazz musician to escape—through legato flights, behind-the-beat musings, and an occasional rushing of his notes—the hidebound four-four beat. He not only educated the Henderson

band but, more important, he educated its star performer—
Coleman Hawkins, who, until Armstrong's arrival, had
been a slap-tonguing vaudeville musician. During the next
four or five years, the recordings Armstrong made with
Earl Hines and Zutty Singleton likewise broke new ground,
and by 1930 every trumpet player in the country was under
his spell. His supremacy lasted well into the thirties (Joe
Thomas and Buck Clayton listened closely to his playing
in the mid-thirties), and subsided only when another listener, Charlie Parker, effected the next musical revolution
in jazz.

During Armstrong's banner years, he created the sort
of celestial art that few men master; transcending both its
means and its materials, it attained a disembodied beauty.
Until the advent of bebop and the new thing, the listener
was equally conscious of the improviser and of what he was
improvising on; there was even a rather slick satisfaction in
ferreting out the outlines of the melody in a solo. But Armstrong's method precludes this ferreting. His means were
better than adequate; he rarely muffed notes and he could
travel easily through all the registers. His materials often
consisted of bad popular songs or hotsy-totsy novelty numbers. Even his accompaniment by various bands was either
cupcake sweet or merely desultory. But one was not
conscious in Armstrong's solos of the tune, of the background, of his specific notes. Each solo was an immaculately
conceived work, a new and beautiful arabesque of sound.

Armstrong's authority was absolute. Listeners sense
fear in a jazz musician as quickly as animals do in men. But
Armstrong worked with the assurance of a Shaw. When he
*did* hit a clam, it was a great clam. This authority rested
equally on technical assurance and on a bottomless fund
of emotion. (Armstrong's technique wavers now, but his

heart is far from dry.) His solos were always climactic—another first in the music. He would start with a subtle restatement of the melody, changing its accents and notes ever so slightly by cutting a phrase short here or lingering over a note there, and then, leaving the melody, he would begin a series of angelic ascensions and swoops that would be occasionally anchored by short, blue phrases—almost desolate sighs—and that would move up steadily from plane to plane. His high notes, which drew lightly on his rich, natural, homemade tone, were eventually used for grandstand effects, but in the early thirties they were effortless reachings toward a majesty that jazz had not yet imagined. Armstrong's outpouring emotion was universal. Some players restrict themselves to melancholy or bravado or comedy, but Armstrong seemed to cover the spectrum in a grand, warm presidential fashion. There were peaks and cloud kingdoms and heavenly pastures in his playing that summoned the listener, elated him, and sent him on his way a better man.

Some of the edifying moments occur on the Victor reissue—namely, in "St. Louis Blues," which Armstrong somehow always gives a national-anthem treatment, in "I've Got the World on a String," and in "Honey Do," all of which were recorded in 1933. Much of the rest of the material, recorded nearly fifteen years later, is indifferent. The early forties were an uncertain time for him, and it was not until late in 1947, when he brought together Jack Teagarden, Barney Bigard, Earl Hines, and Sidney Catlett, that he regained his early brilliance. (There is a sad photograph, taken at a 1944 concert, of Armstrong and Roy Eldridge seated side by side. Eldridge was at the peak of his powers and looks radiant, while Armstrong, temporarily flummoxed by changing musical fashions, looks cadaverous and beat.)

The fifties passed well for Armstrong. Although his band tended to decline steadily—Catlett was replaced by Cozy Cole, Teagarden by Trummy Young, and Hines by Billy Kyle—he remained constant. This is clear in at least a dozen of the selections in the Decca album. One, "King of the Zulus," is done with his own band, and it is superb. Playing in a legato, low-toned way, he constructs a series of seemingly lazy, halting phrases that rival anything he has recorded. They have a relentless but insouciant urgency. The rest of the good selections offer Armstrong in his best setting—with a big band that supplies plenty of supporting organ chords. All are remakes of numbers originally re- corded in the thirties, and there are wonderful patches—the drama of "Song of the Islands" and "Some of These Days," his muted choruses in "Lazy River" and "I Surrender Dear" and "Exactly Like You." Moreover, his voice, which has put on a lot of weight over the years, is well controlled and wholly free of vaudeville effects.

So Armstrong goes on and on. It is hard to under- stand why he behaves when he appears in person like a blackface minstrel. He must be weary, and perhaps this sort of posing is a prop, or perhaps he doesn't even realize he is doing it anymore. Or perhaps it is just his New Orleans "evil" coming out. It doesn't matter. The old Armstrong— the inventor, the beautifier, the champion of emotion—lives safely within.

# Mecca, La.

The first jazz I heard —recordings by Louis Armstrong's Hot Five and Jelly Roll Morton's Red Hot Peppers—hurt my ears. Then I read "Jazzmen," a pioneering history published by Harcourt, Brace in the late thirties, and the pain vanished. Like Thomas Wolfe, "Jazzmen" should be read at sixteen or seventeen and never again. A collection of articles by nine enthusiasts, it offers an irresistible all-American myth of New Orleans as a wild, dark pantheon, roamed by gods like Buddy Bolden, the first celebrated jazz musician, who achieved immortality by going mad during a parade in 1907. Then I discovered that New Orleans jazz was out of fashion. It sank in my estimation beneath swing and the subsequent cities of bebop, cool jazz, and hard bop, and it was an atavistic shock when the current New Orleans revival began a few years ago. (Bebop jammed my senses when the first revival, centered on the trumpeter Bunk Johnson, flared up in the mid-forties.) I had thought that jazz had pretty much died out in New Orleans when Storyville, its notorious red-light district, was closed in 1917, forcing the musicians it helped support to migrate North. But the present revival, it appears, is being carried forward by musicians who have been playing in New Orleans ever since. Many of them are in their sixties or seventies, some are in their eighties, and a few have passed ninety. As the number of new New Orleans recordings swelled, I suspected that the old myth was simply being dusted off and revised. The liner notes on these recordings revere unfamiliar musicians like Sweet Emma Barrett, Kid Thomas, and De De Pierce, new brass bands, and upstart musical temples like Preservation Hall and Dixieland Hall, but their hyperbole is familiar, and with good reason—it is often the work of the surviving contributors to "Jazzmen." Most indicative, the music on the records, though almost always honest-sounding, is rough and halting and frequently out of tune. It could have been recorded in 1925, or even in 1915.

I went to New Orleans not long ago in an effort to find out whether this new edition of the myth has the salt of the old one. I had written to Richard Allen, the curator of the Archive of New Orleans Jazz, at Tulane University, and asked if he would shepherd me around, and he had replied that he would be delighted to. His letter continued, "I am afraid that I do not spend too much time around Preservation Hall or Dixieland Hall, but since a new hall, Southland Jazz Club, has recently opened, I have attempted to give it some of my support until it becomes established. You are fortunate that you are arriving on Saturday, as there is to be a concert on Sunday in the Grand Salon of the Royal Orleans Hotel. A parade will precede it. I hope that we will be able to find some jazz in less commercial surroundings. I frankly have grown allergic to tourists by this time, and enjoy getting away from the French Quarter to brass-band functions, rehearsals, and dance halls."

A few minutes after I had checked into my motel, in the Quarter, Allen telephoned and asked if I was too tired to hear some music. I said I wasn't, and he told me, in a measured Southern drawl, that a band led by a white trumpet player named Tony Fougerat was playing a one-night stand in Munster's. "Munster's is near the river-front, in a section we call the Irish Channel, about sixty blocks from the Quarter," he said. "It's a workingman's neighborhood, and it might be a little rough, but it should have a lot of the atmosphere of the cabarets Buddy Bolden and Joe Oliver worked in."

Allen picked me up in a cab. He is short, round, and bullet-headed, and has thick, graying hair. His face is placid and intelligent. "Hello and good evening, as we say in New Orleans," he said, shaking hands. He had two umbrellas with him, and he handed me one. "The rainy season is upon us," he said. "You'll need this every day."

The French Quarter smells even older than the narrow streets behind the Fulton Fish Market, but the Garden District, which we drove through on our way to Munster's, is full of trees and grass and big, ornate houses, and it smelled green and fresh. Allen pointed out the window at a white blur and said, "I think either that house or the one just around the corner is where Joe Oliver worked as a butler before he went to Chicago in 1918. But I really don't care. It's not the places here that interest me as much as the people. Fougerat, who is sixty-six, is something of a rarity. He played with Papa Jack Laine, who is in his nineties, and who probably had the first white jazz band. He also recorded with Jimmie Rodgers, the old hillbilly singer. Fougerat is an insurance man by trade, but he still plays a lot. He might have a white trombonist with him named Red Margiotta, who's about the same age. Margiotta's right arm is amputated just below the elbow, but that doesn't bother his playing. Munster's is a white bar, and

Negroes aren't welcome. But desegregation is better here than most people think. There never *have* been any truly segregated neighborhoods, and the big hotels, like the Royal Orleans, have been open to Negroes for four or five years. Dizzy Gillespie stayed there a little while ago. The first Negro to eat in the Rib Room in the Orleans is supposed to have left a fifty-dollar tip, and there hasn't been any trouble since. The public swimming pools will be re-opened this summer, but the schools are still a problem."

Our cabdriver, who was a Negro, said, "There's a white private school established here in the Garden District after the Supreme Court decision, and it's so crowded it's spread between two residences about a mile apart." He laughed. "Man, there's a lot of bussing goes on."

Munster's Bar proved to be in a low cement-block building. The air inside was rigid with smoke and the smell of beer. A bar stretched along one wall, and plastic-topped tables were ranged loosely around the three other walls. Large coat hooks stuck out from the walls like elephant ears. The room, which had a cement floor, was jammed with stolid-faced dancers of every age. A tall, red-haired girl hung over an old Brueghel type. A thin elderly lady was with a stocky young man. Some of the dancers were in work clothes, and some were in their Sunday best. Allen led the way to the rear of the room. Fougerat, who has a pleasant, angular face, was seated against the wall, and was deep in "Margie." Margiotta had his trombone tucked deftly under his stump, and his bald head and red face glistened as he played. A beefy drummer with a big Roman nose was drawn up to a historic set of traps made up entirely of a small bass drum, a cymbal, and a snare drum. A bassist and a guitarist, both of them weathered and lanky, rounded out the group. All were in shirtsleeves. Fougerat nodded to Allen and indicated a table near the bandstand. The band broke into "Lazy River."

A lean, brown-faced man with a shock of beautiful white hair bumped against our table. He reared back and smiled widely at us and at a tiny old woman with him. "I'm only seventy-five," he said, and swayed away. A fat-armed, round-shouldered woman in a silk dress and harlequin glasses stood in front of the band, alternately singing and conducting. Her voice was sweet and quavery. "I used to have my own band!" she shouted at Allen. "I could sing like Helen Morgan then, but who cares now?" She shifted into a heavy, one-footed dance, her arms held out like a gull's wings, her fingers snapping. A young man with flat black hair unpacked an accordion and joined the band. The band and the dancers were matched in a way I had never seen before; each group seemed an extension of the other. The music was primitive, unhurried, and perfectly executed. The improvisation was limited to gentle variations and formal flourishes. The tempos were medium, and the tunes ranged from "Girl of My Dreams" to "Hello, Dolly." Fougerat is a blunt, homemade trumpeter. His phrases are short, and his tone is heavy and dark. Like most New Orleans trumpeters, he doesn't solo much. Margiotta does, however, and he delights in melody. His tone is pure and plaintive, and he sounds like a mannerly Kid Ory. The accordionist comfortably plugged the chinks in the ensemble, and the rhythm section kept strict two-beat time.

Allen, who had been rocking discreetly back and forth in his chair, suddenly excused himself and asked Helen Morgan to dance. They moved off to the middle of the floor, and Allen began a slow-motion Twist. The drummer, relinquishing his seat to an intense young man, sat down with me, and mopped his forehead. He was chewing tobacco.

"That snare drum, the strings they come loose on it," he said, in a curious French-Italian accent. "So I have a tomtom instead of a snare. I ask the bartender for a little piece string. No string. I ask Fougerat. No string." He shrugged. "I live fifty miles from here, in Raceland, up Bayou Lafourche way. Raceland, she has the longest main street in the world —thirty-seven miles. I go home tonight, sleep two hours, go to choich, and in the evening show a quarter horse." He shrugged again, got up, and cut in on a plump woman.

Allen sat down. He was beaming. "This is it, isn't it? This is how it all began. A classic atmosphere."

When we left, around one o'clock, the dance floor was crowded and the band sounded fresh. Helen Morgan was singing "Bye Bye Blackbird."

I got to the junction of Basin Street and Canal Street, where the parade was forming, at two o'clock Sunday afternoon. It was warm and sunny, and there were two brass bands—the Onward and the Eureka. I found Allen in a swarm of musicians and onlookers. He had on dark glasses and was carrying a clipboard. "Hello and good day," he said. "I'm one of the sponsors of this affair—it's a Heart Fund benefit—and I have to show Danny Barker, who's the marshal of the Onward Brass Band, the route we are taking to the Royal Orleans. He's a little out of practice. He only moved back to New Orleans six or seven months ago."

Barker, a Negro, has spent most of his career in the North—as a big-band guitarist (Benny Carter and Cab Calloway) and a small-band banjoist (Wilbur de Paris). He has also spent a good part of it writing an enormous autobiography, which, though unpublished, has long been regarded by students of jazz as an invaluable lode of New

Orleania. I hadn't seen him for ten years, but he looked about the same—lean, stooped, his smile crooked and mischievous. He had on a Madras jacket, dark pants, and dark glasses, and he was holding a straw hat. A heavy multicolored sash across his chest seemed to increase his stoop.

"The Eureka Brass Band has Fats Houston as grand marshal," Allen said. "Both bands are running a little large —ten or eleven men. Louis Cottrell and Willie Humphrey are on clarinets and Louis Nelson and Jim Robinson on trombones. Louis Barbarin, Danny Barker's uncle, is on snare with the Onward, and Peter Bocage, who played with Bolden, is on trumpet with the Eureka. He's in his late seventies. The youngest men are Milton Batiste, a trumpeter, and Keith Smith, an English trumpeter who's been here several weeks. English musicians come to New Orleans by the drove and support themselves however they can, and when they've had their fill they go home. It's their Mecca."

Each band fell into rough ranks. The trombonists were first, and the drummers brought up the rear, behind the trumpeters. The two groups had identical uniforms— dark caps, white shirts and dark ties, and dark pants. Allen stationed himself near Barker, and the Onward burst into "Bye and Bye" and started down Canal Street. The Eureka marched in silence not far behind. The second line—a name given to the dancers who appear from the woodwork for every parade in New Orleans, and whose agility and beauty are barometers of the quality of the music—had already collected in front of the Onward. Most of its members were young Negro men. They were dressed in singlets and shorts and sneakers, and half a dozen of them were carrying the traditional open umbrellas. The Onward gathered steam slowly, and so did the dancers. They shuffled along the pavement pigeon-toed, their arms bent and held close to their sides, their umbrellas at shoulder arms. Then the band found its groove, and the dancers obliged. Their knees shot up like those of broken-field runners, and some of them spun around, their hips rotating. They moved up onto their toes, came together in an undulating, umbrella-bumping mass, flew apart, and came together again. A stream of onlookers moved along on each side of the street, carrying with it an Iowa-type matron who jiggled like a truck, and an aristocratic New Orleanian who let loose a skip every ten feet or so.

The Onward fell silent, and the Eureka took up "Bye and Bye." The second line split in two, raced back up the street, and re-formed in front of the Eureka. Two tiny Negro boys in gray business suits joined the dancers, and so did two women. One was fat and gray and had an enormous bust, which moved oceanically. The other was tall and hawk-nosed and rodlike. The large woman rolled and swayed, the thin one moved as if she were on a pogo stick. A beautiful young Negro woman in a close-fitting blue dress danced up to the gray-haired woman, laughed, and said, "They always ask who taught me to dance—ho, ho." Her name, I learned later, is Ellyna Tatum, and she is a breathtaking dancer. Leaning backward, she did a steady, rolling shimmy, her knees bent and her toes curling down. Her arms crooked and uncrooked, and her head, tilted slightly forward, snapped gently from side to side. All the while, she sang in a fine, clear voice. Now and then a couple of men would dance up to her and around her, making mock bows. She would flow between them, and they would peel away, very low to the ground.

Allen held up his left hand, and Barker, who was slippering along backward with a bemused expression, turned into Royal Street, which is narrow and was filled with parked cars. The parade poured into the street like lava. Natives clapped in time on their wrought-iron balconies, and tourists, clustered in the doorways of antique shops, blinked. Royal Street had a miraculous effect on the music. (The Onward was playing "When the Saints Go Marching In.") The walls of the houses collected and compressed it, and the volume doubled. The musicians, probably hearing themselves clearly for the first time, reacted accordingly. The trumpeters let loose a series of high, glistening notes, and the drummers took up the tempo. The second line, squeezed into a space roughly ten feet square, danced perpendicularly, umbrellas chopping up and down. At Toulouse Street, Allen halted the parade, glanced at his watch, and consulted his clipboard. He looked like an official at a track meet. The Onward was playing "Victory Walk," an engaging stop-time number. Like every number played during the parade, it was an extraordinary collective scramble. The nearest thing to a solo was a snare-and-bass-drum duet by Louis Barbarin and Chester Jones. Barbarin played loose, galloping, marching figures while Jones dropped in jarring single and double offbeats. It was superb counterpoint in which the two men at once challenged and supported each other. The rest of the number was given over to intricate, heaving polyphony that suggested Charlie Mingus's more ambitious ensemble ventures. With the exception of several choruses of plunging, bowsprit riffs, each horn went its own way. The trombones snaked ceaselessly around each other, staying just above the sousaphone. The tenor saxophone provided a central monotone, and the trumpeters took turns carrying the lead. Occasionally, one of them would lean back and fire directly at the sky. The clarinet fluttered and swooped and dived. It was a gorgeous rug of sound.

Allen gave a Teddy Roosevelt charge signal, and

the parade oozed around the block, paused briefly in front of the Royal Orleans, and suddenly turned into a flood. The second line swept into the hotel, laughing and whirling and dancing. I caught a glimpse of Allen and Barker sailing through the doorway. Dancers, musicians, and onlookers shot through the dark, cool lobby, leaped like salmon up a couple of flights of stairs, and flowed down a luxuriously carpeted hallway to the door of the Grand Salon, where the whole mass broke over a couple of ladies who were shouting, "No one allowed in without a ticket! No one allowed in without a ticket!" Most of the second line couldn't meet the tab, which was two dollars and fifty cents, and, slowly subsiding, it washed casually down the stairs and onto the street. The bands marched into the Grand Salon—a large, mirrored room full of pillars, draperies, chandeliers, and blue-haired women—and formed a long line in front of the bandstand occupied by a sedate-looking group that included George Lewis (clarinet), Punch Miller and Kid Thomas (trumpets), Cie Frazier (drums), and De De and Billie Pierce (cornet and piano). All three bands roared through a short "St. Louis Blues," which visibly shook the watching cheeks and jowls. Then the Onward and the Eureka blew their way out of the Grand Salon, and the concert began. After the brass and the sun and the dancing, it was a letdown. The music sounded thin and mossy, and it seemed to get entangled in the chandeliers, which repeatedly changed color, and in the massed blue hair. Things toned up considerably when the Onward marched back in, played "When the Saints," and marched out again. I marched out after them, and found Allen by the door.

"Enjoy yourself?" he asked me.

I said the parade had been magnificent and the concert disconsolate.

"But I was glad to see Punch Miller," he said. "Punch

is seventy-two, and he hasn't been well. He came to talk and play at my Wednesday-evening lecture last week, and during a number that reminded him of his childhood he got so sad he broke down and cried right in class. It was pretty upsetting, and I'm worried about him."

Allen had told me that New Orleanians in general don't care about jazz. I stopped in at the New Orleans Tourist Commission on the way back to my motel and asked a pigeon-shaped woman behind a desk where I might hear some good jazz. She looked startled. "I'm sorry, but we can't help you. We don't have anything on jazz."

I had asked Allen on Saturday if he knew someone who could show me what was left of the New Orleans of "Jazzmen," and he had suggested Manuel Manetta. Manetta, he told me, is at least seventy-eight and is a Creole of color, as they say in New Orleans. Manetta plays several instruments, but he is primarily a teacher; his pupils have included Wingy Manone, Red Allen, Kid Rena, and Emmett Hardy, the last of whom is said to have influenced Bix Beiderbecke. He played with Buddy Bolden in 1904, with Frankie Dusen's Eagle Band in 1909, for Lulu White, the celebrated octoroon who ran Lulu White's Mahogany Hall, on Basin Street, in 1910, and with Kid Ory and King Oliver in 1916. "I don't know if Manetta—or Professor Manetta, as I call him—will take you," Allen had said. "But we'll go and see him across the river in Algiers anyway. Negroes haven't been riding in cabs with white people all that long, and he might feel uneasy about it. But he might ride with his old friend Louis Kohlman, a Negro who runs a cab in Algiers."

Manetta's house is small and gray, and beside it stands his studio, a high, oblong structure on stilts. He was in the studio, sitting on a piano stool and smoking a cigarette. A tan fedora with a brim as wide as a running board rested on the keys of a yellow-and-black upright, and he was dressed in a brown business suit and a green sports shirt. Allen and I sat down, and Manetta handed me his card, which read:

"Fess" M. Manetta's
Master of All Instruments

He has a hound-dog face, with a pendulous lower lip that folds up like a drawbridge. His voice is low, and he speaks slowly. He obviously delights in keeping his fires carefully damped. He and Allen exchanged pleasantries for about ten minutes, and then he told Allen, "I don't take but three or four pupils a week now. I stopped regular teaching about four years ago. When I was young, the piano was considered a lady's instrument, a sissy job. I wanted to play the piano, but I didn't have the spunk. Then, one night, my brother took me to the Ping Pong Club, near here, on Brooklyn Street, to hear Gussie Neil. He was playing in the back room, and I couldn't get over it. My eyes were popping. I'd seen a man *could* play the piano and not be made fun of, and when I got home I took a big old lantern and crept into the parlor to the piano and sat there picking out tunes until my brother got home, and said, 'Hey, it's five o'clock. What you doin', Fess?' Well, I been doing it ever since." Manetta gave a soundless chuckle and lit another cigarette. "It's still there, the Ping Pong Club."

I asked Manetta what he remembered about Buddy Bolden, who died in an insane asylum in 1931.

"The first time I saw Bolden was at the Odd Fellows Hall, on Seguin Street. That's gone now. Frank Lewis was

Bolden's regular clarinettist, but he took sick, and Alphonse Picou, who passed just a little while back, came in for the night. He was just about white, and it caused a stir. 'Oh, say, Buddy's got a white man playing with him' was all they could say. Bolden was a ragtime player. Very powerful, but he could play those little trills and runs, too. He was a very nice, fine gentleman, and the ladies' favorite of nights."

Allen laughed, and said, "That reminds me of when I had my record shop on Baronne Street in the fifties, not long after I came down here. The bass player Albert Glenny, who also played with Bolden, came in one day, and I said, 'You must be about the last surviving member of Buddy Bolden's band.' Glenny turned and pointed at the street. 'See that man standing over there at the bus stop? *He* play with Bolden, too.' And he was right. Glenny was a funny man. Another time, a woman asked him for his autograph, and he thanked her and said no, he couldn't do that. 'When I went to school,' he told her, 'they didn't teach us to read and write.' Of course, that would have been in the eighteen-seventies."

There was a knock, and a short man of about fifty with a big paunch and an amiable face came in. "Hey, Fess, how are you feeling?" he said. His voice went falsetto. "Teacher, I'm a little late for my lesson and I forgot my clarinet." He and Manetta laughed and embraced. He turned out to be a former pupil of Manetta's—Freddie Kohlman, a drummer, who has worked in Chicago for the past ten years or so. He is Louis Kohlman's son.

Allen mentioned the tour to Manetta for the first time, and then explained to Kohlman what we had in mind.

Manetta looked guarded, and Kohlman said he'd drive us to his father's house. "I don't know where he's at, but maybe he's left word. Anyway, Fess and I got to arrange about a get-together Thursday."

When we reached the Kohlman house, Freddie Kohlman's mother, who is handsome and bespectacled, offered us a drink in her parlor.

"I'll have just a tall glass of water with a taste of that good stuff in it, and a little sugar," Manetta said. "Freddie knows what I take."

"Fess, you got to hear Mama play her new electric organ," Kohlman said.

Mrs. Kohlman giggled, sat down at a small organ, and played "I'm Getting Sentimental Over You" in a dirge tempo. Manetta stood behind her and coached: "Get at those quarter notes, now. Get at those quarter notes."

"Now, that's what I'm having trouble with," Mrs. Kohlman replied as she played. "My time. I can't seem to get my time right."

When she finished, Kohlman said, "Fess, you know who came by my place in Chicago the other night and sat in? Lil Armstrong. She still plays very powerful piano."

"I first got acquainted with Lil in 1931," Manetta said. "She was married to Louis Armstrong then. Louis had a contract uptown here. I went to see him backstage, and he was shut up in this little bathroom trying to play two trumpets at once, like I used to do." Manetta dropped his voice and growled like Armstrong. " 'Hey, Fess. Hey, Fess. How you do that? Show me how you do that. How you play those two horns at once?' He put the horns back to his mouth and blew, and nothing happened. 'Show me, Fess. Show me.' Well, I tried, but he never learned." Manetta laughed, and finished his drink.

Kohlman senior arrived, a medium-sized man with short, grizzled hair, and ten minutes later he and Allen and

I were waiting in his cab for Manetta, who was standing on the sidewalk talking to Freddie Kohlman.

"They're still setting up their Thursday meeting," Allen said.

"What'll they have left to talk about?" I asked.

"Oh, no trouble. They'll talk about today and the old days and tomorrow."

Manetta heaved himself into the back seat. We passed the Ping Pong Club, a dishevelled one-story building that looked deserted, and recrossed the Mississippi. Kohlman is a cautious driver, and he threaded his way through the tollgate at the bridge as if it were the eye of a needle. We turned off the Pontchartrain Expressway and found Simon Bolivar Avenue. "It's pronounced Salmon Boulevard hereabouts," Allen said. "Just as Socrates Street, in Algiers, is pronounced So-crate-eez, and Tchoupitoulas Street, where Frank Lewis lived, is Chapatoola. Turn into First Street, Mr. Kohlman."

The houses on First Street were low and scattered and dilapidated. The dirt sidewalks were crowded with telephone poles and children. Shaking his head, Kohlman said, "This place ain't changed a bit. Not one bit in fifty, sixty years."

Manetta, who had had a second taste before leaving Kohlman's house, looked shrunken and sleepy beneath his enormous hat.

"There's where Buddy Bolden lived," Allen said, motioning toward a squat brown house. A woman was standing dimly behind a screen door. "This was his address in the city directory for 1902." The screen door opened, and for a second I expected Bolden, who would be in his late eighties, to step out. But it was the woman, carrying a basket of clothes.

We passed Nelson Joseph's Shaving Parlor, where musicians had often been hired. On Danneel Street, which was the old Rampart Street, Kohlman pointed out the Joseph P. Geddes Funeral Home. "That's been there as long as I can remember," he said.

We stopped in front of a big two-story building with a stucco Spanish façade. "This was the Bulls' Club," Allen said. "It now belongs to the Elks. We call that three-story rise sticking up at its rear a camel's back."

Manetta opened his eyes and sat forward. "I played here with Chris Kelly, the trumpeter," he said. "He never recorded, but he was a great blues player. One night, he hired this boy Earl Humphrey on trombone. He still around, ain't he, Mr. Allen?"

"He played in the Heart Fund parade on Sunday," Allen said.

"Humphrey and Kelly were gettin' at each other that evening, I guess over money, and they came out in front right there, and Humphrey was full of wine and lost his mind and picked up a brick from the banquette, which is what we called the old raised sidewalks, and hit Kelly right on the side of his eye. Kelly fell down, and there was a lot of blood, but he was a tough fellow and he went back and finished the night, bandages and all."

We came to a three-story stone building. "Isn't that Masonic Hall, once the Eagle Saloon?" Allen asked Manetta.

Manetta grunted. "Frankie Dusen, Bolden's trombonist, played here every Saturday night, after he'd taken over Bolden's band and it became the Eagle Band. Fellow called Smith ran the hall. He had a floorwalker named Bob Foots, who wore size-fourteen shoes. Foots was a stick-beater, carried a police nightstick to keep down the fights.

And over behind those new buildings—that's the Civic Center now—over there was the Battlefield. A very tough area. Ma Rainey, the blues singer, used to go back in there and work. And right on the edge of it was Louis Armstrong's stamping ground, and the parish prison."

"And that was Chinatown," Allen said, waving toward a group of buildings near Masonic Hall. "Kid Sheik, the trumpet player, told me the sidewalks would be covered with Chinamen, stretched out in the sun like alligators, smoking hop."

We turned into Iberville Street, which had been the northern boundary of Storyville. A raw-looking housing development covers it now.

"Oh, man, I like to see all these demolishings," Manetta said, and sighed. "It's a *new* world."

Allen asked Manetta if any cribs were left. Cribs were rows of small rooms, giving directly off the sidewalk, where the low-priced prostitutes worked.

"No, they all gone," Manetta said. "They was mostly over on Gravier Street. A short-time trick was fifty cents, and rolling around was a dollar a shot. Right down there, on St. Peter Street, in that old building, was my headquarters, where all my musicians hung out." He pointed into the housing development. "And I had a girl, she lived right about there."

We came to the intersection of Basin Street and St. Peter Street. A partly dismantled brick building stands on one corner. "That's what's left of Lulu White's saloon," Allen said. "Her Mahogany Hall was right next to it, where you see the Krauss department store's garage. It didn't come down too long ago. That park over there is Beauregard Square. A hundred years ago, it was Congo Square, and the slaves danced there on Saturday nights. George Washington Cable has written about it."

Manetta yawned.

"You getting tired, Professor Manetta?" Allen asked. Manetta nodded.

"Mr. Kohlman, please leave us off at Chartres and St. Philip, in the Quarter," Allen said.

I paid Kohlman and thanked Manetta. He smiled, and the two men drove away. Only Manetta's hat was visible through the rear window.

After dinner, I persuaded Allen to show me Preservation Hall. It is on St. Peter Street, just below Bourbon Street, in a typical gravy-colored, two-story Quarter house, complete with tall, shuttered windows, a wrought-iron balcony, and a carriageway leading to a back garden. An old trombone case with the word "Preservation" on it in brass letters hangs above the carriageway entrance, and suspended from it is a smaller case, lettered "Hall." The hall, which we looked into from the carriageway, has a high ceiling and is roughly fifty feet square. A bandstand on the street side faces half a dozen rows of benches. There are cushions on the floor between the benches and the stand. The walls are grimy and the floorboards give. Gloomy paintings of musicians hang just below the ceiling. A tubby, stubbled man with wild hair and sleepy eyes joined us in the carriageway. Allen introduced him as Allan Jaffe, the operator of the hall, and then excused himself and said he was going home to bed. I told Allen I would stop by Tulane in the morning to see him.

Jaffe and I sat down on an ornate wooden bench set against one wall of the carriageway. It had three or four gracefully curved armrests. "I bought this beauty, which is a pew, along with a lot of others, from the Church of the Good Shepherd, uptown, before it was torn down," he told me. "It's cypress. I was going to furnish the hall with them, but I was afraid they'd get carved up. We've got a good band tonight—Kid Thomas on trumpet, and George Lewis and Louis Nelson. They start around eight-thirty and finish around midnight. We take contributions at the door—a dollar a head minimum. And we don't serve liquor."

I asked Jaffee how long he had run the hall.

"My wife and I quit our jobs in Philadelphia and moved to New Orleans in 1961," he said. "Sam Charters' New Orleans recordings gave us hope that things were coming to life. We lived next door to Dick Allen, and he suggested to Larry Borenstein, who owns this building, that we take over the informal sessions that were being given here. The hall was an art gallery then. We didn't have any big bang at first. New Orleans doesn't support its own music. It took two years to get the place going even on a month-to-month basis. In the early days, a sideman got thirteen-fifty a night and the leader twenty-six. Now the leader gets thirty dollars and a sideman twenty-fifty."

A tall man with a fringe of white hair, taped-up glasses, and a book in his hand came and sat down beside Jaffe. Jaffe introduced him as Bill Russell, and then said he had to leave us and start taking contributions.

Russell was one of the authors of "Jazzmen." He is a composer, musicologist, and critic, and some of his early jazz criticism is definitive. He was largely responsible for the Bunk Johnson revival, and he has been a kind of amanuensis to Mahalia Jackson. Since 1942, he has spent most of his time in New Orleans, where, in addition to making and selling records, he has amassed an enormous

316

amount of research material on the early musicians. He has biographies of Manetta and Johnson under way. By reputation, he is a lone wolf, an ascetic, and a mild anarchist. He has a gentle, caved-in face, and is a non-stop professorial talker.

"I often open up the Hall at night," he said, taking off his glasses. "I do it to pay back Jaffe, who takes care of Pretty Baby, my parakeet, when I'm away. Pretty Baby —he's named after a Tony Jackson tune—is ten, and if he's lucky he'll live to be twenty. I feed him nothing but vegetables and greens. I live upstairs, and pay Larry Borenstein rent by giving his wife and kid violin lessons."

I asked Russell if the musicians involved in the current New Orleans revival had been simply unable to make the grade up North.

"Yes, by and large they were. But there were a lot of others who just wouldn't leave the city or who died before they got the chance. Joe Oliver tried to get Bunk to join him in Chicago, but Bunk wouldn't go. The music has never died out in New Orleans—even in 1959 and 1960, when Kid Thomas, who's one of my particular favorites, had the only regular band here. During the Depression, there was a one-hundred-piece W.P.A. band. It had twenty trumpeters alone in it. It would break into groups, and they'd play. Most of the musicians had day jobs, too, and many still do. On my second visit to New Orleans, in the early forties, I ran all over the city on trolleys and buses looking for old musicians I'd heard were playing in out-of-the-way places, but I missed a lot of them. Papa Celestin was alive then, and so were Alphonse Picou and Big Eye Louis Nelson, the clarinettists, and Charlie Love, the trumpeter. Tom Brown, who took the first jazz band North, in 1915, was, too. Between 1900 and 1910, New Orleans was twenty years ahead of its time musically. The city was filled with music. When you opened a store or restaurant, you hired a band. When you had a birthday party, you hired a band. Bands advertised their own dances in the streets and then played at them. There was music between the rounds at prizefights. Bands would be made up on the spot out of musicians who rode the old Smoky Mary, a train that ran from near the French Market to Lake Pontchartrain, where there was always a great demand for music."

"I've always wondered if Buddy Bolden had a first-rate predecessor—a kind of Essenic teacher," I said.

"Well, I've looked into that, and all I can find out is that there might have been a guitar player named Happy Galloway. Mutt Carey, the trumpeter, and Bud Scott, the banjoist, mentioned him when I was in California in 1939. Bolden *is* a legend, but sheer massed opinion among the musicians I've talked to who heard him makes it certain that he was good. The tales of his sexual prowess probably stem from the peculiar legend that all trumpet players are oversexed. Bolden may have learned a lot of his music in church, but I don't think it was instrumental music. I once asked the late Baby Dodds about music in the churches here, and he said, 'There was no music, no music, just singing.' Dodds was a purist. He often said the main job of the snare drummer in a brass band is to shade the band—make it play soft or loud, as the need arises. He considered it neurotic to have your name on your bass drum, and he would never use a snare drum that even had paint on it, because he thought the paint would affect the tone." Russell paused for a few moments, and then went on, "Lately, I have been getting disgusted with the way the bands play in the streets. Bunk Johnson played eight-hour parades almost up to the time of his death, in 1949, and he never put his horn down once. Now one or another of the trumpet players is always resting, and sometimes the drums stop altogether. And there are strings of solos, like an Eddie Condon jam session. And what business has a saxophone in a brass band? I can't believe that anyone would be that insensitive. In the old days, the leader never wanted to be a star. In the old days, it was always 'our band.' "

The music had begun, and Russell and I went in and stood at the back of the hall. The cushions and the benches were all occupied, and the standees were three deep. The audience was middle-aged, white, and easy to please. When Kid Thomas managed a triplet, it clapped; when Emmanuel Paul, the tenor saxophonist, held a single note for four measures, it clapped (I wondered how it would react to the twelve-chorus tremolo that Earl Hines tosses in at the end of his "St. Louis Blues"); when George Lewis interpolated the melody of "Oh, They Don't Wear Pants in the Southern Part of France" in a solo, it laughed uproariously. It was hard to see the musicians. Their color and their everyday clothes made them seem part of the décor. The most frequent soloists were Lewis, who is a thin, sweet embellisher, and Paul, who veered continually between the young Coleman Hawkins and a country-club saxophonist. Thomas is a rough, steady performer whose occasional solos reminded me of Yank Lawson, and Louis Nelson is a plank-by-plank melodist. The drummer's time suggested a roller coaster. The band sounded best collectively, when, leaning together like the old houses in the Quarter, it achieved a dense, hymnlike texture that reached affecting heights in soft versions of "Bye Bye Blackbird" and "Just a Closer Walk with Thee."

Most of the audience left at the end of the set. About half bought records at a rack in the carriageway and asked the musicians to autograph them. In five minutes, the hall filled again. Russell had slipped away, but I found Jaffe by the door, and said good night. He held a basket on his lap, like a woman shelling peas. It was brimming with money.

Outside, I was hit by a blast of music from across the street. It was coming from the new Southland Jazz Club. I gave a donation at the door to a peppy blonde in sneakers who resembled a gym teacher. She told me that George Finola was on cornet and Raymond Burke on clarinet. She also told me that Finola worshipped Bix Beiderbecke, that he was only twenty, and that he was from Chicago. She said that Danny Barker was a regular performer, but that he was home ill. The differences between Preservation Hall and the Southland were startling. The band was mixed (Finola and Burke white, and the trombonist, the pianist, and the drummer Negro), the audience was skimpy but mixed, and the room, about two-thirds as big as Preservation Hall, was full of fresh paint and good cheer. So was the music. Finola, who is thin and intense, is surprising. He has Beiderbecke's blessed tone, but he is freer rhythmically. His solos *rush* out of him, and are highly inventive. Burke, who has a reputation that is partly the result of his refusing to leave New Orleans, fits perfectly with Finola, for he resembles Beiderbecke's old friend Pee Wee Russell, minus Russell's stylistic kinks.

Deciding to finish off the big three in one swat, I worked my way several blocks up Bourbon Street, through knots of glass-carrying tourists, to Dixieland Hall. I was greeted there by the Southland gym teacher, who said she liked to help out wherever she could. She gave me a personnel list, and also a folder which stated that Dixieland Hall was founded in 1962, that "numerous television and movie stars flocked to hear its music and enjoy its fantastic 'good-time' atmosphere," and that it is "the only place on Bourbon Street where children may be brought to see and hear in person the old-time bands of New Orleans." Its décor—wooden benches, a peeling ceiling, and an out-of-tune upright—was Preservation Hall, but the band, led by the drummer Paul Barbarin, played with style and verve. Barbarin, who worked with Luis Russell in the early thirties, when Russell had the hottest band in New York, is compact and fierce-looking, and he blew the band along. New Orleans drummers tend to become hypnotized by their snare drums, lavishing on them endless press rolls and barn-door rim-shots. But Barbarin, in addition to a marvellous press roll, in which his sticks come at one another low from opposite edges of the snare in fat blurs, like gulls after the same clam, uses a high hat and ride cymbals to excellent effect. He also flashes about between his snare and his tomtoms, and during a brief ensemble pause in "Bill Bailey, Won't You Please Come Home" he got off a lightning multidrum *poorum* that left him nodding with satisfaction. Louis Cottrell, his clarinettist, is a liquid performer who bastes his melodies, and Ernie Caglanatti, his trumpeter, is a tiny, contented-looking man who admires Red Allen. The Luis Russell band, with Barbarin at the helm, must have been a wonder.

The music was still charging around my mind as a taxi took me to Tulane the next morning, and so was a brief conversation I'd had at Dixieland Hall with a sociologist from Minnesota who told me he had been listening to jazz for forty years. "New Orleans jazz has never got over its marching-band origins," he said during an intermission. "It's still a communal music. And since communal projects, in order to remain communal, abhor the star system, it is also a mediocre music. Of course, this can be comforting, for mediocrity en masse often fools itself as well as its audience. But a superior talent wrecks this cozy ménage, which is why Armstrong and Red Allen and Jelly Roll Morton broke so quickly with their collective origins and became one-man bands. None of them were communal types, and none of them returned to New Orleans." He paused at this point and lit a small cigar. "I've noticed another striking, or diminishing, thing about New Orleans jazz. Its blues have as much color and life as lard. They have none of that old train-whistle keening you hear in Kansas City and New York blues. There aren't even any blue notes—the blue note being an anticommunity, unorthodox note. Maybe jazz was born in New Orleans, as the histories say, but it grew up elsewhere."

The Archive of New Orleans Jazz occupies a small, locked room on the third floor of the Howard-Tilton Memorial Library. Allen let me in, and handed me a sheet of paper headed "Statistical Summary of Holdings." The Archive, it revealed, possesses well over eleven thousand recordings, including twenty-four cylinders; thirty-nine piano rolls; almost nine thousand pieces of sheet music; fifteen hundred taped interviews; sixteen motion-picture reels; four thousand books, periodicals, catalogues, and microfilm rolls; and twelve thousand pieces of miscellany, among them posters, clippings, and photographs. Allen sat down next to a table cluttered with recording equipment, and fingered a pipe. "Bill Hogan, who's a professor of history here, got the ball rolling on all this," he said. "I'd talked to him in the late fifties about doing a thesis on recorded interviews with old jazz musicians. Bill Russell and I had already done a good many interviews on our own, but the cost was more than we could carry. Hogan knew the right people, and by 1958 we had a seventy-five-thousand-dollar grant from the Ford Foundation for starting the Archive. Russell was the first curator and I was his associate. The Foundation has given us over a hundred and fifty-six thousand dollars in all, but it's all gone, and now we're simply part of the library, which pays my salary. I took over in 1965. We can't afford to do much interviewing anymore, so now we're making digests of the tapes on hand. We used to make word-for-word transcriptions, but it was backbreaking—particularly with someone like Slow Drag Pavageau, the old bassist, who speaks an almost unbreakable code of Creole patois and consonantless English."

I remarked that Russell had been gloomy about the music in New Orleans.

Allen laughed. "Bill is always exercised over something, whether it's the Telephone Company or the deteriorating quality of Coca-Cola bottle caps," he said. "The number of brass bands *is* decreasing, and their personnels are often interchangeable. But there are new musicians coming up. I'm always meeting new faces. There may even be as many as twenty or thirty big bands—rock-'n'-roll and swing—which work occasionally in the city. Last week, I heard a marvellous band at Xavier University, and its best soloist, an alto saxophonist, is a *freshman*. And there is a scattering of modern groups. Ornette Coleman lived here a while back, before he got famous. Well, if you'll excuse me, I've got to prepare my weekly lecture. I have three or four students—doctors and the like—and I try to get musicians to talk to them. I've asked Tony Fougerat this week. Have you been to the New Orleans Jazz Museum, over in the Quarter? The director, Henry Clay Watson, may not know all that much about jazz, but he's a genuine, museum-trained museum man. Danny Barker and George Finola work there, too. Let's find some more non-tourist music to-night."

The museum is in a neat one-story brick building on Dumaine Street, and it is an appropriate setting for Watson, a short, precise, fluttery man who talks like an educated circus barker. "This is an institute of casual education," he told me. His hands were clasped across his stomach, and he moved steadily up and down on his toes. "We were founded in November of 1961 by the New Orleans Jazz Club, which still provides most of our support. Tulane is basically *oral* history survey. We are three-dimensional and *visual*. This is probably the smallest and most unique museum in the world. We have twenty to fifty times as much material in storage as is on display—*tons* of sheet music, beautiful William Sidney Mount prints, and the like. We have just acquired thirty full years of *Down Beat*. We are hunting desperately for storage area, and we may get a chance to move into an old bank building near the Royal Orleans Hotel. We authenticate every last piece of memorabilia that is given to us, and we—"

Watson was interrupted by a telephone call. I picked up a facsimile copy of the 1915 *Blue Book*, which the museum sells for five dollars. I remembered having read about the *Blue Book* in "Jazzmen." It was a guide to Storyville, which was probably the only legal enclave of prostitution ever set up in this country, and it listed the names and addresses of the prostitutes (white, octoroon, and colored) and was sprinkled with rosy advertisements for specific "sporting palaces." I turned to the preface:

This Directory and Guide of the Sporting District has been before the people on many occasions, and has proven its authority as to what is doing in the "Queer Zone."

Anyone who knows to-day from yesterday will say that the Blue Book is the right book for the right people.

WHY NEW ORLEANS SHOULD<br>HAVE THIS DIRECTORY

Because it is the only district of its kind in the States set aside for the fast women by the law.

Because it puts the stranger on a proper and safe path as to where he may go and be free from "Holdups," and other games usually practised upon the stranger.

It regulates the women so that they may live in one district to themselves instead of being scattered over the city and filling our thoroughfares with street walkers.

It also gives the names of women entertainers employed in the Dance Halls and Cabarets in the District.

An advertisement for "Miss Grace Lloyd" read:

Off all the landladies of the Tenderloin, there are few better known or admired than Grace Lloyd. Grace, as she is commonly called by all who know her, is a woman of very rare attainments and comes of that good old English stock from across the waters.

Grace is regarded as an all-round jolly good fellow, saying nothing about her beauty. She regards life as life and not as a money-making space of time.

Grace also has the distinction of keeping one of the quietest and most elaborately furnished establishments in the city, where an array of beautiful women and good times reign supreme.

Miss Lloyd recently went to enormous expense renovating her establishment, which had been almost totally destroyed by fire.

A visit will teach more than the pen can describe.

(When I got back to my motel, I totted up the number of girls in the *Blue Book*. There were nine octoroons, two hundred and fifty-four Negroes, and four hundred and sixty-four whites.)

Watson was still talking on the phone, so I wandered around the museum. A giant "Family Tree of Jazz" occupies one wall, and on another is an exhaustive chart tracing the origins of jazz from Spain in 758 A.D. to Dizzy Gillespie and Charlie Parker. A partition in the center of the room has five wall telephones which, when they are dialed, offer recorded lectures and illustrative music. The rest of the room is filled with display cases containing such authenticated memorabilia as a pair of Bix Beiderbecke's cufflinks, contributed by Hoagy Carmichael; one of Beiderbecke's cornets; the bugle that Louis Armstrong played in the Colored Waifs' Home when he was thirteen, and a chunk of the flagpole that stood in front of the home; Armstrong's first cornet, with a mouthpiece notched by its owner to prevent it from slipping; the head of a bass drum belonging to Ray Bauduc when he was with Bob Crosby's Bob Cats; one of Sidney Bechet's soprano saxophones; the guitar that Johnny St. Cyr used with Jelly Roll Morton's Red Hot Peppers; and a clarinet owned by Larry Shields, of the Original Dixieland Jazz Band.

"It's good to see a New York face again," a quiet voice said. It was Danny Barker.

We shook hands, and I asked him how he was feeling.

"I've got the old diabetes, you know, and I haven't been so well. I took a whole lot of tests at the hospital yesterday, and my wife made me stay home last night. She hid my banjo so I *couldn't* play."

I suggested that we have lunch in the Rib Room of the Royal Orleans. When we left the museum, Watson, who was now showing a visitor a copy of the *Blue Book*, unclasped his hands and waved them.

At the Rib Room, we got a table immediately. I caught only one untoward look, and it came from an old man with a napkin tucked under his chin—a vicious squint that may have been nearsightedness. Barker ordered trout amandine, and I ordered a poor boy, the New Orleans version of a hero sandwich. "I've been Jim Crowed in New York as long as I can remember, but I can be slippery here —move around," Barker said. "At one time, if I'd walked in here the customers would have been spilling their water, the waiters mumbling, and the headwaiter stumbling. Now everything's cool. I came back down here because there wasn't any work in New York. At least there's some action here, and I have over a hundred relatives. My autobiography—there's enough for *two* books—is all ready to go. I just need a publisher. It's been turned down by so many that I think I'll get some cheap paper and mimeograph machines, and get all those relatives to crank the handles." Barker smiled and leaned back. "In the winter, there is terrific party-giving here. We have the molasses king, the cotton king, the lumber king. Man, you can make two bills a night. The caterers are Negroes, and they and the musicians are tight. The musicians have their own table and all they can eat and drink. And I work off and on at the Southland Jazz Club."

I asked Barker what he knew of Bunk Johnson.

"Bunk was considered the equal, or better, of King Oliver and Manuel Perez and Freddie Keppard. He was also a great ladies' man and a boozer, and it got him in trouble. Lee Collins, the trumpet player, told me once of some trouble Bunk got in. The Jefferson City Buzzards were an Irish Channel marching club whose members were stevedores, firemen, and policemen, and they loved to ball in the Irish fashion. They were all six-foot Irishmen from County Cork and Galway Bay, and they had some fracases. It was the custom in those days for a committee from the club to decide on the music it wanted for a particular dance or outing. So the committee went to Spannol's, the bar where Bunk hung out, and gave him a deposit to play with his marching band at an all-day parade. This must have been around 1914 or 1915. Came the day, the Buzzards marched without a band, because Bunk didn't show up. So they sent word to Spannol's to tell Bunk he had blowed everything up and that they were going to catch him and put him in a coffee sack and throw him in the Mississippi. Although Bunk said he didn't get any deposit, he sent word back that he was willing to repay it, but the bread of friendship was beyond repair. Bunk was advised to leave town while the anger of the Jefferson City Buzzards subsided, and he went out to New Iberia, Louisiana, and from there he travelled all over the Orient and the world. It was in New Iberia that Bill Russell found him with no teeth and no horn in 1942 and brought him back to play again."

Barker took a bite of his trout. "But there were other trumpet players besides Bunk," he went on. "Buddy Petit, who never recorded, was the diminished-note king. Louis Armstrong plays a lot of his stuff. Petit was acknowledged by all New Orleans musicians as being one of the supergreats. And Chris Kelly was a good blues player. All these musicians played for different types of people. In fact, there was a caste system within the Negroes themselves. The Catholics liked Creole music, which was refined, and the Protestants were closer to blues shouting and spirituals and screaming to the skies and the Lord. In the downtown section, below Canal Street, Chris Kelly would be their boy. Kelly would never be allowed uptown, with all the skintight squeezing and hugging that happened when he played. All the bands had particular sections of society they entertained—high yallers, mulattoes, *comme il faut,* or blue bloods—and particular halls where they played. You'd find Kelly at Perseverance Hall, Petit at Economy Hall, and Sam Morgan at the France Amis. These halls were the homes of the benevolent societies and social clubs, of which there were once a hundred and fifty. The benevolent societies were like Blue Cross. If you wanted to form one, you got a dozen or so people together and went to see the doctor, the druggist, the undertaker. You got sick, needed medicine, or died, it was all paid for out of your dues. And there were yearly bonkeys, or banquets, for the members. Now there are only forty or so societies and social clubs left. The music at the old functions was always easy and free-flowing. It never excited you. Now it has become—in Preservation Hall and such—show business. You sit up there before an audience and you got these eyes on you all the time. You can't even scratch yourself on the bandstand. Most of the musicians playing in these clubs are old men—half blind, half sick. They're hamfat musicians. In the old days, the rough musicians kept pieces of ham fat in their pockets to grease the slides of their trombones or the valves of their trumpets. For every good musician, there was a hamfat. It looks like the hamfats didn't dissipate as much as the good musicians, because this town is full of them, and they're being exploited by smooth operators."

Barker put down his fork and pushed his empty plate away. He took a sip of coffee.

"But I've had the pleasure of playing beautiful music with beautiful people in my life. Now it's just a matter of the buck."

Allen took me on a dizzying tour that night. Our first stop was the front parlor of a Reverend Williams' house, in the uptown section, where a small band was rehearsing for a special church service. I recognized the Englishman Keith Smith, Earl Humphrey on trombone, and Andrew Morgan on tenor saxophone. A young Swede, Lars Edegran, was on piano, and there were a guitarist and a bassist. It was sweet, quiet ensemble music, and it sent the Reverend Williams' wife, seated in a rocker on the front porch, into violent motion and fervent singing. We stopped at the Golliwog Lounge to hear Armand Hug, another white New Orleans musician who has earned a reputation by staying at home. He looks like George Brent and plays like Jess Stacy. We stopped at the big, modern International Longshoremen's Association Hall, where a large rock-'n'-roll band made up of young musicians was pumping away impressively for a formal Negro subdeb cotillion. We stopped at the Haven, a small Negro bar. There was no dancing, but the band, made up of a trumpeter (who resembled Bill Coleman), a country-club tenor saxophonist, and rhythm, had some of the nonchalance of Tony Fougerat's group. And we stopped at Pepe's, a tourist spot in the Quarter, where there was a modern quartet led by the drummer Henry (Pickle) Jackson and including an alto saxophonist, an electric guitar, and a bass. Jackson was fascinating. He looks older than Paul Barbarin, but he plays flawless bebop drums.

"Hello and good morning," Allen said on the telephone the next day. "We're lucky—which isn't quite the right word under the circumstances—because I've just found out there's a funeral this afternoon in Walkertown, in Marrero. That's about eight miles out on the other side of the river, and there will be two bands—the Young Tuxedo and the Olympia. Betty Rankin, who is the associate curator at the Archive now, is taking us out."

On the other side of the river, the three of us drove between low, woolly clouds and flat country anchored by shopping centers and small factories. "The country funeral with brass bands is rapidly vanishing," Allen said. Mrs. Rankin, who is large and cheerful, nodded, and he went on, "The well-to-do and middle-class Negroes have begun to look down on it. They consider it Uncle Tom. It's too bad. There is no ritual like it anywhere in the world—dirge music on the way to the cemetery, and swinging music on the way back. They show death respect and then rejoice in life. Turn left just ahead, onto Ames Boulevard, Betty, and then left again, onto Second Street."

Walkertown is a dirt-poor Negro hamlet. Its one-story wooden houses are set on stilts, and the front yards are shabby. There are almost no trees. The dusty white streets, made of crushed clamshells, are flanked by open drainage ditches with planks for bridges. Mrs. Rankin pulled up near the Morning Star Baptist Church, a long wooden building with a mock-Spanish steeple. An enormous ear-trumpet loudspeaker was fastened to the front wall of the steeple, and air-conditioners jutted out of most of the windows.

Several musicians were milling around in front of the church. One of them strolled past and, seeing Allen, leaned into the car and said, "Hey, you brought yourself! How you feeling?"

It began to rain, and a second musician appeared. It was Kid Thomas. "Man, it rains at a funeral, it means it's washing away the dead man's sins. A really big sinner, it rains like hell." He smiled, showing a lot of gold teeth.

"There will be a lot of repeats from the Sunday parade," Allen said. "Andrew Morgan and Chester Jones and Jerry Green from the Onward, and Earl Humphrey, Papa Glass, Peter Bocage, and Milton Batiste from the Eureka. And Keith Smith, too."

The rain stopped, and we got out of the car. A thin female voice, singing a hymn, came out of the loudspeaker. A static-filled silence followed, and then a man spoke. A series of moans and screams grew louder and louder behind his words.

"The bereaved women generally try to outscream one another," Mrs. Rankin said. "I once went to a funeral where the deceased had a legal and a non-legal wife, and they screamed at each other for fifteen minutes. It was quite a show."

The church door opened, and two women in black and white, their faces wet and contorted, hobbled out on the arms of several men. A file of men wearing Odd Fellows' ceremonial aprons and neckpieces followed. The Young Tuxedo Band and the Olympia Band played a slow "Just a Closer Walk with Thee." Then the Olympia marched past the church and turned into Ames Boulevard, with the Young Tuxedo about fifty feet behind. A dozen Odd Fellows walked between them. The snare drum was muffled and the beat as slow as Big Ben's. "Saviour Lead Me," by the Olympia, was followed by the Young Tuxedo's "What a Friend We Have in Jesus." Dead, soft drumbeats separated the numbers. The second line ambled along quietly at one side of the road, and a long string of limousines nosed the Young Tuxedo. The procession moved between a housing development and a farmyard full of charging guinea hens, between a power station and a field of cows, and after a mile or so it halted at a wooden bridge over a deep ditch. On the other side, a dirt road disappeared into a patch of woods. The Young Tuxedo marched across the bridge, followed by the hearse, which moved cautiously, filling the bridge. The cemetery began on the left of the dirt road, and was a bedraggled sea of small stones, briars, wooden crosses, and long grass. Refuse had been dumped as fill on the other side of the road. A tunnel of trees dripped and whispered. The Young Tuxedo played "Saviour Lead Me" at the grave, and after the service the mourners walked slowly back to the boulevard. The Young Tuxedo suddenly started "When the Saints Go Marching In." The second line materialized in front. The music was thin and loose, compared with the New Orleans parade, and twice as brave. The sun came out, burnishing one of the tubas. The Olympia began a fast "Just a Closer Walk with Thee." In the second line, a fat man dressed in a tight blue suit and a small fedora threw back his head, switched his hips, and strutted through a crowd of leaping, delighted children. The two tear-drenched women from the church danced arm in arm. An old woman flopped heavily in circles, like a turkey with an injured wing, and was joined by an old man, who pumped his knees and trembled his hands. The returning limousines roared past, leaving big white dust devils. The Young Tuxedo played "Bye and Bye." The road was filled with dancers, and when the rain started again there were little screams. I looked down, and half a dozen tiny pistonlike children were sharing my umbrella. Their turned-up faces were split by smiles, and their cheeks were covered with rain.

We moved into Third Street and stopped in front of the house belonging to the head of the Odd Fellows. The old woman danced into a front yard across the street and onto the porch. Both bands, packed into a circle, played "Lord, Lord, Lord." It was a glorious five minutes. Twenty instruments rose and fell in broken, successive waves. The rain let up, and the music ended, stunning us all. The dancers ran down, and I could hear cars on Ames Boulevard. A thin middle-aged man in a cowboy hat came up to me. "That was my papa was buried today," he said, smiling. "Fifty years he was an Odd Fellow."

Mrs. Rankin and Allen and I walked back to the car. "I don't believe I've been to a finer country funeral," she said.

"I share your feelings," Allen replied.

# The Blues Is a Slow Story

One of the high points of the 1965 Monterey Jazz Festival was reached during the final afternoon concert when Henry (Red) Allen, the fifty-eight-year-old New Orleans trumpeter and singer, unintentionally "cut" the three equally celebrated trumpeters who were appearing with him. But it was an uphill effort. All four trumpeters—Clark Terry, Rex Stewart, and Dizzy Gillespie were the others—played in the first number, and Allen came off poorly. His solo was strained and full of fluffs and his generally ebullient, almost vaudeville stage manner was distracted and uncertain. The next number was even less complimentary. In the middle of it, Gillespie and Terry, joined by the singer Jon Hendricks, broke into some nonsense singing; Allen, who is one of the redoubtable jazz singers, was unaccountably left standing alone at the back of the stage, his trumpet swinging idly from crossed hands, a bleak smile on his face. When Allen played again, after a slick, technically perfect Terry number, he suddenly became himself. His characteristic long melodic lines had become airborne and his tone had taken on its usual crackle. It was a slow blues, and in it he constructed three august choruses, sang as many more in a soft, high, husky voice, then closed the number with a climactic, high-noted chorus.

That night, Allen, who had arrived from New York just the day before, flew home. Little else in the weekend matched him.

Allen's ugly-duckling-into-swan performance at Monterey stayed in my mind, and several months later, when I heard that he was nearing the end of a short engagement at Jimmy Ryan's, on West Fifty-fourth Street, I called him at his apartment, in the Bronx, and told him I would like to talk to him. His voice was high and hoarse and singsongy: "Nice. I have to go up to Providence week after next, but I'm not working next week. Why don't you stop up Wednesday, and we'll have a taste and Pearlie May, my wife, can put a little spread on us. Take the No. 5 Dyer Avenue train on the Lexington Avenue and get off at Freeman. I'll meet you. Look for me across the street from the bank. I have a blue Cadillac."

Allen is something of a wonder in jazz. He is, along with Zutty Singleton and Louis Armstrong, among the last of the first-rate New Orleans musicians still at large, and he is the only New Orleans musician who has, barring a few stops and starts, continued to develop. His playing has in recent years been increasingly subtle, and there are suggestions in it that he may listen to such modernists as Miles Davis and Art Farmer. His style was fully formed by 1929. Armstrong hovered in its background, but Allen's originality dominated it. It was an elegant and primitive and fearless style, and it was perfectly balanced. His full, often declamatory tone was suitably crimped by growls or piercing high notes; his basically legato approach was enlivened by rushes of on-the-beat notes; his seemingly straightforward melodic content was enriched by long, sagacious phrases and by a daring choice of notes. Allen was particularly striking at slow tempos. He would linger over his notes, holding them far longer than any other trumpeter, and he would bend them and press them, coloring them with a distinct and disturbing melancholy. His slow solos were often requiems. But this sadness, which lifted at faster tempos, was invariably toughened and guided by a subtle, leashed power. By 1934, he had become a full-fledged innovator; indeed, in his recordings made with Fletcher Henderson, he is a one-man avant garde—a credit only recently granted him. His solos are full of long, roving lines, unexpected off-notes, and free rhythmic turns. It is the sort of I-can-get-all-this-out-in-one-phrase improvising that was perfected five or six years later by Lester Young and Charlie Christian and that still sounds absolutely fresh. Some of Allen's solos with Henderson had such completeness and authority that they were studied assiduously several years later by Harry James when he was with Benny Goodman, and some were scored for whole sections of the Henderson band. Allen's playing changed in the forties. It became brassy and even harsh, and his unevenness, theretofore occasional, became pronounced. He would start a solo with a beautiful, languorous phrase, pause, lose the impetus of it, and wander off into an entirely different mood. But this uncertainty began to decline in the early fifties, and in 1956 he made a startling recording for Victor. It included several long ballads, and Allen converted each one into a luxurious hymn. He literally flowed around his horn (fat lower-register notes—almost trombone notes—would be planted beside soft, high flutters), and the blues underlay almost every passage. He has made equally good recordings since, and gorgeous patches appear in every solo he takes in night clubs or at concerts, no matter how hard he is blowing. Allen has much in common with Pee Wee Russell. Both appear to be inimitable and both have long been lumped with the wrong musical schools—Russell with the Chicagoans and Allen with New Orleans jazz. But both are, in reality, advanced swing musicians who play best in fast, original company. Allen was invariably at ease within the big swing bands of the thirties, and he has since led a variety of comfortable small swing bands. He has recorded well with Russell, and, like Russell, he would be at home with Thelonious Monk.

When I came down the stairs from the subway platform late that Wednesday morning, I spotted Allen's car immediately. It was new and dusty blue, and its license plate read "RA 67." Allen was seated behind the wheel, reading the *Daily News*. He smiled and we shook hands and I got in. He was wearing a dark-blue fedora, its narrow brim turned up, a brown chamois pullover with a wool collar, and brown slacks. He made a leisurely U turn, stopped at a traffic light, and headed west toward Prospect Avenue. He drove quickly, frequently tapping out light, staccato bursts on his horn, and humming a nameless melody. I asked him how Monterey had felt. He shook his head and fired off a horn burst. "Whoof. I got smothered out there. Flew all the way out and back just to play two numbers, with nobody telling me anything or giving me any chance to talk with the drummer and bass player, tell them what little things I'd like to do. The piano player didn't even show up, and Gillespie had to sit in for him. The only reason I called for the blues was I figured everyone would know that. What happened was the drummer and bassist tried to play *my* way, *my* style. It should be the other way around. I always try and fit myself to the guys I'm sitting in with. But I was happy to have the chance to get on there."

Allen turned into Prospect Avenue, a wide street that

is flanked in his block with houses, some of them wood, and with low apartment buildings. He made another U turn and parked across from a five-story yellow-brick building. "There it is," he said. "We got a little climb to make. Five flights." Allen rang his apartment bell downstairs and started up at a fast pace. He is tall, and has become portly in recent years, but he was not winded when we reached the fifth floor. He pushed his doorbell and there was a thumping sound inside. A muffled voice said, "Is that you, Allen?"

"I'm here, Pearlie May. Open up." There were more confused sounds and the word "doing" came through the door. Allen chuckled. "She's putting the dog away. He's a big white German shepherd that we call White Fang after another White Fang we had and he'll jump all over you, cover you with hair. But he's a fine watchdog. When I come in late, I ring the bell downstairs and Pearlie May lets him out and he runs down to meet me."

A chain rattled and the door opened. Mrs. Allen, who is short and plump and has a round, pretty face, was fastening the top button of a house dress. Allen introduced us, and she said, "Lord, that dog is so *curious*. Wants to see what everybody looks like comes in the house and then sits all over them. I put him in the bathroom, where he won't bother anyone."

Allen led the way down a short, dark hall and past a small, cheerful kitchen. A rather bleary Impressionist painting of him hung by the kitchen door, and farther along, on the opposite wall, there was a large counteracting photograph of a thin young smooth-faced Allen dressed in a tight, dapper double-breasted suit and holding an extremely long trumpet. A small room with a day bed and a television set and a couple of chairs was at the end of the

339

hall, and to its left was a larger room, with glass doors. Allen ushered me in. "This is the front room, which is what we call the parlor. I'll close the doors to keep out the dog." The room had a small green sofa, several red chairs, and two end tables. A silver tea service and a pair of tall orange china swans were on one of the tables. A dark abstract painting hung on one wall and another painting of Allen across from it. On the wall near the doors were two plates, one with the message "God Bless This Allen Home." The Venetian blinds at the only window were down, but the slats were open. The room was in pleasant twilight.

Allen sat down heavily in one of the chairs, his legs spread wide, his toes pointing in. His face is a study in basset melancholy. He has a high, narrow forehead and thin, dark hair. A single, ironbound furrow runs across the lower part of his forehead, and it seems to weigh on his eyes, which are heavily lidded and slant down at their outer corners. Two more deep furrows bracket his generous nose and his mouth, and he has a cleft chin. His cheeks are heavy but firm. His smile is surprising; it easily lifts and lights the mass around it. His speech, I had already noticed, resembles the odd, watered-down version of the Brooklyn accent that is found in New Orleans and St. Louis. He is apt to start sentences with "der"—in the manner of the French "donc"—or to use it to fill a pause. Moreover, words like "rehearsal" and "bird" are pronounced "rehoisal" and "boid." Allen yawned, tweaked his nose, and rested his thick, square hands on his thighs. "I don't think I've felt as unsettled as I did at Monterey since my first visits to New York in the late twenties. My first was in 1927 when King Oliver called me to come. I was leery of leaving New Orleans. I'd heard of too many New Orleans musicians getting stranded up in the North. But I went because Oliver had

340

worked in my dad's brass band. It was my first time away from home. I was an only child and I'd had a lot of care. I wasn't accustomed to taking things to the laundry and making my own bed. I couldn't get used to it. I lived in a boarding house with Omer Simeon and Barney Bigard and Paul Barbarin, New Orleans friends and all in Oliver's band. Then I moved in with Oliver and his sister. Oliver and I stayed together like father and son. I used to kid with him all the time and imitate the grand marshal in one of the parades back home and he'd laugh so hard he'd cry. His teeth had gone bad by then and he wasn't playing much, so I'd take most of the solos at the Savoy, where we were appearing, and pretty soon people started calling me King Oliver. Then Oliver was supposed to go into the Cotton Club, but somebody brainwashed him about the money, telling him he should get more, so he didn't take the job. Duke Ellington, who was just starting out, did, and that was the beginning of *that* story. Oliver's band was booked into a park in Baltimore, but we had rough luck there with weather and that job didn't work out either. When we got back to New York, I couldn't take it anymore. I made my first record—with Clarence Williams—and the next day I took off for home. I'd saved my fare money, kept it in my shoe, so I didn't have to send to my father for money. I was only gone two months and I was happy to get back. Even the coffee was bad in New York. In New Orleans it was so strong it stained the cup, but I drank so much of it I got headaches if I didn't drink it. In New York, I drank the same amount but the headaches just got worse, so I gave it up. And I don't drink much of it to this day, unless I'm in New Orleans on a visit."

There was a commotion in the hall and White Fang appeared outside the glass doors. Mrs. Allen grabbed him by the collar and started pulling him back toward the kitchen. Allen laughed. "Let him be, Pearlie May!" he shouted. "Just put that chair against the door so's he can't get in." Mrs. Allen wedged a chair under the door handle. She shook a finger at the dog, and said, "You want to come out, you act like a grown boy." The dog sat down, his nose pressed against the glass. He stared at me a long time, then he stared at Allen, and then he jumped up on the chair and resumed his vigil.

"I joined Fate Marable's band when I got back. Fate worked the riverboats on the Streckfus line, and during the winter we'd stay in New Orleans and play one-nighters. Go up the river a little way and turn around and come back. When it warmed up, we'd head for St. Louis and stop at towns along the way and dock and play dances on the boat. We stayed in St. Louis about three months, and though we played on the boat we lived in the city. You had to go out and find a room—which was called every tub on its bottom, or being on your own. There were some rough places in St. Louis. The Chauffeur's Club was so bad they built a fence of chicken wire around the bandstand to protect the musicians when fights broke out. In 1929, I started getting letters and wires from New York. Luis Russell, who had been with Oliver when I was and who had the band now, wrote me to join him, and Duke Ellington wired me. I knew most of the people with Russell—Pops Foster, who'd been a longshoreman with my father, was on bass; Charlie Holmes was on alto; and old Paul Barbarin, who had instigated my joining Oliver in 1927, was on drums. I knew about J. C. Higginbotham, on trombone, and I'd heard of Bill Coleman and Otis Johnson, who were on trumpets. So I told Russell yes, and turned down Ellington. Barney Bigard was the only person I knew in his band. I believe he hired Cootie Williams instead. Fate Marable said O.K., I could go. He also said, 'Red'—that was a nickname given me because I was light-skinned and my face got red when I blew—'Red, if you see my man Jelly Roll Morton, tell him hello. He used to work for me, you know.' The first time I ran into Jelly in New York I gave him the message. Well, Jelly Roll had a lot of posing and hot air in him, always saying things like 'My car is so long I got to go over to Central Park to turn it around,' and he just stood there and looked around and after a while he said, 'Oh, Fate Marable. He had this big old band that wasn't doing *nothing* and so one time I let him use my name to help him out.'" Allen laughed and rubbed his hands together. White Fang was on the hall floor, asleep.

"That first week back in New York was scary. Teddy Hill, who played tenor for Russell, met me at the train and took me straight to the Roseland Ballroom, where the band was playing. I was to learn it was the kind of band that hung out like a family. It had brotherly love going. It was also the most swinging band in New York; it put the audiences in an uproar. One of the reasons was rhythm. Ellington had switched from tuba to bass and from banjo to guitar and so had Russell. All the New York bass players were taking lessons from Pops Foster, and they even began carrying their basses on their shoulders, like the New Orleans men. Before that, you'd see them in the street carrying that fiddle in front of them in their arms like a baby. Russell did most of the arrangements, and whenever you took a solo there was a lot of fire up and down the band. But it wasn't Russell that made me nervous that first week. It was the after-hours jam sessions. I'd heard a lot about them and about the 'cutting' contests and I didn't know if I'd make it or not. I couldn't look to alcohol or tobacco for support, either. My father had never allowed me to drink or smoke and I obeyed him. I don't believe I took my first strong drink until the forties and I still don't smoke. I hadn't been in New York but a day or two when Alphonso Steele, who was a drummer, began taking me to the sessions at the Rhythm Club, on a Hundred and Thirty-second Street. He used to be a Paul Revere, sending around the news of sessions and announcing a new man in town. They would have trumpet nights and trombone nights and saxophone nights at the Rhythm Club. The first sessions I went to every trumpeter was there—Cootie Williams, Rex Stewart, Ward Pinkett, Freddie Jenkins, Sidney de Paris. I don't believe Joe Smith showed up, but I learned later that when he did you were really in the lion's mouth. Whoever was on piano decided on the key and set the tempo and then everyone soloed. If you wanted extra choruses you stomped your foot. The applause decided the winner." Allen laughed. "I guess I did all right, because I'm still in New York. But those sessions were more than just outblowing someone. They were the only way of getting noticed, they were our publicity. If you made a good appearance, stood on your own, the word got around, and that's where the jobs come from. If you lost out too often, you just wouldn't make it. There were challenges all the time. One night, Big Green challenged Higginbotham. It was late, so Big Green went back to the Saratoga Club, where he was working, to get his horn and had to break down the door, which was locked. He came on back and I believe Higgy took care of him. Another time, the St. Louis clarinettist, Thornton Blue—the 'reputed Blue,' he called himself—took on Prince Robinson and Omer Simeon and Buster Bailey. When Buster got going on 'Tiger Rag,' that sealed it up. I heard Rex Stewart and Bix Beiderbecke battle, but, all due respect for the dead, Rex must have been in better form that night. And of course the bands battled all the time—at the Roseland and the Savoy and the Renaissance. And white musicians came up from downtown to sit in or listen: Jack Teagarden and the Dorseys and Krupa and Red Nichols and Goodman and Bunny Berigan. And there were breakfast dances at Small's Paradise, which began around four or five in the morning and went on half the day. I'd developed a strong embouchure on the riverboats, where the hours were long, so I could stand it."

There was muffled barking, and two little girls in school uniforms appeared outside the doors. "Oh, that's nice," Allen said, and smiled. "Here's the grands, home from school. Their address is with my son and his wife, who are only four blocks away, but they practically live here. They come by every day to do their homework and spend the night. They only go home Saturdays, but their parents stop in most every day, too. That way we get to see them. The grands call Pearlie May Mama and me Papa." The taller girl opened one of the doors and came in and kissed Allen. "This is Alcornette," Allen said. "She's eleven. Pearlie May's maiden name is Alcorn and of course there had to be some mention of a trumpet or cornet. And this is Juretta. She's named after my mother. She's six. They go to a Catholic school nearby. Go change your clothes and get on that homework. Alcornette, ask Mama can we have some ice and two glasses. And close the door. We'll have a little taste, a little Scotcherini.

"I stayed with the Russell band until 1933, when I got a telegram from Fletcher Henderson asking me to meet him at a drugstore uptown. Russell Smith, who played trumpet with him, mainly persuaded me to join. I didn't

345

like leaving the Luis Russell band, which was my home. But I guess Henderson offered me more money and it was *the* band. Most of the arrangements were by Fletcher or Horace, his brother, and they were in difficult keys—D natural and the like. I'd learned all the keys in New Orleans by playing along with records set at every different speed. Each speed would put the music in a new key. I'd try all kinds of things with Fletcher, loafing through the channel of a number like 'Yeah, Man,' with the result that Horace liked what I'd done so much he wrote it out for the brass. Horace would just sketch out the chords for new numbers and you could skate on that. I got accustomed to him. Take my thirty-one bars, or whatever, and get out. I was with the band for a year and during that time Coleman Hawkins left and Lester Young replaced him. He only stayed a couple of weeks. He had a light tone and it just didn't fit with the arrangements, which called for a rich, deep sound. But I was happy for Lester to be in the band because his father and my father had played together in New Orleans. Ben Webster took his place. I got ninety dollars a week when I joined and I made something on the side with small-band dates for Brunswick. They paid a hundred dollars a date. I picked the men, mostly from Henderson's band, and we made popular things like 'Red Sails in the Sunset' and 'If I Could Be Twins' and 'Boots and Saddles.' They sold very well in Europe. Fletcher always had money, even when he said he didn't. It seems he had these special pockets—a two-dollar pocket, a five-, a ten- —because whenever you asked him for a slight advance he'd go to such-and-such a pocket and bring out just the amount. In 1934, things got bad. Henderson couldn't find work. The Mills Blue Rhythm Band, which was fronted by Lucky Millinder, was having trouble, too, but when Lucky sent for

Higgy and Buster Bailey and me, we went. Irving Mills made the proposition of making me the leader of the Blue Rhythm Band, but I couldn't see cutting in on Lucky. I was satisfied to be what I was. Every band I'd been in I'd been featured. I got good money and didn't have the headaches. It's not so easy to relax when you're the leader. Imagine, you have fifteen or sixteen minds going you have to control. I joined Louis Armstrong's big band in 1937, which was coming home again because it was still the old Russell band, but expanded. Higgy came with me. Louis was very good to me. He gave me little solo parts here and there. In fact, it was just the other month Louis and Lucille Armstrong climbed these five flights to come and see me. They'd heard something had happened to me, but it was only a rumor. We had a fine dinner together."

Mrs. Allen put a bowl of ice, two Old Fashioned glasses, and a bottle of Scotch on a table. Allen poured two fingers into each glass and added ice and handed me one. "You hungry, Allen?" Mrs. Allen asked. "I got something coming up in a few minutes." She leaned into the next room, where Juretta and Alcornette were. "Now hurry up and change those clothes," she said. "And, Alcornette, when you finish, set up that card table in the front room."

"I eat around two o'clock in the evening and after work," Allen said. He poured a little water in his glass and took a sip and coughed. "Even though I got to be a leader, the forties were all right for me. John Hammond arranged for me to see Barney Josephson, the owner of Café Society Downtown. We weren't doing all that work with Louis, so I formed my own group in 1940, with Higgy and Edmond Hall. We were at Café Society a year with people like Pete Johnson and Billie Holiday and Art Tatum and Hazel Scott and Lena Horne, who was in the chorus at the Cotton Club, in 1934, when I played there. I took the band to Boston from Café Society for a long gig at the Ken Club. Sidney Bechet played with us. Don Stovall replaced Edmond Hall and Kenny Clarke came in on drums, and later Paul Barbarin. We had another long stay at the Down Beat Room, in Chicago, where we worked with Billie again. She missed a lot of shows and so we'd use a girl named Ruth Jones, who was always hanging around waiting for the chance to sing. I'd announce her—burlesque style—as Dynamite Washington, which later became Dinah when she joined Lionel Hampton. I added Ben Webster to the band. Later, we worked in San Francisco and in Salt Lake City and at the Onyx and Kelly's Stable on Fifty-second Street, and back to Chicago and to Boston. They were all long engagements. I went into the Metropole in 1954. I had Higgy and Buster Bailey and Cozy Cole, and I took Claude Hopkins out of deep freeze and put him on piano. It was a seven-year gig. The owners of the Metropole were very good to me. *They* didn't make us play loud. It was the people. We'd try a soft number or two, and they'd say, 'Now what's the matter with you, Red? You sick or something?' And we'd go up again."

Juretta sidled into the room and handed Allen some homework papers. He held them at arm's length, read through them slowly, and handed them back. He smiled. "That's just fine, darlin'. Lovely. You go and finish now." Alcornette brought in a card table, and Allen heaved himself to his feet and helped her set it up. Then he walked around the room, peered through the Venetian blind, and went back to his chair. Mrs. Allen called from the kitchen, "Alcornette, put on that white tablecloth that's in the chest in your room. And set some plates and glasses and napkins for two, please."

"You got some peppers, Pearlie May?" Allen called.

"I got them right here, Allen," she replied.

I asked Allen how much influence Louis Armstrong had had on his work. "The most influence Louis had on me was on the records he made in the twenties—the 'Savoy Blues,' 'Cornet Chop Suey.' We used to learn those numbers from the recordings in New Orleans. And I'd hear Whiteman recordings that Mr. Streckfus brought back from New York with him. I also listened to people in New Orleans like Buddy Petit and Chris Kelly, who never recorded. And to Kid Rena and Punch Miller. Rena was the first trumpeter I ever heard play high. Those things worked together to make my style and the rest was me. When you play, so many things work together. You have your brain. You have your fingers. You have your breathing. You have your embouchure. Playing, it's like somebody making your lip speak, making it say things he thinks. I concentrate a couple of bars ahead at all times. You have to have an idea of where you are going. You have more expression of feeling in the blues. And you have more time. The blues is a slow story. The feeling of the beautiful things that happen to you is in the blues. They come out in the horn. You play blues, it's a home language, like two friends talking. It's the language everybody understands. You can inject into people with the instrument, I think. I've had nights when it was better than others, but I've been a little fortunate in my loving to play so much."

Mrs. Allen brought in a platter of fried chicken and a dish of boiled cabbage. She put a jar of pickled hot peppers between them. Allen grunted, pulled his chair up to the table, and helped himself. "Bring some of that Rheingold, please, Pearlie." He turned to me. "Try a hot pepper. Birds' eyes we call them. My aunt just sent them from New Orleans. It's what they make Tabasco Sauce from. People live on hot peppers and mustard and garlic in New Orleans."

I bit into a tiny olive-colored pepper. Waves of scalding heat filled my mouth and went up my nose, and my eyes watered. I gulped down some beer and sucked in some air, which felt icy. "You eat them with every meal, you get used to them," Mrs. Allen said. She was standing in the doorway arms akimbo. Juretta stood beside her, staring at the chicken. "All right, a *small* piece," Mrs. Allen said. "Otherwise, you'll ruin your supper. And don't chew all over the carpet."

"I visit my mother and my aunt in New Orleans every year," Allen said. "My mother is eighty-two and spry. She still lives in the house where I was born, at 414 Newton Street, in Algiers, which is to New Orleans what the Bronx is to New York. My father passed in 1952. He was seventy-five. He was born in Lockport, Louisiana. Everyone was in his brass band at one time or another—Punch Miller, Papa Celestin, King Oliver, Louis Armstrong, Sidney Bechet. My father played trumpet. His brother Samuel was a bass player, and a younger brother, George, played drums. The band generally had two trombones, three trumpets, a bass horn and a baritone horn, a peck horn, a clarinet, and two drummers. The trombones marched in front, so they wouldn't hit anybody in the back. The bass and baritone came next, then the clarinet and the peck horn, the trumpets, and then the drummers—bass drum on the left and snare drum to the right. The bass drummer played his drum and a cymbal attached to it, and the other drummer played snares. The two of them got a sound like a regular set of drums. The horn players needed strong embouchures. The roads were rough and if you stepped into a hole you had to hold on to that horn to not break your notes. Maybe that was the reason King Oliver never marched with the band but always next to it, on the sidewalk, where it was smoother. There were generally parades on Sundays, and of course when there was a decease and for special occasions, like housebuildings and the regular outings of the social clubs. I don't know how many social clubs there were—the Money Wasters, the Square Deals, the Bulls, the West Side Friends of Honor. You paid dues and when you passed your club paid for a band and for putting you away. The big men belonged to four or five clubs and they'd have four or five bands. My father had six when he passed. If you wasn't a member of any club, they put a saucer on your chest while you lay in the front room and pretty soon there'd be enough for the proper arrangements. Each club had its own colors and its own banner. In parades, the two men who carried the banner got twenty-five cents apiece, and the man who carried the American flag got fifty cents. And each club had its own button—black on one side and its colors on the other. You'd wear the colors for the regular parades and the black for funerals. The men who played in the bands were stonemasons or slaters or plasterers and such, and their jobs would let them off for a funeral. These funerals went according to the Bible—sadness at birth and rejoicing at death. If the deceased belonged to several clubs, he'd generally stay on view in the front room for three or four days to give all his brothers time to pay their respects. If you were very sacred, you'd stay with the deceased some while, then you'd go through to the kitchen, where they'd have a bousin, which is a Creole term for a party. There would be gumbo and ham salad and burgundy and sangaree, a kind of punch." Allen helped himself to another piece of chicken and more cabbage.

"On funeral days, the club and the band assembled

at the deceased's house and then they'd march to the church. The band played very slow, very slow. The snare was taken off on the snare drum, giving a kettle effect. When the deceased went by, everyone in the street would stop talking and moving and take off their hats and put them over their hearts, and then go back to what they were doing. While everyone was in the church, the musicians sometimes went to a saloon nearby, and it was my job when I was little to run from the church to the saloon when the service was over and get the musicians together. We'd march to the cemetery and the band would stand in the road and wait until the moans and cries went up, which meant that the preacher was saying, 'Ashes to ashes, and dust to dust,' and throwing the dirt on the coffin. Then the drums rolled like thunder and the band would break into a fast 'Oh, Didn't He Ramble' and march back. On a wide avenue, when there was more than one band, the first band would split in half, one half lining up on one side of the avenue and the other on the other side, and the band right behind would march between these lines. The bands would be playing different tunes. Then the second band would split open and the first one would form up again and march through *them*. You could tell by the applause of the onlookers who was best, and the winner would go a roundabout way to the house of the deceased and play there up on the gallery, really swinging, for ten or fifteen minutes, and then go inside and enjoy the bousin. Pearlie May, let me have one more beer!" Allen shouted to the kitchen. He pushed himself back from the table and took a bite of a red pepper the size of his finger.

"Of course we played at dances, too. The men in the band would get three dollars apiece and the leader four and there was a dollar allowed for phone calls and such. And there were building parties. When a man decided to build himself a house it was like the pioneering days. The members of his club and his neighbors would all gather on a weekend on his plot—wives and children, too. The men would put down the foundation and get the frame up. There would be a few kegs of beer or some home brew— Sweet Lucy or Son Kick Your Mammy—and a band to play. They'd build and eat and build and drink and build and laugh and have a fine bousin. The man whose house was being put up would turn around next time a house had to be built and help with that. At Mardi Gras, musicians got scarce in New Orleans, and a week or so before, my father would hitch up a sulky and travel maybe a hundred miles into the country to round up musicians he'd heard or heard about. He took me when I got big enough. The roads were poor, and we never went too fast for fear the horse's legs might get stoved up or swollen. We'd stop and visit every few miles and spend the night with relatives or friends."

Mrs. Allen cleared the table and brought two more bottles of beer. Then she went to the window and looked out, her hands clasped behind her. The room was darker and Allen switched on a lamp.

"I started on the violin. My mother preferred it because most of the boys who took up the trumpet got balls in their cheeks and necks from all that blowing. But I'd practice on my father's trumpet, and he'd keep telling me to tell my mother it would be all right, I wouldn't get those balls in my cheeks, and finally she said yes. From the age of eight I played the upright alto—the peck horn—in my father's band. He'd carry me in parades some of the way and then put me down on a corner and I'd play and a little crowd would gather and he'd tell everybody, 'Sonny's got it, Sonny's got it.' My first teacher on trumpet was Manuel

Manetta, but my father taught me to read. I did pretty nice in school. I had to; my father signed the report cards. He was a serious man, a strict man. I had to obey the New Orleans curfew, which was nine o'clock. It was sounded by a calliope on one of the riverboats. Come nine every evening, you'd see nothing in the streets but children running, this way, that way, like mice. I also indulged in track in high school and I set up a few records in the cross-country. My father was never rich, but he tried to give me everything I'd think of. At one time, I even had a couple of horses—a pacer, which puts down two feet at a time, and a racker, which puts down one foot at a time. They were building a neighbor's house once, and I was sent over the canal into the woods to drag back a cross-style, which was made of six-by-twelve beams, and when my horse got on the bridge over the canal he balked. He wouldn't *move*. I blew a whistle and rang this bell I had and all of a sudden that horse moved. He moved right into the canal, cross-style and all, everything mired down in mud. Sometimes I'd go to auctions where they were selling horses and watch the pep man. He stood kind of backstage and before the horse—it was usually an old nag—came out of the chute to where the people was, the pep man would take a rag soaked in turpentine and whap the horse right across his rump end and that horse would come shooting out of the chute, head up, prancing and looking like a colt, and then, after somebody had bid and bought, he'd sag and his head would go down and he'd look like the used-up horse he was. Some afternoons after school, when my father was still at work, I'd take my horse and ride over to the poolroom—Louis Kohlman's poolroom—and tie him up outside. The horse got so used to the route that once when my father asked me to ride him over to the ferry to

New Orleans the horse got to the corner near the poolroom and instead of going straight to the ferry he turned the corner with me pulling and straining at him and headed right for the poolroom and stopped dead in front of it. My father looked at me and I didn't say anything. He said, 'Sonny, I thought you didn't hang around here.' Then he smiled, and I knew I was off the hook. My father wanted me to be a musician and nothing else, so I was already working in brass bands and in cabarets when I was in my teens. You weren't allowed to wear long pants until you were eighteen—just short pants, knickers they were. Leonard Bocage would bring me home at night or my father would come and get me. He got so set in the habit that when I visited him not long before he passed and went out somewhere and didn't get home until three or four in the morning I found him in the front room waiting for me —and me not a junior anymore but a grown man."

Mrs. Allen was sitting in a chair, her head resting on one hand, watching Allen. "You used to try and get him to stop playing when he got old, Allen."

Allen smiled. "That's right, but you said I was wrong. 'Let him play,' you said. 'It's good for him. He'd suffer without it.' He played right up to the end."

"My father died when I was but fourteen," Mrs. Allen said, "and my mother when I was two. I was born a Creole, the last of three children. My father was a slater. New Orleans was famous for its slate steeples and most of the roofs were slate, too. I went to public schools and then to New Orleans University. My parents were gone, but I had thirteen people on each side of the family and they contributed to put me through. I took a general course and then went to Gillume College for a business course for two years and then went to work teaching in Utica, Mississippi, for a year. I was working for an insurance company in New Orleans when I met Allen. He was playing at the Pelican, a ballroom, and I sold tickets there at night. We were married in New York in 1930, and my son Henry—he's our only child—was born in 1931."

"He's been with the New York police for eight or nine years," Allen said. "Before that he was an M.P. in the Marines in Korea. He plays trumpet, too, and he's good. Pearlie May and I have never been apart much. If I was on the road more than a week, Pearlie May would come and stay. If I was away and had a couple of days off, I'd come home for a quick visit. We're rare ones. Most of the others have been divorced and married three or four times. Pearlie May knows how to carry things on. She's very good brainwise. All my flexible brains are musicwise. She pays the bills and does the taxes. I get the loot."

"If I can close myself up in my room, really get my brain to it, the taxes don't take too long," she said.

"We have relations in Chicago and Michigan and New Orleans and we have a tremendous phone bill."

"A letter's something you keep putting off," Mrs. Allen said. "I'm gonna write, I'm gonna write, I'm gonna write, and then you never do."

"If you do, then you call up the person on the phone and say, 'Oh, here's something I forgot to say in my letter.'"

"We have plans to move out of this neighborhood someday. We've been in this apartment since 1940. Before that we lived at St. Nicholas Place, around a Hundred and Forty-eighth Street."

"One day my boy got tagged up there with a brick," Allen said. "Kids in the street called him out and then dropped a brick on his head from the roof. We lived on the ground and we were robbed a couple of times."

"That's why we live on the fifth floor. I like it here. I know everyone in the neighborhood and they know me. People'll carry your groceries up for you and things like that. Allen can leave his car unlocked and if he's parked on the wrong side of the street, someone calls up and tells him he better move, the policeman's coming."

I asked Allen if he planned to retire. He chuckled. "When I pass is when I retire. I love to play; that horn is good for me. When I'm not working, I sit in front of the television when there is a decent musical show and play along with it. Or I go and sit in at Jimmy Ryan's. A couple of weeks ago, I played at the Dom with Tony Scott on Eighth Street. I think those young cats were a little surprised."

"When Allen's on television the children and I watch. Even that dog sits and watches, turning his head from side to side. When he finishes, we applaud."

"Jobs are scarce now," Allen said. "But this isn't the first time."

"In 1934, Allen told me, 'Let's pull in the belts and tighten up a little.'" Mrs. Allen laughed, showing perfect teeth. "You get a few nickels together in the good times and you survive the bad ones."

"1934 was with Fletcher. We'd been booked to go to Europe and before that we were supposed to go into Connie's Inn. We never made either scene. In fact, I didn't get to Europe until 1959. I'm going to England in February for six weeks."

Mrs. Allen laughed again. "He's got his ticket already and his bags are packed."

"They ask me what I've done, I don't have any regrets," he said. "Pearlie May is happy. She has her grands. I've raised my family even if I don't have a mansion. If

I was anyway fixed financially I would still want to play the music on my way out, all the way. The only thing gets to me once in a while is the dropouts, the guys that are gone. Just yesterday I was listening to a record I made with Lionel Hampton in 1939—'Haven't Named It Yet.' It shook me some when I looked at the label. Sid Catlett gone, Artie Bernstein gone, Charlie Christian gone, Earl Bostic gone, Clyde Hart gone. Just Higgy and Hampton and me left. But I guess we carry on for them. Least, that's the way I like to look at it."

# Index

359

# Index

361

# Index

# Such Sweet Thunder

# Index

ML3561.J3 .B255          CU-Main
c. 1
Balliett, Whitney/Such sweet thunder; forty-nine p

3 9371 00033 1009